MOTIVATION
IN THE
REAL WORLD

MOTIVATION
IN THE
REAL WORLD

THE ART OF GETTING
EXTRA EFFORT FROM
EVERYONE—INCLUDING
YOURSELF

Saul W. Gellerman, Ph.D.

A DUTTON BOOK

DUTTON
Published by the Penguin Group
Penguin Books USA Inc., 375 Hudson Street,
New York, New York 10014, U.S.A.
Penguin Books Ltd, 27 Wrights Lane,
London W8 5TZ, England
Penguin Books Australia Ltd, Ringwood,
Victoria, Australia
Penguin Books Canada Ltd, 10 Alcorn Avenue,
Toronto, Ontario, Canada M4V 3B2
Penguin Books (N.Z.) Ltd, 182–190 Wairau Road,
Auckland 10, New Zealand

Penguin Books Ltd, Registered Offices:
Harmondsworth, Middlesex, England

First published by Dutton, an imprint of New American Library, a
division of Penguin Books USA Inc.
Distributed in Canada by McClelland & Stewart Inc.

First Printing, June, 1992
10 9 8 7 6 5 4 3 2 1

REGISTERED TRADEMARK—MARCA REGISTRADA

Library of Congress Cataloging in Publication Data
Gellerman, Saul W.
    Motivation in the real world : the art of getting extra effort
from everyone / Saul W. Gellerman.
        p.   cm.
    Includes index.
    ISBN 0-525-93468-5
    1. Employee motivation.   I. Title.
HF5549.5.M63G455   1992
658.3′14—dc20   91-38087
                                                            CIP

Printed in the United States of America
Set in Caledonia
Designed by Leonard Telesca

For Pat

CONTENTS

PART IV.

MOTIVATION IN THE REAL WORLD

Acknowledgments

This book could not have seen the light of day but for the efforts of four remarkable women, to all of whom I am deeply grateful:

My agent, Denise Marcil, had the vision to recognize the need for such a book, and both the persistence and the skill to find a publisher who shared that vision. She is also a fine writing coach.

My editor, Alexia Dorszynski, tactfully steered me away from several not-so-wise ideas which, mercifully, will not appear in print with my name on them, and toward a better integrated presentation of my ideas than I could have crafted myself.

My assistant, Peggy England, must surely be the world's most patient typist, as well as an ingenious decipherer of my interminable changes to the manuscript. She and I alone share the embarrassing secret of how many drafts each chapter had to go through before we finally got it into proper shape.

My wife, Pat, to whom this book is dedicated, was more than just my inspiration. She was also my initial editor. When I finally felt that a chapter was ready, she would take her blue pencil to it, mercilessly cutting out my unnecessary parentheses and semicolons, and making me conform to a cleaner writing style than I could have achieved myself. She is the reason why Alexia thinks I am a better writer than I am. She is also the light of my life.

The anecdotes in this book are drawn from my experiences as a consulting industrial psychologist. I must therefore also acknowledge my clients as the source of most of what I have learned about the ways in which people are actually motivated, and sometimes demotivated, in the real world.

S.W.G
Irving, Texas
1991

MOTIVATION
IN THE
REAL WORLD

PART I

THE
MOTIVES
INSIDE
PEOPLE

CHAPTER
—1—

WELCOME TO THE REAL WORLD

What managers like to call the "real world" is, quite simply, wherever work is actually done.

In that all-too-real managerial world, it is seldom very smart to follow simple formulas in your dealings with people, because the formulas hardly ever fit the facts. Nor does it help much to rely on abstract theories, because hardly anyone knows how to actually make them work.

In the real world, the work that people do is sometimes done superbly, but too often it is done atrociously. This book is about the main reason for that difference, which is motivation.

As a concept, motivation is much-abused, overused, and oversold. We're going to treat it here with great respect, the way a surgeon treats a beating heart, because so much depends on it. Motivation is what makes the difference between doing as little as you can get away with and doing everything that you possibly can.

We will define *motivation* here exclusively in terms of its effects on productivity. Motivation is the art of helping people to focus their minds and energies on doing their work as effectively as possible.

NOTE: Unless a pronoun refers to a specific individual, the use of masculine pronouns throughout this book should be understood as referring equally to women and to men.

If you're a manager, you have to motivate everyone, every day, every way that you can. You have to take into account just who those people are, what they are supposed to do, how they are paid, and with whom they have to work, to mention just a few of the things that motivate all of us. There is no motivational technique, simple or otherwise, that works with everyone. People are just too various for that, not to mention just too ornery.

In the real world, motivation is the art of creating conditions that allow every one of us, warts and all, to get his work done at his own peak level of efficiency. Individuals, companies, and countries that can do that consistently acquire enormous advantages over their competitors. The main purpose of this book is to deliver those advantages directly into your hands.

Beware of Bogus Motivation

This introductory chapter has two purposes. The first is to draw a clear distinction between real motivation and four familiar, but oversold, imitations. The second is to preview what you can expect to find in each of the eighteen chapters that follow this one.

In everyday language, *motivation* can mean anything from ballyhoo to bribery. In fact, there are four common misuses for that much-abused word: (1) pumping up enthusiasm; (2) making people happy (or at least, less likely to complain); (3) a few easily memorized formulas that allegedly make people either more reasonable or less ornery; or (4) plain old bribery.

The first three of those "definitions" are much too unrealistic to be useful. To prevent them from cluttering up our thinking, we'll demolish them right now. As for the fourth, we'll only touch on it here. That's because money is so much more complicated than it seems that we'll have to devote all of chapter 10 to it.

Now, for a brief, but hard, look at each of those bogus versions of motivation.

Pumping Up Enthusiasm

Have you ever heard a "motivational" speaker working a group of people into a state of cheering, yelling, arm-waving hysteria? The really good ones brim over with self-confidence as they assure you, in sincere and compelling tones, that if you "really" believed in yourself, you could really work miracles. Most adults would reject that message as childish, if they thought about it at all, because it amounts to little more than a naive claim that "wishing will make it so." But they don't usually think about it, because good inspirational speakers are spellbinders. Consequently, their delivery gets much more attention than their message.

Inspirational speakers can play on your emotions as deftly as any virtuoso ever played the violin. They can start your pulse racing, start the adrenaline squirting into your arteries, and pump up your blood pressure. They are *exciting!* That's why we hire them. But it's also why they are useless, especially if your real purpose is not merely to entertain but to actually boost productivity. The reason is simple: most people can't stand that kind of excitement for more than a few minutes, or at most a few hours. Otherwise they collapse.

When a good inspirational talk ends, most of us will be on our feet, jumping and shouting, caught up in the mass hysteria. But fifteen minutes later, most of us will have cooled off and calmed down. Aside from some pleasant memories, the effects of that allegedly "motivational" talk will have evaporated. That rapid return to normality is precisely where the problem lies. The effect of inspirational talks (or books, or films, or tapes) is just too brief to matter. It's a momentary high that is measured in minutes, not hours. But a manager needs a way to keep people motivated throughout an eight-hour day, which is thirty-two times longer than the average fifteen-minute high. What's more, a really effective manager needs to do that day after day after day. And if you tried to pump people that full of enthusiasm all day long, you'd need a full-time cardiologist to handle all the cases of heart failure you'd be causing.

THE FALSE ANALOGY OF FOOTBALL

Successful football coaches are sometimes asked to share their motivational secrets with business managers. Most of them rely on locker-room pep talks before the game, and again at halftime, inspiring their players in much the same way that inspirational speakers do at sales meetings. But we too easily forget that the coach and the manager face very different motivational challenges. The coach needs to get a supreme physical effort during two periods of thirty minutes each. That's all. What happens after the final whistle blows doesn't matter.

What usually happens is a letdown: not as quick for the winners as for the losers, but a letdown for both nonetheless. For the coach all that matters is that the letdown be postponed until *after* the final whistle. If it comes before the final whistle, all is lost.

But the comparison between football and business doesn't really hold up, because managers face an altogether different problem. For managers, there really is no final whistle. Yes, fiscal years end, and so do sales campaigns, but the next ones start almost immediately. What managers must do is to motivate not for a short-term burst of supreme effort but for a long-term streak of *sustainable* effort. Managers need to provide motivation that lasts for days, weeks, even years. If you'll pardon the pun, that's an altogether different ballgame. It calls for an altogether different game plan, too.

A manager's job, unlike a football coach's, is *not* to get people to play as hard as they can. That's because workers have to work much longer than players have to play. If people put the same effort into their work that football players put into their game, most of them would fall flat on their faces after a few hours, or at most after a few days.

Inspirational appeals can liven up an otherwise dull meeting. They're entertaining and they're fun. But that's about all they're good for. They're not motivational in any practical sense of that word. Inspirational speakers are cheerleaders, not motivators. And that is why you won't read any more about inspiration in this book.

Real motivation is much more than mere entertainment. It's more than antics on a lecture platform, more than bellowing into a microphone. Real motivation is the serious, never-ending task of creating conditions to which the natural response of ordinary people is to accomplish extraordinary things.

And who is a real motivator? Someone who knows which conditions have to be created in order to get that effect.

Making People Happy

The second bogus usage of the word *motivation* equates it with paternalism, generosity, and benevolence. Employers sometimes give people lots of things that they like in hopes of getting a *quid pro quo.* This is the Santa Claus approach to motivation: if we shower you with goodies, perhaps you'll do a little work for us in exchange. For example, we'll provide picnics and posters, discounts and dinners, subsidized cafeterias and supervisors who have been to charm school. We'll provide company newspapers and magazines, bowling leagues and softball teams, and even Christmas parties for the kids. The idea is to make employment fun.

But that isn't motivation. It's distraction. It's the same thing we do to hush crying children. Its real purpose, when it masquerades as motivation, is to make people less argumentative and hostile. That's why many companies strive to convince their employees that they've joined a big, happy family in which we all have lots of fun together.

The technique works pretty well, provided you use it as a supplement to real motivation, and not as a substitute for it. Real motivation is about making people productive, not about making them happy.

THE DAY THEY TOOK THE TURKEYS AWAY

My favorite story about the folly of trying to motivate people with benevolence concerns a man who owned a small manufacturing company during the Great Depression. One year, as Christmas approached, he decided to demonstrate his affection for his employees by presenting each of them with a turkey for their dinner. Altogether about one hundred turkeys were distributed, and in those desperate economic times the gesture was deeply appreciated.

One year later the personnel manager went to see the owner and asked the obvious question: "Shall we hand out turkeys again?" The owner probably did not understand the full implications of that question, because he gave his assent without much thought. After that, of course, the question did not have to be asked again, because the Christmas turkeys had been enshrined as a company custom.

Years passed. During World War II, the company grew into a major defense contractor. Its employees were numbered in the thousands, and so were its Christmas turkeys. After the war ended, the company continued to grow. Turkeys were now being distributed to tens of thousands of employees.

But attitudes toward the turkeys changed. Younger employees resented them as a symbol of paternalism. Older employees felt that the company could afford something more elegant and expensive.

Some employees felt slighted because their turkeys were smaller than those received by their colleagues.

Realizing that the custom had lost its meaning, management squirmed desperately to find a way out. On several occasions they stopped short of canceling it outright, fearing to seem ungenerous at Christmastime. One year they contracted with a chain of supermarkets to distribute the turkeys for them. But employees persuaded store managers to let them stock up on detergents or paper towels instead, or even to give them cash in exchange for their turkey vouchers. Finally, management acknowledged that the annual turkey distribution had lost its meaning, and canceled it. As they feared, a great hue and cry went up from the employees, many of whom complain to this day about "the day they took our turkeys away."

Of course, there's nothing wrong with trying to make people happy, by giving them turkeys or anything else, as long as you have no unrealistic expectations about being rewarded for it in return. If you're one of those managers who is happiest amid laughter and smiling faces, go to it. Just remember that a manager's job exists in the first place for an altogether different purpose. Managers exist to make people productive. That's why we'll say no more in this book about making people happy.

Motivational Cookbooks

The honest answer to all questions about whether any particular motivational technique really works always begins with the same two words: "It depends." Remember that. It will save you from being misled by attractively packaged recipes that will work only some of the time if at all.

Nothing works all the time. People are too varied and complicated for that. Instead, some techniques work some of the time. There's no magic to motivation, no miracles, no amazing results. Anyone who promises you any of these is either a naive fool or a con artist. Motivating people is hard work. It takes thought, attention to detail, know-how, and, perhaps most of all, flexibility.

Nevertheless, there are lot of simple "motivation" recipes. For example, the "sandwich" recipe for delivering criticism ("Slip in a thin slice of criticism between two thick slabs of praise"). Or the "family" formula for lubricating your working relationships ("Your work is awful, your attitude is rotten, and your future here is hopeless; but by the way, how is your wife?"). Or the "positive thinking" recipe, which encourages you to ignore mounting evidence that something is drastically wrong with your assumptions about some chronic mischief-maker. That's like beating your head against the wall in the serene hope that the wall will crack before your head does.

There are also some serious recipes. There is, for example, the "One-Minute Manager" formula: to motivate people, you let them know what you expect, that you'll praise them immediately for doing their work well, and that you'll reprimand them immediately for doing it badly. There's more to Blanchard and Johnson's recipe than this, of course. But the whole premise of their book is that following a simple set of rules with everyone will motivate them all.

As recipes go, this is one of the best. But does it work? The answer is, as always, "It depends." Among other things, it depends on whether the people you're trying to motivate have been selected so that their abilities are matched to their jobs, on how they've been trained, on how they are paid, on their prospects for advancement, and on how many of them are really tough to motivate.

If simple motivation formulas work only part of the time, why are they so popular? Precisely because they *are* simple. What makes them so attractive is that it's a tough world out there, full of people who march to different drumbeats. Some managers find that diversity scary, so they cuddle up to a recipe that is at least understandable, no matter how drastically it oversimplifies the truth.

Real motivators are not dismayed by differences between individuals, or by inconsistencies in the same individual. They thrive on it. They would rather give their minds a good workout than a good rest. That's why they don't need cookbooks, and it's also why you won't encounter any motivational recipes in this book.

Motivating with Bribery

The fourth bogus way to define motivation is as a purely economic transaction. We assume that effort is for sale and can be bought if the price is right. If that were true, and you wanted to motivate extra effort, all you would have to do is cross someone's palm with silver. Motivation would be a simple matter of haggling over the price, striking a bargain, and then making sure that the bargain was kept.

This is where economics and psychology get all tangled up with each other, so let's try to get them disentangled. Economic theory assumes that people act rationally in their own self-interest. Of course, most economists know enough about psychology to realize that this is a proposition that "ain't necessarily so." But trying to factor human irrationality in all its varied forms into an already complicated theory would make it too horrendously convoluted. Instead, economists assume that the effects of irrationality will come out in the wash, that my irrationality will be canceled out by yours. If that were true, economists could safely neglect both of us.

But the premise is not true. Most people are *not* irrational about money, but their logic is subtler than the logic of economists. Of course, most people wouldn't mind receiving more money, as long as they don't have to pay much for it in time, effort, risk, or forgone pleasures. That's why lotteries and other forms of cheap entertainment are so popular.

But there's a limit to how much people are willing to give up just to make more money. That's especially true if the extra money comes in relatively small amounts. To motivate people with money, you have to offer them a *very* good deal. Lots of extra money for a small increase in effort should do the trick. But that, of course, would be uneconomical for the motivator. And there you have the paradox.

The great irony in trying to use money as a motivator is that it is by far the most expensive and inefficient of all motivators. It takes a lot of money to buy a little extra effort. The limit on our ability to motivate with money is financial, not psychological. Money motivation just costs too damned much. It's as simple as that.

Money is a wonderful communicator, a great attention-getter, and an excellent recruiter. And, alas, it's an all-too-effective corrupter. But a great motivator it is not, and that's chiefly because of its cost. For the moment, just remember that money *alone* is not going to buy you a lot of motivation. We'll look at some more efficient ways of motivating with money later, in chapter 10.

What Motivates a Motivator?

A motivator knows how to get people to stop sitting on whatever they're sitting on and start doing what must be done. If you can do that, you'll have a big head start in the race for top jobs and the perquisites that go with them. Here's why: Most companies spend between 20 and 40 percent of their revenues on their own employees. That's their bill for wages, salaries, and benefits. Simple economics guarantees that if you can boost the return on that big an expense, you'll be singled out for favorable attention. If you can help other people to consistently put all the care, effort, and common sense into their work that they can, those people will build an eye-catching track record for you. Multiplying other people's effectiveness is a rare skill, and smart companies will gladly pay for it.

Good motivators tend to be well paid. But that's only one of the ways to motivate them, and it's rarely the most important. There's also the challenge of figuring out how to bring out the best in someone who's been turned off, or who was never turned on in the first place. There's the satisfaction of knowing that you've made a major difference in other people's lives. But perhaps most important, there's the simple fact that for some of us, motivating other people can be fun. When all is said and done, doing something because you like to do it is the best motivator of them all.

A Word About Words

It's time to sharpen our definition of *motivation* by distinguishing it from *motives* and *motivators*. These terms are not quite identical. The rest of this book is organized around the distinction between these three words, so now is the time to get it straight.

If we see you persistently seeking certain results, we assume that you want those results, and we call your desire for them a *motive*. If, for example, you are what is commonly called a workaholic, you have a motive to immerse yourself in work. No one has to create or arouse that motive, because it's already in you.

In addition to internal motives, there are also external forces that can influence your actions. We're going to call anything that is not part of you, but can affect your behavior, a *motivator*. Some motivators are inanimate, like money. Some people are motivators, although relatively few are good at it.

One of my motives in writing this book is to motivate you to master motivation. That is, I want you to want to learn how to get other people to do what you want them to do.

So much for semantics, at least for the moment. From time to time we'll have to invest a sentence or two spelling out the distinction between other definitions. But I promise to do that as rarely and as briefly as possible.

What Every Motivator Should Know

This book is divided into four parts, each of which looks at a different aspect of motivation. This and the three chapters following comprise part I, "The Motives Inside People." Part II, "The Motivators Outside People," will cover the main external motivators in the next seven chapters. (There's that distinction that we just emphasized.)

Then we'll tackle some of the more challenging motivational problems in the five chapters comprising part III, "The Hardest People to Motivate." Finally, in part IV, "Motivation in the Real World," we'll pull together all of the varied themes that are considered separately in the preceding chapters. To illustrate the way in which many motivators work together simultaneously, we'll include an in-depth look at one of the most successful motivation systems of modern times. Then we'll close with some answers to the toughest motivational challenge of them all: how to keep *yourself* motivated when all of the external motivators are working against you.

Now for quick previews of each chapter.

After this, part I continues with "Winners' Motives." We'll focus on two motives that are found chiefly in people who are likely to become effective leaders. The chapter will tell how to pick winners who can serve as your lieutenants, and how to be picked as a winner yourself.

That alternation—between motivating others and motivating yourself—recurs throughout the book. Sometimes the emphasis will be on you, the motivator of other people. Sometimes it will be on you, a unique individual with motives of your own. But whenever I'm about to switch from one emphasis to the other, I'll let you know.

The next chapter, "Survivors' Motives," focuses on two motives that drive practically all of us to at least some extent. Survivors' motives are the keys to winning the trust and confidence of those whom you would lead. It does not overstate the importance of these motives to say that if you don't know how to satisfy them, you'll be out of the motivation business before you start.

Chapter 4 is concerned with the three main "comfort motives." They are "what is left to want" after the survivors' motives have been well taken care of, as they usually are. They will round out our survey of motives that are deeply implanted in most of the people whom you might wish to motivate, long before your first chance to try your hand at it.

In part II we will look at seven external motivators.

In chapter 5 we consider communication, which is the vehicle for most attempts to motivate. This is notoriously easy to mismanage. The problem with communication is not that people don't listen well, or that they don't express themselves clearly. Rather, it is that good communication is inherently expensive, and management persistently tries to buy it on the cheap. The chapter will show you how to communicate well, even if you're not especially glib or articulate yourself.

The next two chapters deal with careers. Chapter 6 focuses on the most important career in the world, which is, of course, yours. We'll stress the importance of *managing* your own career, instead of leaving it to chance. The chapter highlights the four major phases of most careers, and what your strategy should be during each phase.

In chapter 7 we'll look at the management of other people's careers. That is usually the most powerful way to motivate the most effective people in most organizations. The chapter will give you some yardsticks by which to evaluate how well your present company, or any company you might be working for in the future, handles this vital function.

Chapter 8 is concerned with the most studied, most written about, but least understood aspect of motivation—leadership. This chapter will have to clear away a lot of mythology. The point to be grasped is that leadership is *not* a gift that certain people are blessed with while others are not. Instead, it's a special relationship that you can create between yourself and other people, under the right conditions. The chapter will spell out those conditions.

The ninth chapter is about the effect of jobs on motivation. Unfortunately, too many jobs just bore people to distraction, because the work can be done with little thought, or even with none at all. But certain kinds of jobs can motivate certain kinds of people. The trick is to give people work that stretches their talents. We'll offer some practical advice on how to do that.

In chapter 10 we consider that great icon of contemporary American life, money. It has been so overmythologized that the basic facts about it are no longer easy to find. We've already touched on the fundamental problem: money is too expensive to be a practical motivational tool for everyone. But under the right circumstances, money can be a far more effective motivator than it usually is. We'll explore both the problems and opportunities that money creates for motivators.

The eleventh chapter explores an almost universal ritual in large American companies, the performance appraisal. It usually gets an unenthusiastic reception from managers, because they consider it much too easy to mishandle. The position taken here is that those apprehensive managers are probably right, and that performance appraisal should be used with great discretion if at all.

We then turn to part III, in which we address certain people who present special motivational problems.

Chapter 12 is written primarily for someone who is not part of a minority group but has to motivate people who are. The chief problem in motivating minorities is for motivators themselves to make sure that their own attitudes toward minorities do not get in the way of their task. Consequently, this chapter will lead you into some candid self-examination.

Chapter 13 addresses people whose own motives make it difficult for other people to motivate them. These include alcoholics and drug abusers, the emotionally disturbed, and chronic absentees. You not only need to know what has to be done to motivate them, which is the easy part, but also how to motivate yourself to do what must be done, which is not so easy.

Chapter 14 addresses a common problem that hardly ever gets addressed: the bad boss. It's a hot potato that no one really wants to handle. That's a pity, because there are effective ways to handle a bad boss. But read the chapter before you sign up your own boss for the treatment. It will tell you what a bad boss really is, and is not.

The fifteenth chapter looks at the conflicts that often erupt between members of the same organization. Don't jump to the conclusion that all conflicts are bad. Some of them are actually good for the organization. The trick is to manage them. You want conflicts to produce the motivational effects you're looking for, but without hurting anyone seriously, or getting out of control.

Chapter 16 deals with a problem that is too often relegated to philosophy books, but really belongs in practical management books like this one. That is the problem of managerial misconduct, or more briefly, ethics. It is an important, overly preached about, much misunderstood problem. Perhaps the most important thing to be said about ethics is that it is a problem in motivation, not in morality.

That brings us to part IV, and the three chapters that try to pull together all of the separate strands that preceded them.

Chapter 17 introduces the concept of "motivation systems," which recognizes that in the real world, motivators act together rather than separately. This is where we'll consider what it takes to keep most Americans in top motivational condition. To understand how the people in a given company are being motivated, you have to look at all of the major motivators that are operating, and not just at the few that happen to interest you.

In Chapter 18, we do exactly that with regard to one of the most successful motivation systems of our time, namely IBM's. It presents a candid, in-depth, unauthorized, and uncensored view of how the premier growth company of our time motivates its almost one-quarter of a million people.

The final chapter was written especially for those awful periods of our lives when staying motivated does not come easily and we have nothing to rely on but our own inner resources. I've been there a few times, and I imagine you have, too. Knowing how to manage your own motivation can be the most valuable skill you ever acquire. Think of it as do-it-yourself lifesaving. Knowing how to motivate yourself is the first essential step, but not the only step, on the road to becoming an effective motivator of others.

That's what's in store for you in the rest of this book. Now, let's jump in and take a hard look at two very important motives. They are important for many reasons, not the least of which is that you probably have a pretty strong dose of both of them yourself. Otherwise you probably would not be reading this book in the first place!

CHAPTER
2

WINNERS' MOTIVES

If you've been out of school for at least a few years, you've probably noticed that your classmates have started to sort themselves out. Some have begun to pull away from the pack. They've advanced farther and faster than anyone else, into better-paying jobs that offer more promising futures. Some of your other classmates, however, have not kept up with the rest. They're having trouble getting started and are beginning to fall behind the pace set by the others.

But setting aside those two extremes, the great majority of the class are probably bunched pretty closely together and are performing more or less "as expected" for this stage of their careers. Because so much of the class fits between the leaders and the laggers, we can call them "the mass in the middle."

Here's what's likely to happen next. Most of those leaders will pull even farther ahead of the rest of the class, although a few of them will fall back into the mass in the middle. Some late bloomers will emerge from the mass to join, and even surpass, the early leaders. Later in this chapter, you'll learn who these come-from-behind winners are likely to be.

Meantime, at the lower end of the scale, a number of the slow starters will manage to pull themselves together. They'll move up into the mass, or occasionally even higher. And a few of those who had originally kept up with the mass will start to fall behind among the laggers. What you see taking shape is something approximating the familiar bell-shaped curve that you learned about in your statistics class. The most important thing to note about that curve is that it is probably *permanent*.

That's not as scary as it may seem. The fate of individuals is not sealed. Those of us who dare can still be the masters of our own destiny. But (and this *is* the frightening part) the fate of large groups is pretty much at the mercy of the laws of chance. It's a rare group that slips out of the iron grip of statistics and that awesome bell-shaped curve.

We see this, for example, in the sales records of stockbrokers, or in the revenues generated by management recruiters. After a break-in period, each of them assumes a position in the performance distribution relative to all of his colleagues and, with rare exceptions, doesn't vary much from that position. The actual dollar volumes produced will go up and down with the economy and other external factors, but relative positions will in most cases stay pretty much the same.

In this chapter we'll look at why that almost inexorable bell-shaped performance distribution defines the careers of most members of most groups. We'll also make some educated guesses as to who will lead, who will lag, and who will dwell in the mass in the middle. Finally, we'll answer the question you've probably been asking yourself since you began reading this chapter, which is how you can use this knowledge to your own advantage.

Brains and Schools Don't Matter

Let's begin by getting rid of some common assumptions that fall apart rather quickly when you stand them up against the facts. Some company's recruiters put a lot of emphasis on college grades and aim to do most of their hiring among the top 10 percent or the top quartile of the graduating class. But the only thing that college grades predict with any reliability is graduate school grades.

True, being admitted to certain schools in the first place, and managing to graduate from them, are hurdles that you have to get over to enter certain occupations. But the actual grades that students earn in those schools bear almost no relationship to their subsequent success, or lack of it. Top students do not necessarily stay ahead of the pack after they graduate. In fact, most of them will turn up in the mass in the middle.

The same thing is true of "intelligence," to the extent that we know how to measure it at all. Intelligence test scores are a pretty good predictor of school grades, but not much else. Once they are out of school, smart people do not necessarily surpass ordinary people, or even dumb people, in the race for income, power, and position. Some intellectuals profess to see a great injustice in this, as if the economy should reward people for their ability. Fortunately, the economy rewards accomplishments, not ability.

It's true that you will find some very bright people in executive suites. But you will also find them among plateaued middle managers who are unlikely to rise any higher, and even among those who never made it to the first rung of the executive ladder. You will also find very successful executives at senior levels who are nowhere near brilliant, and whose academic records were at best mediocre. This is not really a paradox, except to those who have fallen for the demonstrably false notion that the brains we were born with and the schools that we went to completely determine our futures.

The quality of your mind and of your schooling are unimportant except to the extent that you apply them both in a focused, persistent way. Those two qualities—focus and persistence—are all that really distinguish the leaders from the laggers and, for that matter, from the mass in the middle. *Focus* is the extent to which you can concentrate everything inside your head—your attention, your memory, your accumulated wisdom, and above all, your creativity—on what must be done. *Persistence*, in this sense, is an unreserved commitment to give the task whatever time it takes to do it in the way it should be done.

Those otherwise unremarkable people in the executive suite, who have to call on more articulate people to write their speeches for them and on more scholarly people to dig up the information they need for their decisions, have earned their positions at the top of the executive hierarchy through focus and persistence. Let's look at how you can out-accomplish people who may be more gifted than you, and better educated than you, mainly by focusing whatever abilities you have more persistently and effectively than they focus theirs. Then we'll discuss how we can predict which people are most likely to develop those two vital qualities.

More About Motives

Psychologists have a deceptively simple answer to the first question. They'll tell you that those who use their abilities more efficiently than everyone else have different "motives" than the rest. More precisely, they'll explain that those who achieve the most have a strong dose of certain motives. Further, that nearly everyone else possesses those motives to a much smaller degree, if indeed they show any trace of them at all.

That may sound like a neat explanation. But when you dig into it you'll find that instead of explaining, it merely describes, in different terms, what we already know: that some people are persistently more successful in their work than everyone else.

The truth is that motivation is a bit of a mystery. Most people, even if they're being totally candid, can't give a clear or convincing account of what they're up to, or why they've done what they've done. And we can't really peer into another person's head to see what's going on there. Instead we have to infer the reasons for behavior from behavior itself. So when we see someone repeatedly acting in ways that usually lead to a certain result, we draw the common-sense conclusion that this result is what that person really wants. And that's all we really mean by a "motive." It's a psychologist's way of saying that most people, most of the time, probably get what they want. Not necessarily what they deserve, or what's good for them, but what they want.

Can that be true? What about people who consistently fail? Can that really be what they "want"? The short answer is: yes. A somewhat longer answer will be given in chapter 13, in which we'll discuss some of life's losers, and how you can motivate them. This chapter, however, is about winners.

What motivates winners? Winning, of course. But there are two kinds of winners. Those who thrive on their own accomplishments are motivated by a process that occurs inside their own heads. It consists of setting and then pursuing their own goals. We call that process the "achievement motive." Those who thrive on getting others to pursue greater-than-usual goals are motivated by their ability to invigorate others. We call that process the "power motive." We know a lot about both of these "winners' motives."

Achievers' Motives

If you have a strong achievement motive, these would be some of your attributes: You have learned, mainly through trial and error, just where the limits of your *controllable* accomplishments lie. And that's where you set your goals. Not so high that you'd need to be lucky to get what you want, because achievers are not gamblers. Not so low that winning would be a cinch, because there's no satisfaction in an easy win. But high enough that you're going to have to use every trick you know to achieve it.

What's more, you've become an achievement addict. You're constantly setting goals for yourself, even when you're not working. You are so focused on them that some friends may think of you as single-minded. And once you accomplish whatever you were after, you just set another goal and take off after it. After a while, you accumulate a long string of tough tasks that you've undertaken and accomplished.

Another characteristic: you like to know how well you're doing. You tend to choose occupations, such as sales, in which the results are self-evident. You're willing to go after long-term goals, but along the way you like to have some proof that you're not on a wild goose chase. That's why you're very demanding of your bosses. You want them to be up to date on what you're doing, to evaluate it, and to tell you candidly what they think of your work. You're not particularly interested in being patted on the back. What you're looking for is information that will help you get where you're headed.

So the four most reliable earmarks of a strong achievement motive are: setting tough but attainable goals; pursuing them relentlessly; restarting the cycle whenever a goal is achieved; and hunting for reliable indications that you're on the right track. Next, let's look at the kinds of careers in store for most achievers. You may be in for some surprises.

The Fate of Achievers

People who have strong achievement motives move out of the starting gate *fast*. That's because they're already in the habit of going all out in pursuit of demanding goals. That pattern dates back at least to their teen years, and probably even earlier. Their work has been important to them for a long time, and it shows in their tendency to become preoccupied with it.

They make *very* efficient use of their time and their abilities. As a result, their performance records are usually spectacular, easily outstripping those of nearly everyone else. They come to management's attention quite early in the game and are likely to be earmarked as high-potential candidates for rapid advancement. This is why it is not unusual for them to garner two or even three promotions before their colleagues in the mass in the middle have had their first.

But that fast head start may not carry them very far. Here's why: people with strong achievement motives can get much more done by themselves than most other people can. Consequently, they learn to rely only on themselves and not on others. They become great proponents of that old saw, "The only way to be sure that something is done right is to do it yourself." While that kind of self-reliance may not seem harmful to their careers, in an insidious way it sets a limit on their potential for promotion.

At first, achievers flourish in lower-level managerial jobs, because at that level their own know-how and efficiency can compensate for any inefficiency among their subordinates. But as they rise higher up the management ladder, they acquire more and more subordinates in the chain of command. And increasingly, more and more of those subordinates will be unmotivated, for the simple reason that nobody is motivating them. They'll be nonperformers.

Eventually, even the most prodigious achiever finds it impossible to offset the nonperformance of all of the unmotivated people in the groups that report to him. The problem, of course, is that people with strong achievement motives are so good at motivating themselves that they seldom bother learning how to motivate anyone else. If you put a highly motivated achiever in a leadership role, you run a risk that his self-absorption and single-mindedness will alienate, and even demotivate, most of his subordinates. This is why achievers as managers tend to breed nonachievers as subordinates.

Sooner or later, management comes to realize that this particular star performer has been doing most of his department's work himself and has gained little or no leverage over the performance of the rest of the people in the department. Of course, managers are not hired to *do* other people's work. Managerial jobs exist in the first place to amplify the value of what other people get done. So we've encountered a paradox here: to be highly motivated oneself is no guarantee at all of being able to motivate other people effectively.

The manager's superiors will have a simple solution to the problem. They'll just give him no more assignments in which motivating subordinates matters very much. There may be interesting, well-paid assignments with lots of professional or technical challenges, but they do not offer much more movement up the management ladder.

And this is where another ironic twist is likely to occur. People with strong achievement motives tend to be ultra-realists. They'll read the tea leaves for themselves, and see that their upward movement is stalled. It has probably also dawned on them by now that the only way to get rich on a corporate payroll is to rise to the top. With that path blocked, they might as well try the other royal road to wealth, which is self-employment. So they become entrepreneurs, and start businesses of their own. These ventures are likely to thrive, at least during the launch phase, because achievers will put in incredibly long hours and apply the full force of their prodigious capacity for work. As the enterprise grows, however, they will once again run into their own limits as motivators. At this point, they'd be well advised to call in a professional manager to run the business for them. Their best choice would be someone with a strong *power* motive.

The Power Motive

Here comes another brief detour into semantics. The "power motive" was misnamed when it was first discovered, but the misnomer has stuck and it's too late to change it now. *Power* suggests compelling people to work, which is something that any idiot with a whip would be able to do. What is actually involved here, however, is finesse.

If you have a strong power motive, you like to orchestrate the work of others. You've learned that by far the easiest way to do that is to do it subtly, by eliminating obstacles to cooperation and by creating conditions in which collaborative work comes naturally. You have become a self-taught deal maker. You've mastered the art of finding out what others want, and then finding ways to give that to them—*provided*, of course, that in return they give you what you want.

It takes a while to learn this elegant art. But those who master it acquire a huge advantage. They can multiply the effect of their own abilities many times over by enlisting the abilities of everyone they can influence. The necessity of going through that "apprenticeship" phase is why managers with a strong power motive get off to a slower start than their colleagues with strong achievement motives. But eventually it's the people with strong power motives who are likely to surpass the frontrunners and then climb all the way to the top of the management ladder.

Individuals with strong achievement motives are masters at motivating themselves, while those with strong power motives are masters at motivating others. The achievements of those who can motivate themselves are ultimately limited by the boundaries of their own abilities, but the achievements of those who can motivate others are limited only by the number of people they have an opportunity to influence.

A word of caution is in order here. The distinction we have drawn between these two motives is a little too glib. The real world isn't divided into people with achievement motives, people with power motives, and people with neither. You occasionally run into people who carry a good strong dose of *both* motives in their makeup. They tend to be the really big winners. What's more, even if you are not heavily endowed with these motives yourself, it's possible to teach yourself to do the things that come naturally to those who are well endowed with them.

That may be exactly why you're reading this book. In that case, bear in mind that becoming a better motivator is really no different than learning to play a decent game of tennis (or golf, or whatever) even if you are not a natural athlete. All that it takes is lots of focus and persistence. But—and this is a big *but*—neither of them is abundant. You have to supply your own.

That's why, in the real world, we encounter something on the order of 10 percent who have really strong achievement motives, somewhat fewer who have strong power motives, and fewer still who have plenty of both. As for the rest, their productivity depends largely on how wisely they are managed. We're going to take a good hard look at them in the two chapters following this one.

Why That Bell-shaped Curve Forms

The curve describing the usual distribution of performance is a direct result of the relative scarcity of self-motivation. That quality is concentrated disproportionately among those with strong achievement motives and power motives. People who are abundantly endowed with those motives are likely to pull ahead of the pack almost regardless of what is or is not done to motivate them. Thus the upper end of the performance distribution, which is usually displayed on the right side of the chart, will show that small group running ahead of all the rest. That small, self-propelled group will probably outperform the rest of the pack, and by a considerable margin.

Meantime, at the left end of the chart, the weakest performers in the group will be trailing behind the pack. These laggers will usually include three kinds of people. Some of them will simply be in over their heads and should really be reassigned to something less demanding. Some of them will be marginal performers whose records have not been searchingly assessed, mostly because it

LAGGERS   THE MASS IN THE MIDDLE   WINNERS

THE BELL-SHAPED CURVE OF PERFORMANCE

would embarrass management to do so. Some will be people whose own motivation is rather marginal and who have not been effectively motivated by management.

In times of severe financial stringency, management reluctantly comes to grips with the difficulties that these people present. In the absence of such pressure, it is easier to overlook or tolerate the problems that they create than it is to address them. That's why a budgetary crunch can actually make a company stronger; it forces management to confront issues it could previously afford to ignore.

Strictly speaking, the performance curve is seldom really bell-shaped. Instead, it will be skewed a bit toward the high-performance end of the scale. That's because of preselection and attrition. Not everyone who applied was hired, and most of the truly disastrous failures have already been culled out. Nevertheless, the analogy of the bell curve isn't bad at all. You'll have a minority of leaders who outperform the rest, a smaller minority of laggers bringing up the rear, and the majority clustered together between the two extremes.

What we have to do now is to explain the motivation of the mass in the middle. From a motivational standpoint, they are by far the most important group, for two reasons. First, it's the group you'll be dealing with most of the time, if only because that's where most people are. Second, if you want to improve a *group's* performance, this is the only group that deserves your attention. The leaders are already running as hard as they can without your motivational help. The laggers call for an administrative, not a motivational, cure. So the mass in the middle is where your best motivational opportunity lies.

The Mass in the Middle

How does someone wind up performing pretty much the same as everyone else? We've already noted that job performance is not so much a matter of your abilities as of *how hard you are accustomed to working your abilities.* So the key question is, how does that "custom" form? It's partly learned and partly an adaptation by the individual and the company to each other.

First, let's look at the learned part. During the first few months on a new job, you learn more than just methods and routines. You also learn the job's gain-to-pain ratio. On the gain side, you'll discover whatever rewards come with success. That's more than just keeping your job and receiving your pay. It also includes having your ego massaged. You'll feel capable and confident because of your successes. On the pain side, there's the toll that the job exacts from you, in terms of pressure, exertion, and fear of failure.

You tend to set your effort level at the point where gain and pain are in rough balance. You learn not to pursue opportunities for success beyond the point where they seem to be outweighed by the risk of failure. This is why the first few months on a job are critically important. Coaching by seasoned "old hands" can be very helpful at this stage. After a few months, however, the habits are set.

This is where mutual adaptation (of the company and the employee to each other) enters the picture. The company tends to set its standards at levels that most employees can meet. The employees tend to set their effort levels in a "comfort zone" within those standards, with goals they can meet without having to risk much pain. The company tolerates these levels of performance, and the employees tolerate the rewards and the pressures they experience at those levels.

What you get is a standoff. Even though greater rewards could be had if the employees were to toil a bit harder, they won't because it won't seem worth it. They're comfortable with what they can earn without straining themselves. Therefore it would take a much greater reward to make any added strain seem worth enduring.

The mass in the middle fills up with the majority of any group because the critical early months on the job are left to chance. That's why we get a performance distribution that approximates a bell-shaped curve. Mathematically speaking, a bell-shaped curve simply depicts an unmanaged, uncontrolled, *chance* distribution. Am I saying that most organizations and managers leave the development of most employees' motivation to chance, by letting them sink or swim during their first few months on a new job? Yes, I am.

What would happen if we concentrated all available resources on coaching all employees during their first few critical months on a new assignment? You'd still get a bell-shaped performance distribution. But it would be a lopsided bell: a lot narrower, and shifted heavily toward the high side.

Would that narrower, lopsided performance distribution be

worth that massive, one-time investment? You bet it would, because the payoff would continue for as long as those people held those jobs.

How to Pick Winners

The next two sections are written for you, the motivator.

The higher you rise in an organization, the more you're going to have to depend on your lieutenants. You'll need people you can rely on to carry out your decisions, and whose standards of performance are as high as yours. You'll need sharp, savvy people who can keep you up to date on what you need to know.

As you start to move up yourself, keep your eyes peeled for other winners whom you can gather around you some day to form an unbeatable team. Only a weak manager would regard such people as competitors. A strong manager regards them as potential allies, and thus wants to help them get ahead.

Picking winners is an art, not a science. That's because the most important data is subjective. Those who advance in a company, and for that matter, those who don't advance, do so on the basis of the *impressions* they make on their superiors. Performance records may bring you to their attention, but what convinces most decision makers is your ability to make them feel secure. They have to decide whether to bet the company's fortunes, and their own reputations, on you. For them, that's a very intestinal decision. It's not cerebral at all.

However, it isn't an altogether subjective process, either. Let me share an experience with you, to illustrate my point. Years ago, a marketing director for one of my client companies made an impassioned presentation to the CEO. He was convinced that the company faced a once-in-a-lifetime opportunity, and he wanted a major commitment of funds. "Prove it," growled the CEO. "Show me your facts."

"Boss," said the marketing director, "there are no facts, because this is all too new. But I've been in this business for thirty years. And I've got this *gut feeling*. I've never felt so certain in my life!"

The CEO stood, glared at the marketing director, and snapped, "Now, get this straight. If we're going to run this company with viscera, it's going to be with *my* viscera and nobody else's. Get out, and don't come back without some facts!"

The CEO's point, of course, was that you use facts and logic to screen out the alternatives that aren't worth considering. Once you've narrowed the choices down to a few that can stand up under analysis, you make your choice from among them by using your intuition. That doesn't mean that intuition is superior to logic. It only means that we all have to be able to sleep at night, and intuition is a surer guide to whatever makes you feel secure than logic could ever be.

The same mixed logical-and-instinctive process is used in choosing people for critically important jobs. There are two variations: the external approach, used by executive recruiters; and the internal approach, used by sophisticated personnel departments. You can adapt elements of both to your own continuing search for future members of your own winning team.

When executive recruiters are asked to conduct a search, they first create a pool of qualified candidates. The more candidates there are in that initial pool, the better. That's because the chances that the pool includes some real winners increase as the pool itself expands. However, that's only true if demanding standards are used to qualify candidates for the pool. Top-flight job performance is taken for granted. What the recruiters look for is something that *distinguishes* an individual from other top performers. So they'll look for someone who has caught the eye of knowledgeable peers. They'll ask as many well-informed people as they can speak with to propose individuals who really know their stuff. Then they'll check those names out with other sources.

What they're looking for is a *consensus*. They want candidates who are highly regarded by their fellow professionals. Only after they create a pool of such well-esteemed people do they begin to narrow it down, trying to figure out which will have the most intuitive appeal to the executives of their client company.

To use a baseball analogy, good executive recruiters are like good batting practice pitchers. The objective is to throw a pitch that the batter can hit. Similarly, the recruiter wants to present the client with a small group of candidates who are all likely to handle the job well. That way, it doesn't matter which one of them the client intuitively prefers.

Intuition is usually right about whether you're going to feel comfortable working with someone. But your intuition about that person's job performance is not nearly as reliable. That's why recruiters use a "best of both worlds" approach: facts and logic to identify the "short list" of qualified candidates, and intuition to determine whether there's a compatible match between them and the key players in the client company.

Applying the Laws of Human Nature

Internal searches can be terribly haphazard. Usually, a few trusted confidants of the decision maker are asked to nominate candidates. Not surprisingly, they nominate people who have impressed them favorably, or of whom they've heard good things said by people whom they trust.

It really does pay to come to the attention of these trusted "gatekeepers," if that's the kind of system your company uses. But I hope it isn't, because it's worse than unfair. It's inefficient. It doesn't capitalize on two tremendous assets that any large organization has in abundance.

A few paragraphs back I mentioned "sophisticated" personnel departments. Those are the ones that not only understand the laws of human nature but also know how to apply them. The two "laws" that matter most, as far as picking winners is concerned, are these:

1. *The behavior of mature adults is reasonably consistent.* That means that if you know someone's history for the past few years in some detail, you can make some educated guesses about the way that person will handle similar situations in the next few years.

2. Because of that consistency, most of us have a behavioral "signature." That's a set of qualities that defines us as individuals, and distinguishes us from everyone else. *If we ask enough observers to define that signature for a given individual, we can eventually discern a consensus among those descriptions.*

Beyond a certain point, adding more observers does not change the consensus. That consensus is the best available forecast of how someone who may never have seen that individual would describe him, after having had an adequate opportunity to look him over.

In other words, our behavior is more or less consistent over periods of at least a few years. So are the impressions that we make on those who see us in action. If you put those two kinds of information together, you can make a well-educated guess about how someone will fare in the next few years, provided only that the situations in which they'll be operating won't be terribly different from those in which we've seen them until now.

That's why a sophisticated personnel department compiles detailed histories on the people in whom it takes an interest. The detail you want is seldom on paper, but it *is* in people's heads. You look up as many people as possible who've seen your candidate in action. You don't ask them for adjectives, but for verbs. You want to know what that person did: what problems he faced, what methods he used, what the results were.

In that way, you compile a comprehensive record of that person's recent performance. What's more, you look at that record through as many pairs of eyes as you can enlist for this purpose. That's because the more observers you get, the more likely you are to see that all-important consensus emerging.

The most valuable information for picking winners is dispersed among the many people who've already seen them in action. That's why you want to garner as many views as you can of the people in whom you take an interest. You have to be discreet about this, of course. But if you know how to listen hard while keeping a poker face, you can actually learn more from casual comments than you ever could from answers to direct questions.

A question gives away your interest and distorts your respondents' answers by putting them on their best behavior. So the trick is to listen to everything, write down (or record) what you want to remember as soon as you are alone, and above all, avoid doing anything that might inhibit your sources from telling you more.

One of the best mentors I ever had made that point graphically to me years ago, when I was just starting my career. "Son," he said, "the good Lord gave you two ears and one mouth, and He probably intended that you would use them in that ratio."

Being Picked as a Winner Yourself

This section is written for you, the manager of your own career, with full responsibility for satisfying your own ambitions.

If your superiors decide to recommend you for promotion, they'll be betting their reputations on you. If you want them to take that big a risk, it goes without saying that your job performance has to be outstanding. But outstanding performance in itself isn't enough.

That point is so important that it's almost impossible to overemphasize. I've counseled more disappointed promotion seekers than I can count who complained that they felt betrayed. They'd played by the rules, done a great job, and then were patted on the head and passed over for promotion.

To make sure that doesn't happen to you, remember this: doing your job well is only the beginning of an effective campaign to promote your own promotion. There are at least three other things you have to do. First, you must distinguish yourself from all of the other good performers. Second, you must become known outside the immediate context of your job. Third, and perhaps most important of all, you must learn how to manage your luck.

To distinguish yourself, you have to be recognized for something *other* than just doing your job well. You have to make it clear that you're not just another great (insert your present job title). You have to demonstrate that you're a broad-gauge individual who can do a lot of things well. The important thing is to avoid being stereotyped by your present job.

That's precisely what happens to most of the people in any line of work, including many of those who outperform the rest. Management is delighted to have a lot of solid, reliable, steady performers whom it can take for granted and forget about. You mustn't let that happen to you. If you have a strong interest outside your job, make it known. If you don't have such an interest, develop one and make it known. If you have a skill that your job doesn't utilize, make it known. Get involved with groups that give you a chance to excel off the job. It could be a theatrical group, an athletic team, a barbershop quartet, local politics, anything. The important point is to do something *besides* your job very well, and not to keep it a secret. If you can, star in more than one off-the-job activity, all the while keeping your job performance up to top-notch standards. You want to create the impression that you can outshine everybody in anything you set your mind to. That kind of impression gets around. It makes decision makers sit up and take notice.

Next, make sure that your reputation isn't confined to the part of the company in which you work. Get to know people in as many other departments or divisions as you can. Nearly everyone takes a break for lunch, so use that time to get widely acquainted. A side benefit is that you'll soon be able to speak knowledgeably about the world beyond your own little department. But the main advantage is that you'll be networking. The more people you know, the more people you can meet through them.

You needn't seek out the powerful or the influential. You want as many people as possible to know you and have a high opinion of you. After a while, that reputation will precede you. Even those who haven't met you yet will know that you are highly regarded. That kind of reputation will get to the powerful and influential by itself. They're always looking for *potentially* powerful and influential people who can join them.

Finally, how do you manage luck? Louis Pasteur once said, "Chance favors the prepared mind." By definition, luck is purely random and eventually presents each of us with roughly the same number of good and bad breaks. What is not random, however, is the ability to move quickly to exploit a lucky break, or the ability to limit the damage caused by misfortune. That calls for alertness, and above all, for knowing the difference between a golden opportunity and an opening that probably leads nowhere. So you can, in a sense, make yourself lucky.

Managing your luck is especially important with regard to job opportunities. You should prepare for these the way a good infielder readies himself for a ball that may or may not be hit toward him. The infielder thinks through what he should do if the ball comes high or low, to the left or the right, so he will not have to think as the ball races toward him.

Similarly, you think through the things you should look for, the questions you should ask, the minimum limits of acceptability, *before* that opportunity presents itself. A decision that can critically affect the rest of your career is much too important to be made impulsively. If you think through the critical parameters of that decision before you have to face it, you'll know whether to leap at that opportunity when it presents itself, or bide your time patiently, waiting for a better break.

Nothing is guaranteed in this life (except, of course, death and taxes). But if you plan your advancement strategy around these principles, you'll be tilting the odds in your favor. And in the long run, the odds favor those who make the odds.

The next two chapters are concerned with the motives you'll have to learn to work with in your subordinates. We'll return to the question of motivating winners in chapters 6 and 7, which deal with careers.

CHAPTER
3

SURVIVORS' MOTIVES

For all the ballyhoo that we lavish on success, most people pursue it only fitfully, if at all. The relatively few success addicts among us are those who carry a strong dose of the achievement motive and/or the power motive. As for the rest, most would welcome success if it fell on them, but they are not about to put much effort into pursuing it. That's one reason why gambling is so popular.

The mass in the middle, and for that matter, the laggers as well, have other priorities. Their relative lack of desire for success does not make them inferior; it just makes them different. They have to be motivated externally if they are to be productive, because their own motives point them toward other ends. You probably have a very different set of motives than they do. Nevertheless, these are the people who get most of the world's work done. Therefore, you can't be an effective manager unless you know how to motivate them. To do that, you have to learn to respect those who, unlike you, ask relatively little from life.

The wise motivator does not disdain those whom he would motivate. Here's why: unless you've missed your calling, and should really be on the stage, scorn shows. No one likes being put down. That only invites retaliation, usually in the form of doing as little as possible of what you want them to do.

If you can't respect the people whom you would motivate, you'd better fix your own attitude toward them *before* you try to motivate them. Disrespect defeats the motivator's purpose. That's especially important when we consider the question of motivating minorities, which we'll look at in detail in chapter 12.

How can you motivate people to get their work done well, when their priorities may not include getting work done at all? Rest assured, it can be done. You have to find out what they want and find ways to give that to them, provided that in return they give you what you want. In other words, it's a swap, but of a much more subtle kind than merely trading money for labor. You have to make their work into an instrument for getting what they want. And most people want a great deal more out of life than just money.

There are six common motives that tend to be stronger, both among the mass in the middle and the laggers, than either the achievement or power motives. These are the likeliest candidates for what they (the mass in the middle) want. We'll divide those motives into those that are concerned with economic survival, which we'll deal with in this chapter, and those that are concerned with comfort, which will be the subject of the next chapter.

The survival motives include security, dependency, and conformity. To understand how these motives work, brace yourself for an encounter with the irrational aspect of human nature. Are you ready? Here goes. The security-motivated individual conjures, *out of thin air*, a benevolent entity (or person) that is powerful enough, and committed enough, to protect him against whatever he fears most, come what may.

The truth is that it's a cold, scary world out there, and many people find these inventions indispensable for preserving their sanity. In the case of the security motive, that protective entity is "the company," or, more generally, any unfailing source of cash. In the case of the dependency motive, the protector is anyone who will relieve you of the necessity of making decisions. In the case of the conformity motive, the protector is a group of people like you, to whom you can attach yourself.

Such notions of safety are all pure fiction, of course, but that doesn't stop people who are driven by these motives from taking these inventions for granted, or from acting as if they were real. That's why the realistic motivator can't afford to ignore them. These inventions are, so to speak, the mental road maps with which the people whom you would motivate are trying to navigate their way through life.

Before jumping in to analyze these motives, one more *caveat* is in order. Virtually everyone shows at least a trace of all these motives. (That's right: even you and me.) However, in any given individual, some motives are typically emphasized more than others. And that's all that we really mean by a "motive": a recognizable tendency to give some goals priority over others, regardless of whether they are rational or something else. The people we'll be describing here differ from you and me only in that they have a stronger dose of the survival motives, and probably a weaker dose of winners' motives, than we do. The difference is only a matter of degree.

The Security Motive

You probably did not grow what you will eat for dinner tonight, or stitch together the shirt on your back, or nail down the roof over your head. Instead, you bought those necessities from people who grow, stitch, and nail for a living.

That's why cash flow is indispensable for survival. It doesn't matter whether it comes from a paycheck, a welfare check, a commission, a dividend, or your rich uncle's legacy. One way or another, we all need a reliable source of cash with which to pay our bills. The security motive is all about making sure that your economic lifeline is firmly fastened to a steady source of cash.

There are few comforts in life more reassuring than the on-time arrival of a check. It's so reassuring that as long as our cash arrives on schedule, we prefer to take it for granted. On the other hand, there are few miseries worse than not knowing where your next check will come from. That's why, if your cash flow is inadequate, or threatened, or, worst of all, cut off, your security motive will probably vault right over all of the others to become your number-one priority.

When their security motive is agitated, most people have trouble concentrating on their work, or, for that matter, on anything else. That's why salaries, pensions, and even union contracts had to be invented. They are all devices for ensuring that you won't suddenly find yourself cut off from a steady supply of cash. If your security motive is stirred up, the best way, and perhaps the only way, to get your attention again would be to offer you a plausible new way to guarantee your cash flow.

Your security motive is a creature of extremes. It is either a berserk monster or a lovable pet. If it is threatened, it acts like an enraged beast, angrily shoving all other motives out of its way. But if it's satisfied, it cuddles up in the corner like a teddy bear, and just hibernates, sometimes for years. Obviously, most of us would prefer to let the beast hibernate. So we play games with ourselves about how "secure" we really are.

That's why "psychological contracts" crop up in the back of many people's minds. These are inferences, usually backed by nothing more than wishful thinking, that one's cash flow is somehow guaranteed. The so-called guarantee is nowhere but in their heads. It is not on paper and would never stand up in court. Nevertheless, in their minds it has the force of a real contract, because as long as they believe it to be real, the beast sleeps peacefully in its corner.

Typically, a psychological contract takes the form of a belief that "the company" will look after you, come what may. If you have the good fortune to live your entire life during peaceful, prosperous times, free of mergers, acquisitions, and bankruptcies, your company may very well do exactly that.

But you and I do not live in such times. That's why psychological contracts are too often the prelude to personal tragedy. They leave the individual defenseless and devastated when the company can't, or won't, live up to its part of the unspoken "bargain."

If they are so dangerous, why do people conjure up these fictitious contracts in the first place? Because the truth about economic security is just too stark for most people to contemplate. The unspoken, unwritten "contract" is a refuge, pure and simple: a place to hide from the appalling fact that life is really a great deal riskier than many of us care to acknowledge.

The Truth About Security

As we head into the last years of the twentieth century and the beginning of the twenty-first, we see more and more companies downsizing by getting rid of older employees, because they are paid more than younger ones. We see more and more companies trying to wriggle out of their pension commitments, because the cost of funding them has turned out to be staggering. For those who are already older, this comes as an awful shock. For those who are not yet older, it has rather dismaying implications.

The truth is that *your only real security lies in preserving the marketability of your talents.* This fact of life has two important implications. For yourself, it means that you should *always* keep your skills sharply honed, your contacts well cultivated, and your eyes open for better opportunities. You should never fall into the trap of assuming that anyone, or any organization, no matter how well meaning or benevolent, has entered into a psychological contract with you. You are by far your own best friend when it comes to preserving your economic security. We'll have more to say about this when we discuss career motivation in chapter 6.

People differ in their ability to cope with that hard, cold fact. Therefore you can't treat all of them alike. For those who are tough enough to contend with an awakened beast, your best approach is along these lines: "If the lifeboat sinks, it's going to be every man for himself. So let's all do all we can to keep it afloat." For those whom that harsh reality would terrify and immobilize, your best approach would be something like this: "This is a stout ship, and our captain is an expert sailor. So let's all pull steadily on the oars, and the captain will bring us out of this all right, just as he always has."

This double prescription raises two questions. With any given individual, how can you tell which approach would be best? And isn't that second approach deceptive, and therefore manipulative and unethical?

Gauging someone's ability to cope with heavy stress is always a judgment call. If you have seen that person deal with rough times in the past, you have at least some notion of how he might react to another time of troubles. Otherwise, you're thrown back on your intuition. Unfortunately, for most people, "intuition" is nothing more than a glorified guess. That's why the best advice on how to use your intuition is to use it conservatively. When in doubt, don't do anything rash. That means that with most people, most of the time, you're going to be reassuring them about how stout the ship is. That's a lot smarter than spreading anxiety among those who might be panic-prone.

But isn't that deceptive?

Not unless the ship is in imminent danger of sinking. There's nothing to be gained, and a lot to lose, by getting security-minded people unnecessarily alarmed. Scaring the hell out of them for no better reason than a short-term productivity gain *is* manipulative and unethical. Keeping their emotions well below the panic point, when there's nothing imminent to be panicky about, is not manipulation. It's responsible management.

Of course, if the risk of real disaster (bankruptcy, for example, or a plant shutdown) has increased from merely "possible" to "probable," they'd be better off alarmed and agitated than they would be if you left them in blissful ignorance. But until and unless the company's fortunes really start to plunge, keep them rowing calmly and steadily. That may even help to stave off the plunge.

MANAGING A LAYOFF

Some problems have no painless solutions, and managing a layoff is a good example. It's an exercise in damage control. You try to minimize the harm to both the employees and the company, but you can't fully protect either. There are various ways to do it, but some are more elegant than others.

Several years ago, a defense contractor on the West Coast completed a major government contract and was unable to replace it with another. Several hundred workers became redundant. The company could transfer some of them to other projects, but most would have to be let go. So an excruciating decision had to be faced: precisely who could stay, and who would have to leave?

In this instance, the employees were not unionized, so management was not obliged to dismiss the least-senior workers first. The only advantage of seniority is that it is entirely objective and thus eliminates the possibility of favoritism in decision making. Management recognized that if seniority was not used as a basis for selecting who would stay and who would leave, judgments would have to be made. And judgments, of course, can always be challenged by those who are not judged as they might wish to be.

Management decided to turn the decision over to those who would be directly affected. The employees were asked to discuss the matter among themselves and to assign a "priority number" to everyone. The only restriction was that management would only accept the resulting list if it had unanimous support. Otherwise, management would draw up its own list, and the employees would have to take their chances with management's views of how dispensable, or indispensable, each of them was.

There was a lot of gallows humor, but the procedure worked. Those who were best able to cope with reentering the employment market agreed to leave. Many admitted that they would have objected strenuously if that decision had been forced upon them. Although the method might not have worked as well in a less sophisticated group, it demonstrates that blows to the security motive do not have to be delivered with a meat axe.

"Manipulating" the Security Motive

More than two hundred years ago, Samuel Johnson wrote, "It concentrates a man's mind wonderfully to know that he is to be hung in a fortnight." He was right then and he'd be just as right today. Your security motive can really get your full attention, and quickly, when it's switched on. Knowing that, some shortsighted managers try to exploit it. That's nearly always a mistake.

Sure, you can "concentrate" someone's mind on what you want him to do, merely by implying a threat to his economic lifeline. All that you have to do is demand that he do what you want, "or else." What's more, you'll probably get your way, at least in the short run. But only the most superficial manager would consider that a smart motivation strategy, because the effect does not end there.

People who have been successfully coerced have a serious problem. They've been forced to do, under duress, what they would not have done freely. Their dignity has been stripped away. They've been the victim of a moral outrage that differs only in degree, but not in kind, from rape. Their problem is whether to just accept their loss or to try to restore what has been taken from them.

Most choose the latter (as indeed you would, and I would, in the same circumstances). The most common way to restore violated dignity is to search for safe ways to retaliate. The safest ways are indirect and unobtrusive. For example, those offended folks could minimize their production, or withhold their cooperation, or "misunderstand" your orders, or "neglect" to notice their errors, or do whatever else they could to decrease the value of their work. There is almost no limit to the ingenuity with which outraged people can find ways to feign stupidity or ineptitude in order to frustrate someone who demeans them. Indeed, they often take pride in these stratagems, and laugh amongst themselves at the overbearing martinets whom they have cut, subtly and undetectably, down to size.

Instead of retaliating directly against you, they may be motivated to retaliate against what you are paid to produce. That way, they would hit you right smack on the bottom line of your performance appraisal. That's why trying to manipulate the security motive is a boomerang. No matter how tempted you may be, don't fool with it.

The Dependency Motive

People who are "dependent" shun decisions and rely on others to tell them what to do. Their underlying purpose is never to have to answer for a mistake, because that would risk the loss of their boss's (or the company's) approval and protection. Psychologically, someone with a really strong dependency motive is a living relic of the feudal era, when serfs did their local baron's dirty work in exchange for his protection against the other barons.

Of course, the easiest way to avoid mistakes is to make no decisions. People with a strong dependency motive "delegate upward" if you let them. They will seek your guidance and approval for every action that isn't explicitly spelled out in the rulebook. They make no exceptions, because that would require a decision as to whether an exception was really warranted.

The manager who expects subordinates to adapt and improvise will find dependency-motivated people maddening to supervise. For a customer or a client, especially one who expects to be treated as an individual, they are utterly exasperating. But for a manager cut from the same cloth, who fears having to answer for what a subordinate may have done, they are a joy to supervise. That's because they follow orders to the letter and never do anything that has to be explained.

Dependency Motives in Strange Places

What's that? A dependency-motivated *manager?*

Yes, you can find this motive in some surprising places. It is not uncommon among managers, especially at the lower and middle levels of old, established companies that face little competition. If their survival is not threatened, too many companies become inward looking and complacent. They start to value loyalty over decisiveness. In that kind of organization, promotion is really a reward for keeping your nose clean.

Dependency-motivated managers prefer to promote dependency-motivated subordinates, because they are perfectly predictable. You don't have to lose sleep worrying about what they might do, because they won't do anything out of the ordinary. That preference drives off employees with initiative (in most cases, straight into the arms of more imaginative employers).

In time, such a company's management team becomes a vast pool of expert decision avoiders. A side effect of this shortsighted policy is that not enough people with winner's motives make their way into the upper ranks of middle management. That forces the company to import most of its top executives from the outside. Depending on how much competitive pressure the firm faces, a dearth of winners in the upper ranks of management could also lead to an inglorious takeover by a more aggressive firm, or even to bankruptcy.

DEPENDENCY-MOTIVATED RETAILERS

You can even find people with strong dependency motives among the ranks of entrepreneurs and independent businessmen. Contrary to popular mythology, they are not all rugged individualists by any means. I stumbled onto that surprising insight a few years ago, when one of the large distilling companies asked me to study a key link in their distribution chain. They wanted to know what actually happened between liquor wholesalers, who were their immediate customers, and the retail liquor store owners through whom their products eventually reached the public.

My client had two objectives. First, distillers saw smaller, individually owned stores as their natural allies, bulwarks against market domination by chain stores. They wanted to avoid too much concentration of buying power in the hands of a few chains, since that could enable chain store buyers to dictate prices. So the client was interested in ways to encourage the survival of more individually owned retail stores.

Second, the client was concerned with the high cost of introducing new products, and with the low survival rate of those products. It takes a lot of time and money to find out whether a product can carve out a profitable niche for itself. The client sought to shorten that time by learning more about the decisions that move new products through the distribution chain.

To get at both questions, I conducted "focus group" interviews with ninety liquor store owners in eleven cities. Other than asking them to talk about their relationships with wholesalers, I provided no directions, and simply jotted down as many of their comments as I could. There was a great deal of similarity in what each group had to say, so I felt that I could risk some generalizations.

Broadly speaking, these retailers could be classified into two groups: a majority who were clearly dependency-motivated, and a minority who were achievement-motivated. Their attitudes were so different that they could easily be distinguished from each other.

The *dependency-motivated* retailers bought unsalable products that the wholesalers wanted to unload. Thus they committed two of the cardinal sins of retailing: tying up both their shelf space and their capital. However, these store owners did not lack for business acumen, and neither were they deceived. They did these foolish things knowingly, precisely to be seen by their wholesalers as "nice guys." They hoped that in return for these favors, the wholesaler would also keep them supplied with salable products.

This kind of retailer welcomed the visits of the wholesaler's salesmen, even though most of them were equally dependent, unassertive "order takers." The salesmen seldom provided advice or information, but instead played hard on the retailer's sympathy, pleading for orders to save their own jobs. The retailers were susceptible because they readily identified with a fellow underdog. Besides, they enjoyed an opportunity to commiserate, philosophize, and garner a few morsels of flattery. So they curried favor with their wholesalers and granted favors to the harried salesmen. For both reasons, the movement of merchandise from the wholesaler to the retailer did not accurately reflect consumer demand. Instead, it fed false signals back through the distribution chain, deceiving distillers as to how the market was really responding to their products. You could say that the economics of this particular market were distorted by the psychology of the smallest players in the distribution chain.

But that was not the only effect. The retailer's folly also minimized their working capital and exposed them to severe price competition from the better-financed chains. The retailers had to match those prices in order to stay in business. They survived only because they were willing to settle for slender profit margins.

In brief, dependency-motivated retailers were willing victims, human sheep who attracted human wolves in the same way that honey attracts flies.

Achievement-motivated retailers, on the other hand, were feisty and assertive. In their view, the wholesaler was a mere convenience, and a dispensable one, at that. They resisted pressure to absorb failed products. When threatened with reduced shipments of fast-selling products, they counter-threatened that they would just seek other suppliers. As one of them put it, "If I let him do it, the wholesaler would make me into a warehouse, which is his job, not mine. The wholesaler is going to have to learn to respond to demand, instead of thinking that he can manipulate it."

Similarly, the achievement-motivated retailers had no use for sales-men who were mere "order takers." They considered the salesmen's prime function to be providing them with information, and when that was not forthcoming, they did not hesitate to go over the salesmen's heads to get it. They had their own ideas about what makes a product sell, and did not assume that the wholesaler, or for that matter the distiller, knew more than they did: "The distillers think that their ads are powerful enough to pull products off the shelf all by themselves. But you need a retailer to *sell* a product. I guarantee you that I can cut the sale of any product, no matter how it's advertised, just by putting it where my customers can't see it."

Motivating the Dependency-Motivated

How can you motivate someone whose primary motive is dependency? Frankly, if the motive is strong enough to be noticeable, you've got better things to do with your time than attempting to remake that person. You *can't* convert that person into what he or she has never been. That would be magic, not motivation.

We all become whatever we are through the long process of growing up, and the results are extraordinarily difficult to change. Even psychotherapists don't remake people. As the late Karl Menninger wrote, "It is much easier [and] more logical . . . to help a child grow up with love and courage than it is to instill hope in a despondent soul. What mother and father mean to them is more than psychiatrists can ever mean."

In other words, the die is pretty well cast by the time we are old enough to work. That's why the realistic motivator works *with* what he has to work with, rather than trying to undo and remake what someone's life has already made him into.

In the real world, motivation is not the mysterious art of radically transforming personalities. It's the realistic art of creating conditions in which the personalities that people already have can function at top efficiency. To motivate people, you give them tasks for which their strengths are important and their weaknesses are not. You don't create a new set of strengths for them, or pretend that you can obliterate their weaknesses.

Most of the so-called motivation problems of this world are not caused by the deficiencies of individuals, but by expecting people to do well in tasks that demand qualities they haven't got. Instead of exhorting them to become what they are not, it's wiser to concentrate on tailoring their jobs to match their limitations. That's why the trick to making dependency-motivated people productive (not self-reliant, mind you, but productive) is to give them jobs in which their strengths matter a lot, and their weaknesses don't.

That means keeping dependency-motivated people out of managerial and entrepreneurial jobs, if you can, because otherwise they reproduce the catalog of disasters outlined above. On the other hand, they can do quite well in jobs that don't demand a wide-angle view of how their role fits into a larger context. They may have the *brains* to do all of these things, but a strong dependency motive puts severe limits on how much of those brains they will ever put to actual use.

Other experts (an "expert," in this case, being anyone who writes a book) will assure you that with enough determination, enough zeal, enough belief, you can transform dependency-motivated people into winners. This expert's hard-nosed advice is to save your time for more promising pursuits.*

---

*Here I can not resist quoting my favorite dog show judge, who, when asked by disappointed dog owners why a prize was not given to their dog, replied, "You asked for my opinion, and now you've got it."

The Conformity Motive

The conformity motive is seen in the attempt to resemble others in appearance, action, and professed beliefs. It is one of the most common and powerful of all forces affecting human behavior. To see it in action, you have only to look around you, or even at yourself when you are among other people. For most of us, most of the time, what we consider appropriate in dress, conduct, and speech is defined by the expectations of whomever we are with at the moment.

The tug of conformity is not unlike that of gravity. To test its force, just try going to work in your pajamas, or showing up for a formal party in your swimsuit. Rugged indeed is the individualist who is not driven back into line, and quickly, by fear of seeming to be conspicuously out of line.

The underlying aim of conformity is to seek safety in the acceptance of one's peers. It is as if the crowd could somehow protect you from misfortune, and you must therefore seek its embrace. It is easy to scoff at the conformity motive, and indeed it does have its ridiculous side. Nevertheless, its power is awesome. Consider the way in which conformity shows up in such diverse events as absenteeism, attitude surveys, and strikes.

The oldest and most persistent plague in labor-management relations is *absenteeism*. (It is also one of the most underrated. Absenteeism does far more harm to productivity than turnover or even strikes.) But there is a little-known aspect to the problem: absenteeism tends to vary consistently from one department to another. In some departments, absenteeism stays well above the company average; in other departments, it stays well below.

So what? you may say. Well, the really interesting thing about departmental absence rates is that when someone is transferred from one department to another, his absenteeism is likely to rise (or fall, as the case may be) during the first year or so, until it approximates the departmental average. It is as if a certain level of absence is expected, or tolerated, in each department. Most individuals seem reluctant to be conspicuously out of line with that average.

Supervisors usually swear that no such "expected" rate is ever discussed, at least not openly. So it appears that absenteeism is, among other things, a conformity effect. The implication is that one of the best ways to lower absenteeism is to lower the perception of how much of it is acceptable. More about that in chapter 13, on "problem people." For the moment, note that conformity has a strong influence on what people think they can get away with.

When *attitude surveys* are used with large groups of employees, we usually analyze the results along various demographic lines, to see whether people in any particular group (for example, white male college graduates) express attitudes that are different from those of other groups. If you massage the data this way, you'll usually find that one dimension is more important than race, sex, and all of the other "demographics" in influencing what one professes to believe. The great fault line, along which people's attitudes tend to be divided most of all, is age.

When you look at the attitudes of new employees—say, those who have joined the company in the last year or two—you'll usually find a jumble of opinions. Almost every conceivable point of view is supported by at least a few people. But after a year or two of employment, opinions start to homogenize. A "party line" begins to emerge in the survey responses. After those two years or so, whatever unique or individual points of view that people may once have had begin to blur and blend with those of the group to which they now belong. Don't underestimate the effect. These people are not merely parroting what they hear, they are convinced. They have been converted and won over.

From about this point onward, people begin to look at most issues in much the same way as those around them. From about four years or so onward, except for the rare nonconformist, virtually everyone will be marching to the same drum. The drum may change its beat, but if it does, the marching will change with it, and in unison.

We find another example of conformity in connection with strikes. Before a strike is actually called, while it is only a possibility, you can talk to workers privately, one to one, and many of them will tell you that they really don't want it to happen. They will cite various reasons, which are usually well thought out, why what they might gain would not be worth what they might lose. You will also encounter some hotheads who are eager for a strike, but there are seldom as many of them as of those who are worried and cautious.

Based on such a finding, you might be tempted to conclude that a strike would have little support and would be ineffective if it were actually called. But that conclusion would probably be wrong, because it does not take into account the galvanizing effect of a strike call, or the overriding need to support one's group in a crisis. Rather than risk losing the comradeship and approval of their fellows, most union members will simply swallow their misgivings and start walking the picket line.

What makes workers change their absence habits when they transfer from one department to another? Why do they gradually adopt the same views as those of other workers in their departments? Why do workers who are convinced that a strike would not be worth its cost go on strike anyway? The answer is that something more important than their own habits or their own ideas is involved. That something is the approval of the group, or, more precisely, avoiding the rejection of the group. These people *need* each other, because they are convinced that their strength is in each other and not in themselves.

Does this kind of submission to group dominance actually occur in America, the land of the free and the home of the self-reliant? You bet it does, and it's so common that it's as American as apple pie.

Motivating Conformity-Motivated People

How can you motivate people who need each other's approval more than they need yours, even if you are their manager, with power over their livelihoods and their security?

You can take a cue from Japanese wrestling. To overcome a larger opponent, you push him in the direction toward which he is already leaning. If he is leaning toward you, you step aside, trip him up, and push him forward over your foot, flat onto his face. In this case, the direction toward which the group is leaning is to follow what each member thinks is the will of every other member. So you have to find a way to change the norm to which the group conforms, because the group will *always* conform to one norm or another.

Here's where Niccolo Machiavelli puts in his cameo appearance. (Weren't you expecting him to show up, sooner or later, in a book about motivating people? Incidentally, the wise old Italian wasn't really evil: he was merely an extremely shrewd observer of human foibles. Some people never forgave him for that, and that's why he's had a rotten reputation for almost five hundred years.) What Machiavelli would say you had to do was to subtly—ever so subtly—change the group's core ideas. Those are the beliefs that everyone in the group thinks that everyone else embraces.

Like a Japanese wrestler, you do that by using the natural dynamics through which a group consensus is formed. You can see those dynamics at work in fashions, fads, and the efforts of marketeers to launch a new product. What's involved is the *pace* of change, the minimum level at which change is *noticed,* and above all else, *mimicry.*

If you want a fad to catch on, you have to plan for a fairly rapid buildup. Slow change isn't noticed by anyone but historians. So you need to pry the group open, and find within it a cadre of people who are open-minded enough to try your new fad (or in this case, willing to listen to a new idea). That small nucleus within the group need not be large, but it must be large enough to be noticeable. Something on the order of 15 percent should do the trick—if your converts are respected and influential. It might take 25 or 30 percent if they are not.

To induce a conforming group to begin conforming to a new idea, you must first take the measure of the individuals in the group, choosing the few whom you'll try to influence. Then you work with them patiently—*very* patiently. Don't try to shift the group's ideas too radically. The way to execute a 180-degree turn is one degree at a time.

It may take quite a while for them to see your point. But once the ice breaks, change amongst your small group can be built rapidly. That is when you want to encourage them to openly advocate what they now believe.

When the change begins, you'll want to fan the flames, because speed is now the key. If each member of your small group of disciples starts conforming to the other disciples quickly enough, the rest will sense that a change is occurring. Change then acquires a momentum of its own. Not wanting to be left out, they'll follow. The bandwagon effect will occur fairly rapidly. The group will then be leaning, in unison, your way.

Is that "manipulation"? Only if the result is clearly contrary to the group's best interests. And that isn't likely to happen, because while dependency-motivated people do not tend to be rugged individualists or original thinkers, most of them are not fools, either.

Motivating the Unadventurous

You can't send a security-motivated, dependent conformist to school, or even to an "executive development program," and expect to change anything but his vocabulary. You could even hand him this book, and tell him to read it. (Better still, you could tell him to go out and buy his own copy.) But having read it, he'll be a much more sophisticated security-motivated, dependent conformist. In the real world, in other words, people are not so easily transformed.

The way to motivate these people is not by remaking them, but by adapting to them. Keep their anxieties down and their group loyalties up, and keep the group's performance standards high. Their performance will seldom be spectacular, but it should be steady and reliable. If you've taken care to be sure that the work they've been given is what most needs to be done, that level of performance should be good enough, and then some.

CHAPTER
4
COMFORT MOTIVES

The survival motives are devices used by the people whom we have referred to as the mass in the middle to fend off their worst nightmares. By contrast, comfort motives are devices for avoiding nuisances. The main comfort motives are the pursuit of fairness, friends, and "rank and respect." (The pair can be treated as a unit.)

Survival motives pack more of a motivational wallop than comfort motives. You can put up with an annoyance if you have to, but you won't quietly tolerate a threat to your livelihood. Nevertheless, it would be a mistake to ignore the comfort motives, because of a quirk in human psychology that was first described some fifty years ago by a psychologist named Abraham Maslow.

He noted that if a motive is well taken care of, it simply becomes dormant. For example, if you're content with the arrangements that "guarantee" your cash flow, your interest in income disappears from the center of your mental "stage," but is promptly replaced by another motive that until then had lurked quietly in the wings. And that new motive turns out to be just as demanding as its predecessor had been.

Maslow's point was that it's human nature to never run out of motives. People who don't have something important to worry about will find something not so important to worry about. And whichever motive is number one for the moment is really number one, entirely apart from whether you or I would consider it cosmic or inconsequential. We are motivated by what we want *now*.

So the best way to motivate anyone is to find a way to satisfy the motive that currently predominates, and to offer that as the prize for getting done what you want done. But that "motive of the moment" is a moving target. It won't be the same for everyone, nor will it stay the same for any particular individual. Virtually any motive can be someone's number-one motive, at least for a while. And that's why, regardless of "theory," you have to be prepared to deal with the comfort motives, even though they are secondary (in theory) to the survival motives.

The Fairness Motive

Executive recruiters have a preference for pursuing people who are not on the job market, precisely because their employers have a high enough opinion of their work to want to keep them happy. Once you identify a candidate like that, and verify that he really is that good, your next problem is to lure that person away. You have to make him *un*happy with his present job. To do that, you have to dangle the prospect of a job that is a great deal more attractive.

The motivation in this case would come from the contrast between the rewards of the two jobs. A fat, munificent, more-than-ample reward can become skimpy overnight if two conditions are met. First, the contrast between the old and the new reward must be strikingly in favor of the new one. Second, that new reward must be believable. Put both elements together, and you've got a potent motivational tool.

Here's where we encounter another quirk of human nature. You might call it the "ingrate effect." If you learn that another job offers many more goodies than yours does, you'll become discontented with your present job. But suppose it's the other way around. Suppose you learn that your job is much better rewarded than someone else's. That might be worth a yawn. You might note, with mild satisfaction, that things are as they should be; and then promptly forget about it.

So the motivational effect of any given reward can vary quite a lot, depending on whether it's perceived as fair or unfair. That sentence says so much that we'll devote the next four sections to taking it apart and putting it back together. Exactly what is "fair" and "unfair"? What are their motivational effects? And most important of all, what can you do about it?

The Fairness Equation: What You Contribute

If you sit down and think hard about "fairness," you'll find that it's not so easy to define. I've talked to lots of people about what they think is "fair," and tried to work out the mental processes they used. My best guess is that when most people talk about "fairness," what they really have in mind is a kind of "input-output" formula. That is, if the value of what they had contributed to an arrangement was at least roughly balanced by the value of what they got from it, they would consider that arrangement fair.

Here's where the plot starts to thicken. There are all kinds of contributions, and all kinds of rewards, so unless we do a little oversimplifying here, we may never find our way out of this chapter. I don't want to insult your intelligence by suggesting that all human minds actually follow the same neat little formulas. Thus, what follows is just an approximation of what really happens. Most of the time, though, it won't be too far off the mark.

There are at least four ways in which most people think about what they contribute to an arrangement from which they benefit (such as, for example, employment).

First, your entire *history* comes to work with you every day. Your education, your previous work experience, and for that matter, the talents and gifts that you were born with, are all stored inside your head and are available to your employer. Whether your employer is smart enough to tap into all that ability and wisdom is another question entirely. The point is that you've invested a lot of time and trouble in acquiring all those qualifications, and you will quite properly want to earn a return on your investment. So your first contribution to any arrangement involving the use of your time and talent is *everything on your résumé.*

Your second contribution is your job. Every job is a certain fraction of the total *responsibility* for running the company. When you're pretty far down on the totem pole, your share is rather slim. When you're the CEO, you're responsible for everything. As you are promoted up the corporate ladder, the CEO is in effect delegating a larger chunk of his responsibility to you. You would quite properly expect your share of the total rewards to be proportional to your share of the total responsibility for generating those rewards. So your second contribution to the arrangement is *everything in your job description*.

Your third contribution is your *performance*. How well do you actually meet the demands of your job? There's also quite a range here. While you're still learning a new job, your performance may be well below the minimums that would be acceptable for an experienced person. Afterward, your performance rating could be anywhere from "barely acceptable" to "above and beyond the call of duty." A complication is that performance appraisals are nearly always someone else's subjective opinion, a problem we'll explore in chapter 11. Your rewards are based in part on how well your actual job performance matches what we normally expect from someone at your experience level. If your performance is well above what was expected, your rewards may be inadequate. On the other hand, if your performance is below the expected level, something is wrong and will have to be fixed. Either way, your third contribution to the arrangement is *whatever is on the bottom line of your performance appraisal*.

This brings us to your fourth contribution, which is your willingness to put up with inconveniences, pressures, hazards, and whatever other nonsense is built into your job. I call this the "E factor," because it refers to things in the *environment* that you have to *endure* in order to get your work done.

If you work in a plush office, doing stimulating work among pleasant people, your "E factor" will be negligible because your work is rewarding in itself. If you work in a smelly, dangerous environment, among unreasonable people, doing work that you hate, your "E factor" would be pretty high. To induce you to do such work, and do it well, we'd either have to hold a gun to your head or compensate you for all that you had to endure. That's why people who work at night or on weekends are usually paid more than those who do the same jobs during normal hours. So your fourth contribution to the arrangement is *everything that the job compels you to tolerate which you'd really rather avoid*.

In assessing whether a working arrangement is fair, the four elements that you'd probably list on the "contribution" side would be your history, your responsibilities, your performance, and any noxious features you might want to list under the "E factor." Now, here comes another interesting twist of human nature. In deciding which of the four should be given the most weight, we all tend to choose (surprise!) our own heaviest element.

Thus, if I really don't have much to do, and don't even do that very well, but have done it for years and years, I'll argue that you really ought to pay me primarily for all that experience. Or if I am saddled with heavy responsibilities, but have had relatively little experience, I'd probably argue that people should be paid for what they have to do now, and not for what they did or did not do in the past. The bottom line is that "fairness" is a highly subjective matter. (That's one reason why so many companies try to keep their salary distributions secret. Otherwise they'd be forever explaining and appeasing.)

The Fairness Equation: Your Rewards

On the other side of the "fairness" equation are the rewards you are given in exchange for your contributions. Once again, we're going to have to oversimplify a bit. I'm going to divide all rewards into two groups, financial and nonfinancial.

The truth is that financial rewards come in many varieties. To name only a few, there are bonuses, stock options, and company-paid insurance. (The IRS keeps a great big list of all the different forms of income, and the list keeps getting longer all the time.) For that matter, nonfinancial rewards come in an even greater variety. They range from simple things, like convenient working hours, all the way to esoteric things, like the exhilaration of surpassing your own previous accomplishments. In order to prevent this chapter from expanding into a book, I'll lump all elements in each group together, as if all of them really had the same effects. That isn't quite precise, but it's close enough for our purposes.

A word about nonfinancial rewards. We have to add them to our equation in order to make the equation predict, with reasonable accuracy, what people actually do. That's because in the real world, money never operates alone. It's always mixed in with other motivators, and it's the *total* mix of all of them that determines how you're going to react. If you ignore nonfinancial motivators, you could never explain why, for example, people who enjoy a small-town lifestyle turn down big raises that would require relocation to Chicago, New York, or Los Angeles.

So now at last we've got all of the elements in your "fairness equation." On the contribution side, we've got your history, responsibilities, performance, and your "E factors." On the reward side, we've got your financial and your nonfinancial rewards. The concept of an equation really fits, because we seem to perceive fairness when the two sides are more or less in balance; and we see unfairness when they are way out of line.

Calculating Your Fairness Balance

One more question remains to be answered. How can you actually determine whether the two sides of your own personal equation are about equal? After all, only one of the elements (your pay package) can be defined objectively. As for the rest, opinions will differ as to how valuable your background really is, how important your responsibilities really are, how your performance matches up to expectations, how bad those "E factors" really are, and how wonderful or awful an effect those nonfinancial elements really have.

Before we can answer that question, we'll need to digress for another close look at human nature. When a question is sufficiently important, the lack of a logical basis for answering it, or a lack of objective information (or even of any information at all) *deters no one*. Logic and facts are just no match for a compelling human need. That's why you have to be willing to confront a certain amount of flakiness if you really want to understand human behavior.

The truth is, *most people are logical and realistic only when that suits their purposes*. The fashion, advertising, and gambling industries all grasped that truth many years ago. If you grasp it now, you'll be way ahead of most other people in dealing with human reactions to the fairness issue.

If people want an answer badly enough and have no logical way to get it, they concoct an illogical way. And if they have no reliable information, or no information at all, they invent the missing information. The concoction is then treated as if it made perfect sense, and the invention is then treated as if it were true. The "answer," of course, may be pure fiction. But it's better than no answer at all, *if* having no answer is intolerable. That's the "logic," so to speak, of abandoning logic.

For example, there is a debate among the experts as to whether it is better for a company to keep all details of its pay program secret, or to reveal enough of them so that individuals could determine whether their own pay was fair. Of course, the more that you reveal, the more arguments and challenges you are going to get. On the other hand, when you ask people who don't know the facts to guess at the pay of others in their organization, they tend to assume a tighter pay distribution than actually exists. In other words, there is probably more incentive in a concealed pay system than most of the people in that system would assume. But because they don't know the facts, they *act* as if there was not much reason to strive for a pay raise. Unless you open a pay system to scrutiny, with all the risks that entails, the people who are affected by the system will treat it as if it were penny-pinching and boring. So the choice is between having unmotivated employees and tranquil administrators, on the one hand, or motivated employees, some of whom will probably annoy the administrators, on the other hand. In practice, the choice is made by the administrators, and, unsurprisingly, they usually choose the former over the latter.

Back to our question. How can you actually determine whether the two sides of your personal fairness equation are more or less equal? You do that by comparing your equation with someone else's equation. Since you probably don't know the elements in that person's equation with any accuracy, you guess at them. You probably don't assume that the two equations have to be identical. But you want the "price" that you are paid for your contribution to be no less than the price that others are paid for theirs.

For example, if you estimate that my contributions are worth about 10 percent more than yours, simply because I'm older and more experienced than you are, you'd expect my reward package to be about 10 percent greater than yours. *But not more than that.* If you guess my rewards to be about 10 percent above yours, you'd conclude that both my rewards and your rewards are fair. So the practical (not the logical) definition of fairness is your belief that *no one has a better deal than you have.* If you believe that, you'll be happy with your rewards—at least until you find someone else who you think has a better deal than you have.

Aggravating the "Unfairness" Issue

But suppose that actually happens. Suppose you are convinced that someone else is getting a better deal for his contributions than you get for yours. Let's also assume that more than just a negligible difference is involved, that the other guy's deal looks much better than yours. Your immediate inference is that your contributions have been devalued. Your employer seems to think that you are not worth as much as you think you are worth.

That's very bad news, and it's definitely going to motivate you. That is, it's going to make you *do* something. That special sensitivity in each of us to being compared unfavorably to others is about to become inflamed. The "unfairness" issue, which always lurks somewhere inside your head, is about to become highly aggravated.

Your overriding motive is now to restore fairness. One of your "secondary" motives has jumped into the number-one position. It's going to dominate your thoughts and actions until you resolve the issue, one way or another. But there are only three ways to do that:

1. You can demand a better deal from your present employer. That will work sometimes. But if you're working for a large organization that is all tied up in policies and procedures and budgets, and in which managers at your boss's level don't have much authority, it probably won't work.
2. You can resign, walk away from an unappreciative employer, and seek your fortune elsewhere. But this is a radical step. Better jobs may not be so easy to find. You might wind up agreeing with my favorite Shakespearean character, Sir John Falstaff, that "Discretion is the better part of valor."
3. That leaves you with the third alternative, which is by far the most commonly used (because the first two are so unpromising). You can deliberately shrink the value of your contributions until they match the value of your rewards. That solves your problem, because fairness has been restored. Of course, it creates a whole new set of problems for your employer, because your productivity has been cut. But that's his problem.

How do most employers deal with employees who withhold effort, who put a lid on how much they'll produce, or let others produce? The answer may surprise you. They tolerate it. They seek productivity gains through capital investment—that is, through bigger and better widgets—rather than through better use of their people.

But that strategy misses a point that has not eluded the Japanese. In fact, it's one of the main reasons why they compete so effectively against us. The point is that the actual productivity of a piece of capital equipment depends mostly on the care, or lack of care, that humans give to it. When equipment fails, "human error" is the most common diagnosis. That's a polite term. Some of the time, it really amounts to humans not giving a damn, or humans not paying attention, or humans figuring, "If the boss doesn't complain, why should I worry?"

And *that's* why we can't afford to let people conclude that they haven't got a fair deal. If that conclusion is realistic, we have to either give them a better deal or a convincing reason why we can't. If it is unrealistic, we have to straighten them out. How can you do that, especially with people whose views of their own fairness equations are unrealistic? You have to do it gently, but firmly.

Most of them have never gone through the analytical exercise that you've just been through. The whole concept of an equation, and of factoring both sides of it, will probably be Greek to them. Unless you're dealing with a sophisticate, don't even mention equations. Instead, ask them to give you their reasons for believing that they deserve a better deal. Be sure to let them talk for a while, because they may have more than one reason.

Then, gently, give them the facts. They may brush those facts aside, or hear you saying things that you're not saying, or not hear you at all. Just persist, gently but insistently. If they've become so fixated on one part of the equation that they've overlooked the rest of it, ask them to step back and look at the entire picture. (It's common to overlook the nonfinancial rewards.) Don't expect them to go away convinced after your first effort. Your job is to plant the seed of doubt. Repeat the treatment as often as it's required.

In most cases you will be dealing with people who are honestly misinformed. Their most common reasons for being unrealistically upset are overstating the value of their own contributions, choosing someone inappropriate for comparison, or just guessing wrong at the size of other people's rewards.

Sometimes you'll be dealing with a professional malcontent who reflexively disagrees with anyone in authority. Debates with such people are fruitless. For this kind of person, tying you up in debate is an end in itself. Make your point as well as you can, and if necessary make it again. Then make it clear that you're not interested in endless repetition and that you have nothing to add, *period*. Your adversary will be frustrated, and you'll have time to get some work done. That's not an ideal result. But under the circumstances, it's not so bad, either.

The Friendship Motive

Most of us like to be liked. But with some of us, it's a passion. People with a strong dose of the friendship motive spend a lot of time ingratiating themselves, doing favors, and trying to be popular. They usually succeed, since only a confirmed grouch would dislike them. Their underlying motive is to make their private world as safe as possible, by disarming every potential adversary in sight. In most cases, this is a harmless, socially valuable motive. But there is one big exception.

That exception is a leadership role. The motivational purpose of a leader is to provide whatever his subordinates need to make them productive. For most people, that does not include being spoiled or flattered. If we selected managers through popularity contests, a lot of these forgiving, indulgent, friendship-motivated people would be elected. It's just as well that in the real world that doesn't happen very often. And for an excellent reason.

People with a strong friendship motive don't mind being manipulated. That's because they can't stand having to disappoint anyone. They make all kinds of exceptions in order to gratify whoever asks for one. But that puts a lot of other people's fairness equations out of kilter. Those who are not in the habit of requesting favors will quickly realize that requesters get whatever they want. So they'll line up for their share of the favors, because in their minds fairness is at stake.

Ultimately, to keep the peace and to avoid having to frustrate anyone, friendship-motivated managers have to give away the store. They lose discipline and productivity, as well as any credible means for trying to regain them. Their plight becomes hopeless rather quickly. That's why it's much better to prevent this kind of calamity than to try to fix it after the fact.

The fact of the matter is that the friendship motive leads to a well-intentioned but inappropriate tendency to reward people just for being nice. The right way to do that is to be as nice to them, in your own way, as you can. The important point is not to go overboard (as they would, if the roles were reversed). Management jobs should never be handed out as rewards. They should be given to whoever shows the most promise of growing into the job description. And every managerial job description, alas, includes the occasional necessity of displeasing someone.

You've no doubt got a bit of the friendship motive in you, too. So do I. It's part of what makes us charming and civilized. It also makes it much easier for the rest of the world to tolerate us. But could either you or I properly be called *primarily* friendship-motivated? Not unless fear of offending someone would stop us from doing what we knew had to be done. That's an important distinction.

Your principal problem with your own friendship motive is to manage it. Don't let it send you off on guilt trips for taking a necessary action that someone else didn't like. Steel yourself, if you must, with the thought that if tough decisions have to be taken, it's better that they be taken by a decent, civilized person like you, who will work hard to minimize any unavoidable harm.

It might help you to recall General Douglas MacArthur. His ego was monumental, and his friendship motive must have been vanishingly small. Nevertheless, he prided himself on campaigns that were planned to achieve their objectives with minimal casualties to our side. You were more likely to survive under MacArthur than under several better-liked generals. In that sense, at least, he set a fine example for all decision makers.

People with strong friendship motives make wonderful followers. They're easy to motivate, because they want nothing so much as to please you. They'll actually search for ways to be helpful. That's why you'll have to be careful not to show undue favoritism toward them. Be sure to let them know that you appreciate the extra effort they'll nearly always give. But let it go at that. You won't want your other subordinates to conclude that you're an easy mark for a flatterer.

In most cases, people with strong friendship motives are not really currying favor. They're not trying to please you for the sake of gaining some reward. What they are really trying to do is to disarm you. They want to be sure that you won't hurt them, because as a manager you have the power to do that. The way to keep them motivated (and unagitated) is to speak to them in terms of a continuing deal. If they continue doing a good job for you, you'll continue doing your best for them.

The Rank and Respect Motives

Rank, in the sense that we are using it here, could also be expressed as "prestige." *Respect* needs no translation. We can consider them together because they represent the two ends of a single dimension—namely, the value that we assign to another person.

Rank

When we are considering whether to bow before someone (figuratively speaking), and if so, how low, we are concerned with rank. That is, we are weighing someone else's importance relative to our own, which in turn determines how much deference we ought to show. Rank is always relative to where you stand in the pecking order. It is a question of whether your own rank enables you to look someone straight in the eye, obliges you to look upward, or permits you to glance downward.

Do we really have to worry about such things in a country founded on the proposition that all men are created equal? You bet we do. But we call it etiquette or protocol, or explain it away with the old army saying that "rank has its privileges."

There is something in human nature that likes to line people up in hierarchies. Perhaps that's because all of us, even in democracies, were born into a hierarchy called a family. We all began our lives looking upward at a minimum of two people who were much higher on the totem pole than we were. Whatever the explanation for our fascination with rank, remember this: you trifle with someone else's rank at your peril.

Rank is indicated by various external symbols, and most people take theirs *very* seriously. (I can still remember being promoted from second lieutenant to first lieutenant. I promptly changed the return address on all letters I sent home from just "Lieutenant" to "*First* Lieutenant.") Rare indeed is the person who scorns status symbols and can claim, with Cyrano de Bergerac, to "wear my garlands on my soul." In fact, most of us prefer to wear them on our calling cards.

For most people, by far their most important "status symbol" is their job title. A sensible title tells the world what you do and how much authority you have. Outsiders need to know whether they're dealing with a decision maker or the decision maker's assistant. But titles are often inflated, partly to flatter you and partly to flatter the people with whom you deal. For example, some "district sales managers" are actually the only salesperson in the district. But if I am your customer, it inflates my own sense of importance to have the district sales manager call on me personally.

Some status symbols can pump up your own ego while simultaneously deflating a lot of other egos. Some examples are reserved parking spaces and separate dining facilities for managers. Unless these are very discreet, they imply a caste system. What they really do is confront the unprivileged with their own lack of status. That only creates resentment and undermines other efforts to provide positive motivation. This is why consultants often advise that these practices be quietly abandoned. But if you really want to see a knock-down, drag-out fight in the executive suite, try putting that recommendation into effect.

True, the proposed change is only cosmetic—but appearances count for a lot. Interestingly, opposition to these proposals does not come from the few genuine snobs in management. They *know* that they are superior, and they don't need a reserved parking space to prove it. Instead, the most ferocious opposition comes from people who have accomplished little that they can be proud of. Consequently, they need all the status symbols they can get to prop up their self-respect. Some cynical observers have suggested that the reason these controversies heat up company politics so intensely is that so little is at stake.

The executive who has to make this decision is in a tough spot. Should you ever find yourself in that spot and have to decide on whether to keep or dump flagrant distinctions between various ranks of employees, here's my advice: dump them. They do more harm to those they demean than whatever good they may do for those they flatter.

Respect

When you are considering whether someone of lower rank is worth your time and attention, or can be disdained or even ignored, the issue concerns respect. That's a critical issue for everyone in a leadership position. It is never so important as when you detach yourself from your erstwhile peers and take your first step up the ladder of rank. That's because, as long as you are on that first rung, you'll be in more intimate contact with lower-ranking people than you'll ever be again.

Unless you're up from the ranks yourself (which is increasingly rare), there are going to be some gross demographic differences between yourself and the people you'll be leading at this stage. First, a lot of them will be older than you. That's because they haven't been going anywhere for a long time. Ninety percent of the workforce never gets its foot on the rung of the ladder where your foot now rests.

Many of them will think, as they look at you, "Oh, God, here's another callow, know-it-all, brand-new manager that we've got to educate." For your own sake, you'd better hope that they do a good instructional job. That's because the reputation that you eventually earn with them will follow you as you mount the ladder. You're going to be known among the troops (including many you have never actually led) either as someone who is excessively impressed with his own brilliance or as someone who is smart enough to listen. If you ever have to ask masses of employees to make sacrifices for the good of the company, you'd really prefer the latter reputation to the former.

Another difference between you and your first subordinates will probably be in formal education. For most of us, the die is cast between the ages of eighteen and twenty. Those who go to college and don't drop out will mostly move into the fast lane for income, status, and managerial opportunities. (That's why college enrollments keep rising, even though tuition rates climb even faster.) However, the psychology of those who did not go to college is exactly the same as it is for those who did. We all tend to make much of whatever advantages we have and to belittle the advantages of others. Thus your subordinates will probably think—until and unless you prove otherwise—that you spent four years in college having your head stuffed with big words and useless theories. For your part, you will probably think—until and unless you are smart enough to realize otherwise—that they are unsophisticated and ignorant.

Your problem is to avoid thinking in terms of stereotypes. As long as you do, you'll be the adversary and not the leader. *Leaders and followers must be on the same side.* Otherwise, the followers don't follow. You must also prove to them that you don't fit their stereotypes, either. The tactics for doing that can be whatever comes naturally to you for expressing the world's most important attitude. It's the attitude that makes the tactics effective, and it's all summed up in that one hackneyed word: respect. It's hackneyed only because its importance has been obvious to thinking men and women for centuries. If you want others to give you all the effort they are capable of, you have to make it clear that you are looking them straight in the eye with a level gaze. You're not better than they are, and you're not worse, either. The whole issue of comparative worth is irrelevant between leaders and followers. That's because you can't condescend to anyone and still expect, in return, a wholehearted effort to do whatever you may ask of him.

CONNIE DOESN'T CARE

My most dramatic encounter with the principle of respect came several years ago, when a company that I will call Consolidated Steel Fabricators asked me to study a plant that had just had a ruinous three-month strike. As you might expect, there were lots of theories as to why the strike had lasted so long. But they tended to be self-serving, which left top management both skeptical and mystified. For example, the staff at corporate headquarters suspected that the plant's management must have been heavy-handed and insensitive in its dealings with the workers. Not surprisingly, the plant's managers disagreed. They felt that the strike was prolonged by internal dissension within the union. The leadership of the union local, which had lost control of its own membership during the strike, was just as perplexed as management.

About the only point on which everyone agreed was that the issues on the bargaining table could not, in themselves, explain why the

strike had dragged on for so long; the differences between management's last prestrike offer and the actual final settlement were relatively minor. Still, *something* had inflamed the workers to the point that
they were willing to endure severe economic hardships in order to
continue their strike. My task was to identify that "something."

A strike, especially one that, like this, involved several thousand
people, is a complex event. No single explanation can really suffice.
The truth is that a lot of factors combined to prolong the strike. But I
will concentrate here on only one, because it turned out to be really
important, and also (of course) because it illustrates my point.

I got one clue from the strikers' informal slogan, which appeared
on many hand-lettered signs that were carried on the picket lines. The
workers' nickname for the company was "Connie," and their slogan
was "Connie Doesn't Care." When I asked workers about that, they
explained that the company seemed to view them with contempt. (As
you can well imagine, they expressed that thought with rather more
vigorous language than I can use here.)

The next clue that caught my eye was a preoccupation with safety
hazards in the plant. Granted, this was strictly a hard-hat operation,
but there were also elaborate precautions to prevent accidents. The
actual accident record was about average for plants of this type.
Nevertheless, most workers professed to enter the plant each day with
dread and to leave with relief that they had not been maimed, or
worse. I wondered why. After lots of interviews with both workers and
their supervisors, I finally grasped the origins of both the slogan itself
and the belief that the plant was unusually dangerous.

Supervisors had the authority to shut down operations if critically
important equipment had to be replaced. The most conspicuous
examples were the steel cables suspended from the overhead cranes.
These carried heavy objects from one part of the plant to another, and
in the course of normal use they eventually frayed. It then became a
judgment call as to when to replace the cable. To be super-safe, that
could have been done at the first sign of fraying. But supervisors
claimed that wasn't really necessary, because a margin of safety had
been built into the cable. They also stressed that they could tell when
it really had to be changed. Their strongest argument was that no
cable had ever actually broken while being used.

But the workers, glancing upward uneasily as huge loads passed
directly over their heads, were not reassured. What upset them the
most was a belief that in the year or two preceding the strike supervisors had deliberately competed with each other to see who could put
up with a fraying cable the longest. As one of them put it, "Those
bastards are playing 'chicken' with our lives." There may have been

some truth to that. Management had informally encouraged each of the three shifts to try to outperform each other. Supervisors would carefully calculate whether a cable would last long enough to force the supervisor of the next shift to deal with it. Eventually, of course, the necessary action would be taken by one of them. Until then, the game went on, and the workers grew increasingly alarmed. Still, it was a long way from supervisors competing over production records, on the one hand, to the workers' conviction that the company was actually indifferent to their safety. What could have caused that gross exaggeration of reality to become a widely accepted belief?

I found the final clue to the mystery in the way in which supervisors had been selected. Most had come up from the ranks. They seemed to have been chosen as much for a certain attitude as for their work records. They considered themselves to be more serious and businesslike, and above all more individualistic, than the rank and file. They also tended to regard their subordinates as, frankly, rather dumb and lazy. They were convinced that their subordinates would work no harder than they were made to work.

Workers knew that they were scorned by their bosses. That was the ultimate basis for their misreading of the safety issue. To them, it was entirely believable that seemingly arrogant foremen would literally gamble with workers' lives. That only reinforced other negative beliefs about the company, most of which (like this one) had at least a germ of truth to them.

And that, I concluded, was one of the main reasons why the strike had lasted so long. It was not really over economic issues at all. It was a retaliation for badly bruised dignity. The workers had simply chosen to punish the company for as long as they could afford to inflict the punishment. They did that partly to even the score and partly in hopes of conveying an unforgettable message. They were terribly, grievously offended at not having been treated with respect.

You may wonder at "Connie's" subsequent record. With regard to employee relations, it has been in the range of fair to mediocre. It has never been one of their strong suits. They continue to pay a heavy price for that deficiency. Technically, however, they are a recognized leader in their industry, and they continue to take great pride in that.

PART II

THE
MOTIVATORS
OUTSIDE
PEOPLE

CHAPTER
5

GETTING YOUR
MESSAGE ACROSS

If you're serious about changing other people's behavior, you've somehow got to get three ideas into their heads. First, you have to spell out what you want them to do. That's the easiest part of the motivation process, but unfortunately it isn't enough. You also have to reassure those people that if they're willing to try, they really can do what you've asked them to do. But that isn't enough, either. The final, crucial part of the motivation process is to convince them that it's very much in their best interests to try. That is by far the most important of all the ideas you have to get across. And every time you try to motivate someone, you must somehow convey all three of those ideas.

Now, to put all of that in a nutshell: if you want to motivate, you have to communicate. Communication is indispensable to motivation. In fact, motivation is unthinkable without it. But communication is not easy. If it were, there would be no speech writers, no advertising agencies, no public relations outfits. And there would be a lot more good motivators walking around than there actually are.

Communication is notoriously hard to get right. Most people are not very good at it. That's why those who can communicate well tend to acquire power. If that's what you want, you're going to have to acquire the power that comes with knowing how to get your message across.

Contrary to popular myth, the shortage of competent communicators is not caused by skimpy vocabularies or by underdeveloped speaking skills. You don't have to be eloquent to communicate. But you do need a different skill, and you also need to know how communication really works.

The skill you need is knowing how to *listen*. The knowledge you need is of which *methods* of communicating work well, even if they are used clumsily, and which methods don't work, even when they are used expertly. If you can master that skill and understand those methods, you won't have to be especially articulate to get your message across. Of course, if you happen to be handy with words, that's an advantage. But it's not as big an advantage as many unwordy people think. After all, we express our contempt for the unconvincingly wordy by likening what they say to the stuff that farmers shovel out of bullpens.

Getting Attention

If communication were a cake, a fancy vocabulary would only be the icing. The cake itself would be the art of seizing and holding your audience's attention. That's because what you say and how you say it won't matter one bit if your audience isn't listening to you.

An old story illustrates the point. A lady was driving through Missouri and came upon a farmer who was beating a mule over the head with a two-by-four. Indignantly, she got out of her car and demanded to know why the farmer was abusing the poor beast. The farmer sighed, and then explained that he was just trying to get the mule's attention.

To get the attention of people, your methods have to be a lot subtler than a two-by-four. Your problem, unlike the farmer's, is not the thickness of a mule's skull. Your problem is the high activity level of the brains inside human skulls. You must never forget that the minds you are trying to reach have already been stuffed with lots of other ideas.

Your immediate challenge is to help your audience tie what you want them to think about to what they are already thinking about.

That's because people make sense out of incoming messages by relating them to what they already know. If they can't do that, they either ignore those messages or reject them as nonsense.

An embarrassing lesson drove home for me forever the importance of getting people's attention. As a young consultant, I was sent to Paris to make a presentation to the managing director of a French subsidiary and his staff. The MD was a member of the French nobility: he was tall and thin and a baron, no less. He sat at one end of a long table with his eyes closed and his long fingers pressed against his forehead. I stood at the other end of the table beside my trusty flip chart.

His staff sat on both sides of the table, and I noticed that they were all looking at him and not at me. Undaunted, I launched into my best high-energy, high-confidence, highly positive and assertive presentation, the same one that had wowed executives in Chicago and Los Angeles. When I finished, I expected my audience to rise to their feet, cheering and applauding, the way they had done back home. To my surprise, the managing director still sat silently, with his eyes closed; his staff also sat silently, still looking at him and not at me. Slowly, my surprise changed to chagrin, and then to agony.

Finally, with an exquisite sense of timing, the baron opened his eyes. With great boredom, he waved his long fingers toward a chair. "You may be seated, young man," he said. If there had been a hole in the floor, I would gratefully have fallen right through it. I had totally ignored the French deference to status. What was uppermost in the staff's mind was not to please me, but to please their boss. I had blithely overlooked what mattered most to them, and they had simply returned the compliment.

Fortunately for me, what was uppermost in their boss's mind was the tiresome necessity of teaching yet another upstart American a lesson he would never forget. Here's that lesson: you start your attempt to communicate by showing that you understand and respect the views of those whose views you hope to change. And if necessary, you adapt your style to one they are comfortable with, even if you aren't.

That's why knowing what your audience already believes is the key to making them accept what you want them to believe. If you know what is in your audience's mind *before* you start sending messages, you are already more than halfway home. Whatever is already in their heads will either block your message, if it looks strange or scary, or welcome it, if the message seems familiar and friendly. So you have to make sure that your message is recognizable and that it looks reassuring.

> A lawyer friend of mine tells a story that demonstrates the point of knowing your audience. He was assigned by the court to defend a man who had been arrested for peddling drugs. So he told his client, "Now, listen carefully. Whatever you do before the trial, you must have *absolutely* nothing to do with drugs in any way. Is that clear?" "Yes, sir," said the client. To make sure that his client had really understood, the lawyer added, "OK. Now, tell me in your own words what I told you." "Don't do nothing with drugs," said the client. "Good," said the lawyer.
> Two hours later, the lawyer was informed that his client had been arrested again for peddling drugs. Furious, he went to see his client in jail, and demanded to know why he had disobeyed him. "Well, you see," said the embarrassed client, "what I thought you really meant was that I should be careful. And I guess I wasn't careful enough."

We all sift incoming ideas through the filter of our prior information. Sometimes our filters are so clogged with old ideas, or so swamped by desires or delusions, that the incoming ideas are bent beyond recognition. That's why the best communicators always take pains to find out what their audiences already believe before they attempt to convince them of anything.

Keeping Attention

Once you've got the attention of your audience, you've got to keep it. And that isn't easy, either. If the people you're trying to reach believe that your mind is open to their ideas, they'll return the compliment, and you'll get a fair hearing. But if they believe that you think you know it all, and that you're here to tell and not to listen, they'll return that compliment, too. They'll sit quietly, with their mental hearing aids turned off, and let you prattle on.

Communication can only happen in a two-way channel. People who sit for too long at the end of a one-way channel will sooner or later turn it off. The human mind wasn't made to swallow endless gulps of incoming information; it either processes that information and feeds it back through an outgoing channel, or it wanders away in search of something more interesting to do. That's why grade-school teachers give their pupils a recess every forty-five minutes or so, and why college professors schedule classes for an hour and a half at most.

You've got to make it clear that you welcome questions, comments, criticisms, even contrary ideas. When no feedback is coming your way, you've got to actively seek it, to go out and ask for it. If you want people to hear you out, you've got to hear them out.

The most dramatic example of the principle of reciprocity that I ever encountered involved an executive in one of my client companies. One day he addressed a meeting of all of his field managers. His topic was his pride and joy: a major cost-reduction campaign that he had personally engineered. He went on at some length, citing economy after economy that he had found with his eagle eye and his sharp pencil. When he finished there was some polite applause. Then a grizzled old veteran stood up. He was nearing retirement, and felt he could afford to be candid. "Sir," he said, "maybe you've pushed this cost-cutting business too far. The men are starting to grumble. They say their workload is getting too big. They say they don't have enough time to do the job right any more."

The executive was tired. He'd had a bad day. He was not in his best form. So he exploded. "Damn it!" he said. "That's a bunch of crap! Anybody who says that doesn't know what they are talking about! Every one of these cuts is absolutely justified! Do you hear that? Nobody's workload is too heavy. You're just listening to a bunch of lazy guys making lame excuses. I don't want to hear any more of this nonsense! Do I make myself clear?"

He had indeed, and he got his wish. After that, none of the field managers passed on reports about the rising tide of resentment and dissatisfaction in the field force. About a year later, the executive was flabbergasted when hundreds of field employees signed a petition demanding the formation of a union. They had returned the compliment. The executive had cut himself off from feedback, which is something that no manager in his or her right mind should ever do. It's about as smart as standing on your own oxygen tube.

Changing Minds

The most difficult of all communication tasks is to change people's attitudes, especially when they are strongly held. You can't do that with a frontal assault, because that will also be viewed as an attack on their judgment, or their values, or even—ultimately—on their self-esteem. So you don't begin by challenging their beliefs, or by exposing what you regard as their faulty reasoning. Instead, you begin by agreeing with them.

Later, you can try to get them to see things in a broader context. While continuing to agree that what they regard as the central facts are facts, you'll begin pointing out that other facts have to be taken into account, as well. Your purpose is to broaden their perspective. Some people, of course, are easier to reason with than others. So you concentrate on those who can follow your argument. Those who can't, or won't, will usually follow behind those who can, if only for the sake of conformity.

Something like this strategy was used during the racial integration of many southern factories. Typically, the attitudes of white workers varied from skepticism to outright opposition. The managers who achieved the smoothest transitions began by acknowledging that employment in skilled and better-paid jobs had until then been the exclusive province of the whites. That nod toward precedent, repeated over and over again, reassured the workers that the managers understood how they felt.

But afterward, managers began to draw a distinction between acknowledging historical realities and endorsing them as right. They also pointed to the political and legal realities, and to the necessity for change. Their purpose was not to make converts of the workers, but to prepare them to live peacefully and even gracefully with the change that would inevitably come.

Of course, what really changed attitudes, to the extent that they have been changed at all, was not the arguments of the managers but the experience of working in integrated plants. But that could not have happened if managers had not won over the more accessible workers, and isolated the hotheads. And what made that rather delicate transition possible was the demonstration that the managers did not dismiss or devalue the workers' ideas, but that on the contrary, they understood them.

The first rule of communication is that you *must* get the attention of your audience. You can only do that if you first find out what is already uppermost in their minds. That's why *listening* is the key skill in communicating.

Listen First, Talk Later

The ideas that are already inside people's heads have a momentum of their own. Once your attention latches onto something, it doesn't let go easily. We see that in the preference of most people to continue thinking about whatever they're already thinking about, rather than shift their attention to what you or anyone else wants them to think about.

That's why *every attempt to communicate is an intrusion.* Unless you can contrive to make your message a welcome intrusion, it will probably be brushed aside. Most failures to communicate occur at the very instant when they are attempted, because the message seems irrelevant to whatever the audience is already concerned with. If your message has no obvious relationship to what worries or pleases your audience, you'll be lucky if they ignore you politely.

The key that opens another person's mind to your message is knowing what he is concerned about. To find that key, you have to either know people very well (which is the secret of being an effective politician) or make it your business to study them (which is the secret of being an effective motivator). You have to know how to *listen.* Even more important: you have to want to listen. Your mind must be as open to their thoughts as you want their minds to be open to yours.

The Art of Listening Hard

When someone speaks to you softly, you have to listen hard to hear what he is saying. You have to focus your attention entirely on that person. You have to screen out all irrelevant noise, and concentrate totally on what that person is saying. That is why some shrewd motivators will at times deliberately lower their voices, precisely to induce that effect.

Even when someone speaks audibly, his *message* may not be

loud. Meanings are easily concealed by one's choice of words, or by timidity or civility. (This is what drives Americans crazy when negotiating with the Japanese. The Japanese want you to infer their meaning, while Americans want them to come right out and say it.) But Americans don't always tell each other what they think in clear, unmistakable terms, either. That's why you always have to listen hard to know what is already important to your audience, regardless of whether they have expressed their views openly or indirectly.

Listening hard means listening for meanings, and meanings do *not* lie in the dictionary definition of words. Meanings are in the intentions of whoever utters those words. So listening hard means listening for clues as to what your audience believes and wants. And it means listening to tones of voice as well as to words. Whenever someone's tone of voice changes, it signals a shift in his intentions: for example, from being literal ("What I say is what I mean") to exaggeration ("Don't take this too seriously"), or vice versa.

Listening hard also means searching for the premises from which your audience's views could be logically derived. Everyone's views make sense to *them*. When they don't make sense to others, that is because the views of others are derived from different premises. You have to figure out the bedrock assumptions that your audience starts from, the ideas that seem so glaringly obvious to them that they feel no need even to express them. Once you have figured that out, you've gone a long way toward knowing what your audience will believe and what they'll reject.

One trick that I learned a long time ago is to pay attention to humor. Humor persists for two reasons: it is fun, and it has survival value. That is, humor helps us to cope with our vulnerabilities. Whatever we fear seems less fearsome if we can laugh at it. Most groups share certain in-jokes that are not especially funny to outsiders. So if most of the in-jokes in a group of workers are about the stupidity or deceitfulness of managers (or salespeople, or minorities, or whomever), that is probably what bothers them most.

Listening hard also means picking up hints about how much trust your audience is willing to place in you. Open, candid, unambiguously expressed views imply trust. Guarded, antiseptic, obliquely hinted-at views imply distrust. In that case, you have to figure out whether your audience considers itself endangered, or whether it sees you as the problem.

Most important of all, listening hard means knowing the difference between what people are saying to you and what you want to hear. You need to know enough of your own psychology to at least become suspicious when everything you hear simply reaffirms your own views. There has to be somebody, somewhere, who disagrees with you. If you're listening hard, you rise above the petty issue of who is right and who is wrong. The real issue is that you have to understand what that other person thinks if you want to have any hope at all of communicating with him.

Understanding someone means more than merely parroting back, verbatim, what has been said to you. It means knowing which experiences have shaped the bedrock assumptions of the people you're listening to. It means recognizing the logic of their views, once those assumptions are granted. Listening hard means doing your level best to get inside someone else's head in order to view the world through their eyes. Until you can present a defensible case for those views, no matter how much they differ from your own, you haven't listened hard enough.

A psychiatrist friend once told me, "Nobody leaves the mirror dissatisfied." And that, dear reader, includes you and me and everyone else. We all maintain our sanity by contriving to interpret everything that happens to us in ways that make us look innocent, justified, and even (occasionally) noble. There's nothing wrong with that, as long as you don't let it distort what other people are trying to tell you.

As long as I am telling psychiatrist stories, here is one for which I am indebted to the late Irving Janis, who was a psychologist at Yale. It concerns a rabbi who had a nosy wife. She had the terrible habit of listening at the keyhole while her husband gave confidential counseling to the members of his congregation. One day she heard a man complaining that his wife didn't understand him, and the rabbi replied, "Well, I think that you are absolutely right, and you have my complete sympathy." Feeling comforted, the man left.

Moments later, that man's wife arrived, and complained to the rabbi that her husband didn't understand her. "Well," said the rabbi, "I think that you are absolutely right, and you have my complete sympathy." Feeling comforted, the woman left.

At this point, the rabbi's wife could contain herself no longer. She burst into his study and said, "What kind of a rabbi are you, anyway?

They can't *both* be right!" The rabbi reflected for a moment. Then he said, "You know something? You're right, too!"

When the people you are trying to influence don't regard your views as the wisest revelations since the Bible, don't take that as a challenge to debate with them. Instead, take it as an opportunity to see the matter from their perspective. They just might return the compliment. And who knows, you might even learn something from them.

So before you start telling other people what you want them to do, invest some time in listening hard to what they think they are already doing and what they think they ought to do, and to what rewards they think they deserve for doing that. Even if your ultimate purpose is to change their minds, you're not going to do that with a frontal assault. You have to get their attention, and you have to get their guard down. You do that by demonstrating that you know and understand the way they think.

At this point I had better say a few more words about "manipulation." Some people profess to believe that behavioral scientists have developed nefarious ways to deceive people, and that if you practice these evil arts, you can actually trick people into doing things that they would not do if they understood your real intentions. There are two things to be said about that belief.

First, it's baloney. The gullible have always been with us, and so have the unscrupulous people who gull them. But nobody has ever figured out how to fool people in their right minds into doing things they wouldn't do anyway.

Second, the essential first step in communication is going out of your way to understand the minds that you're trying to influence. Initially, in other words, the people you are trying to reach will affect your behavior much more than you affect theirs. So if you bend over backward to understand them, who is manipulating whom?

Manipulation, in brief, is the most overpublicized nonissue in communication. That's why we'll say no more about it.

Methods Matter, Mastery Doesn't

When is communication effective? It's effective when a message is *received* by the people for whom it was intended, *understood* to mean what the sender thought it meant, *remembered* for reasonably long periods of time, and—here comes the acid test—*used* the way the sender wanted it to be used. We communicate to motivate. A message that doesn't affect the way people think or act doesn't communicate. If your message doesn't pass all four of those tests, you're not communicating. You're just making noise.

That's true regardless of whether you were intelligible or tongue-tied when you said whatever you said. The method of communication that you use matters more than how expertly you use it. A public relations expert whose message isn't received, understood, remembered, and used is simply making eloquent, expensive noise. True, if our p.r. genius actually does touch all four of those bases with one message, it's likely to be quotable, memorable, admirable—all of those good things. But it won't be more *effective* than a plain, everyday, rather dull message that hits the same four bases. And if a message isn't going to be effective, there's no point in sending it in the first place.

There's one method of communication that is far ahead of all the others when it comes to effectiveness. It isn't used often enough, because it has three dreadful disadvantages. First, it's old—probably as old as civilization. Second, it doesn't involve any breathtaking new technology. (It's not only low-tech: worse still, it's no-tech!) But the last disadvantage is the real killer. It's time-consuming.

In fact, this method has only one advantage to compensate for all those awful handicaps: it works. Nothing else works nearly as well. If you use it, you will probably get your message across most of the time. If you don't use it, you're going to strike out more than you should. Smart motivators just make up their minds to swallow those three disadvantages. The third (the time cost) is the only one that really matters, anyway.

Here we have to confront the famous distinction that Peter Drucker made between efficiency and effectiveness. To be efficient, you simply minimize the cost of whatever you do. Being efficient has survival value in a competitive economy, which is why managers tend to become obsessed with it. Unfortunately, that obsession sometimes blinds them to the larger issue of effectiveness, which means doing only those things that produce results worth having. Alas, you can be efficient without being effective. You can do the wrong things well. Managers do it all the time, especially when they are trying to communicate.

The most efficient ways to communicate are also the most ineffective. They produce results that aren't worth having, but at very low cost. The savings, of course, are irrelevant. Consider, for example, the memorandum. With a good copying machine, you can send one of your memos to literally every in-basket in your company at a very low cost per copy. That's efficient. But how many memos have you filed away forever in your "I'll read this when I get around to it" file? How many have you simply skimmed without reading them carefully, because you had better things to do with your time? How many simply wound up in your wastebasket? One of those three fates is the most common destiny of most memos. They don't cost much, but they don't get many messages across, either.

Or consider another highly efficient method of communicating: the speech. For a nominal cost per person, you can hire a hall, fill it with as many people as the Fire Department will permit, put your beloved CEO on the stage in front of a microphone, and hand him a speech to read to the assembled throng. You can even go high-tech, and put him on a satellite TV hookup that broadcasts his message all over the world. Lots of people will hear exactly the same speech at the same time. That's efficiency for you. But is it effective? That depends on how many people were listening in the first place, and on how many listened all the way to the end. The rule of thumb is that the more people there are in the audience, and the longer the speech, the lower the percentage of people who get the message.

Good communication is inherently time-consuming. To do it well, you'll have to concentrate your attention on a limited number of people, and invest a lot of your time in communicating with them. To free up that time, you'll have to delegate a lot of your less important tasks to others. And you'll have to leave the task of communicating beyond your close circle of associates to those associates. To become a good communicator, you'll just have to learn to do everything else more efficiently, so as to leave plenty of time for the inherently inefficient process of getting your message across. That's where the bulk of your time has to go. Face it: ineffective communication is worse than inefficient—it's useless.

Now, then: what is this old-fashioned, no-tech, time-consuming, inefficient method of communication that gets your message across more effectively than any other method? It's *frequent, face-to-face dialogue.* Why does it work so much better than anything else? Because the human brain processes incoming information much more efficiently when it arrives via that channel. We were made to be conversed with. We are not well designed to be anyone's passive audience. Neither television nor copying machines nor the word processor on which I am writing this book has changed that.

Frequent, Face-to-Face Dialogue

Let's take this best-of-all methods apart and look at its components. Why does communication have to be *frequent* to be effective?

Because people have short memories. As soon as your message to someone ends, other messages from other sources start crowding in to compete with it. Psychologists have been studying human memory for more than a hundred years, and they still haven't found anything that works better than plain old repetition to make a message stick. That's why advertisers want you to encounter their messages everywhere you look.

The problem with simply conveying your message once, and then forgetting about it, is that your audience will do the same. Managers who are reluctant to be repetitive sometimes ask if their audiences won't get tired of the same old message. The answer is that it's better to risk that than to risk having them forget. Say it differently each time, say it creatively or amusingly or seriously, as you prefer: but keep on saying it. For how long? For as long as you want them to remember it.

How about that *face-to-face?* Why is the best communication one-on-one and eyeball-to-eyeball? Because your physical presence, right in front of someone, is far more arresting and unignorable than your face on a television screen, or than any piece of paper that you have signed. And the gesture of going to see someone, and investing something as precious as your time in speaking directly to that person, is a tangible, dramatic proof of how much importance you place on speaking to him.

I was lucky enough to learn that lesson when I was just beginning my career. One morning, a few months after I had joined my company, I entered my office, which in those days was little more than a partitioned-off cubicle. To my utter astonishment, the president of the company was waiting for me in my tiny office. "I read your report last night," he said, "and I just wanted to stop by this morning and tell you that it was great." He shook my hand and left. The entire gesture took him about fifteen seconds, and today, many years later, I still feel good about it.

Finally, why dialogue? Why is it necessary to let people communicate right back at you, in order to communicate effectively with them? There are four good reasons. First, Marshall McLuhan was right: the medium is the message. The particular method of communication that you choose sends a message of its own, entirely apart from whatever you may choose to say. Thus, if I choose to communicate with you via a one-way lecture, that choice suggests that I have many more important things to say to you than you have to say to me. That's one reason why it's so hard to concentrate on a lengthy lecture: the lecture itself is an implied insult. And it's why smart professors pepper their lectures with requests for questions from their students, or by putting their own questions to the class. On the other hand, if I invite you to help me to arrive at a conclusion that satisfies us both, the gesture shows respect for your point of view.

The second reason is that dialogue holds the attention of your audience. That's partly because the outcome of a two-way discussion is never entirely predictable, so they'll be curious to see what happens next. It's also because one never knows when he'll be expected to speak, and so he has to remain alert.

The third reason for the superiority of dialogue is that it gives you a chance to make instant corrections. If people have misconstrued what you said, or if what you said just wasn't clear to them, you'll detect that in their comments. You can fix that before the wrong interpretations are etched into their memories. (This is one of the main disadvantages of all forms of written communication, including this one. You can't ask a document what it means, and a document can't ask you whether you understand it.)

The fourth reason for the superiority of dialogue is that you have to touch that fourth base. That is, your message must motivate: it has to be converted into appropriate action. You have to demonstrate to your audience that it's in their best interest to do what you've asked them to do. Dialogue helps to remove their doubts, because it gives them an opportunity to express those doubts, and gives you an opportunity to reply to them. And dialogue gives them a stake in making whatever is agreed upon actually happen, because the plan that emerges from a dialogue is partly of their own creation.

So, how can you communicate effectively, regardless of whether or not you are particularly gifted in the arts of language? First, listen hard to know what is already on the minds of those whose minds you would change. And second, engage them in direct discussions, and repeat them as often as it is practical for you to do that. You'll find that this approach to communication is going to eat up a lot of your time. But if your purpose is to motivate, there isn't a better way for you to invest your time.

CHAPTER
6

THE BEST-KEPT SECRET IN MOTIVATION

The best-kept secret in motivation is that most people care a lot about their careers. Granted, that isn't really a secret. But careers get so little emphasis in comparison to more highly touted but less potent motivators (like money and leadership) that a bit of poetic license helps to make the point.

Until you get up into your fifties, and sometimes even later, you're going to care more about where a job might lead you than about its fairness equation—unless, of course, that equation is grossly out of balance. Otherwise, until you start staring retirement in the face, your hopes of what the future may have in store for you can usually out-motivate whatever rewards you are collecting now. That's why we tolerate jobs that sometimes leave a lot to be desired, as long as we believe that something a lot better may be in store for us, down the road.

In this chapter, we'll deal with the most important career in the world—yours, of course. The main point here is that you can't afford to let your career merely happen to you. On the contrary, you have to actively *manage it*.

In the next chapter, we'll look at how companies use, and misuse, the career motivation of their employees. This will give you an opportunity to weigh how well your own company is managing the most important career in the world. That chapter will also give some advice on what you can do, as a manager, to put the career motives of your subordinates and associates to work for you.

But our concern here and now is with your own career, and with your efforts to motivate other winners by influencing their careers.

Managing Your Career

I assume that you are reading this book because you want your career to carry you as far as your talents and your luck will go, and that you want to get there as quickly as you can, and stay there as long as you can. If that's the case, the sooner you face the following fact, the better off you'll be. *There is an inherent conflict of interest between you and your employer.*

There are only two exceptions to that rule. First, if your company happens to be in a rapid growth phase of its own, its growth needs may be more or less synchronized with yours, so there'll be no conflict. But if your timing is wrong, because you joined the company too soon or too late, that rule applies to you. Further, most companies, most of the time, are not growing all that rapidly. So most ambitious people have to face that fact of life, and deal with it.

The second exception is if your company is managing the career motivation of its employees intelligently. Some do, and some don't. If your company isn't doing this, that conflict is inevitable.

Here's why. To your company, you are an investment. It paid the cost of finding you, hiring you, and training you. It buys the supplies and equipment that you use, and pays for the people who help you. Added to all that, your company had to pay your salary and benefits until your productivity reached the break-even point. That's when your accumulated accomplishments finally pay back the accumulated investment.

Depending on the nature of your work, that payback may take months or even years. It's only after that point is reached that your company begins to cash in on its investment in you. And isn't that the whole point of any investment? To get a lot more out of it than had to be put into it?

So if your company looks at you objectively and unsentimentally (as it should), it has a vested interest in keeping you in the job for which it's trained you. How long? For as long as possible *after* you repay its initial investment. That's what makes its investment in you profitable.

You can see why a non-growing company's motives fit neatly with those of employees who are content to stay put. And there are lots of people who aspire only to years and years of nonstop employment by the same employer, all the way to retirement. I presume, however, that this description does not fit you.

If maximizing your own career potential is your principal aim in life, you have to regard your company as a means to an end. It's either a ladder to be climbed or a bridge to a better ladder in another company. If you can't foresee it serving either purpose, you're in the wrong company. If that's the case, you really have to look at your company no less objectively and unsentimentally than it looks at you. Why? Because you definitely want to avoid the middle-aged, middle-management trap and the sudden job death syndrome, both of which I'll describe for you in a moment.

Playing Hardball With Your Career

You should be just as hardheaded in thinking about your company as it is in thinking about you. Both parties to the bargain are out to get all they can from each other. Ten or twenty years from now, your company may well be playing hardball with people your age. The folks who will be making decisions then about your career are the same tough characters who decide which departments should be folded, which plants should be shut down, and which older employees should be involuntarily retired. (And that's not the picnic you may think it is, because all of those too-early pensions must be cut drastically.)

So you have to play hardball, too. You can't afford to leave your career in the hands of those tough characters who will quite properly put the company's interests first, with yours a distant second. You have to start making decisions now that will keep the top cards in your hands throughout your career. That's your best defense against getting stuck in a classical career rut as a stalled, overpaid, clearly dispensable has-been—right about the time when your marketability starts to evaporate. That's the middle-aged, middle-management trap, and you want to stay out of it at all costs.

When a company accumulates too many such managers, its

bloated payroll attracts the attention of corporate raiders, or of bright young management consultants with sharp pencils, looking for jobs to eliminate. That's when the sudden-job-death syndrome puts in its appearance. Your job will suddenly be deemed unnecessary, and therefore, regrettably, so will you. If that happens, your own security motive, which slept so peacefully for so long in its remote corner of your brain, will suddenly lurch to its feet, shake its head, and begin to growl.

If you trust your company not to do that to you, consider that most of the fine managers who inspire that trust today will be retired by the time you become exposed to the syndrome. Consider also that the smart young consultants who will be gunning for your job then are probably still in diapers today. The old saw is absolutely true, and it applies to you, too. The only thing that doesn't change is change itself.

How can you tell whether you're really exposed to being eased out, or bounced out, of your company, ten or twenty years down the road? You can't. At least, not with any certainty. But here are some indicators to look at.

How does your company treat people today who are ten, fifteen, and even twenty years older than you are, and who once held jobs that were comparable at that time to yours? Are they actually being allowed to use all that knowledge and experience, or have they simply been moved aside onto comfortable, well-paid plateaus where they have little to do, and can do that indefinitely? Is being bought off in that way any way to spend your most vulnerable years? What will happen to you then if your company should get into serious financial trouble? Finally, the most important question of all: *What makes you think the company will treat you any differently, when your time comes?*

That's why in the long run, and possibly even the short run, your motives and your company's motives are probably on a collision course.

What About Company Loyalty?

Many companies like to encourage the notion that you've finally found a home with them. If you'll just do your job right and stay out of trouble, they'll take care of you from here to eternity. That's a pleasant thought, but you have to consider the company's motives for implying all those good things. (*Implying* is the right word. The company lawyers would never let them put that in writing.)

First, knowing the havoc that an aroused security motive can wreak with labor relations and with productivity, the company will wisely try to keep that sleeping beast asleep. Second, there's that investment to protect. If you should decide to decamp too soon, with all that valuable training inside your head, the company's bottom line with you could well be below its "hurdle rate." (That's whatever its in-house financial experts consider the minimum acceptable return on any investment.) Third, your company's personnel department may well suffer from a common delusion that might be called "turnover phobia." That's the erroneous belief that voluntary departures reflect unfavorably on all of the things that personnel departments do.

So the company's motives in encouraging your loyalty are not altogether altruistic. (I should add that there are many well-intentioned souls in personnel departments who haven't a cynical bone in their bodies, and who have simply never considered the economic advantages to their companies of encouraging employee loyalty.) Nevertheless, the device may work all too well with you. You may get twinges of guilt from even contemplating the possibility of seeking your fortune elsewhere. Is it really fair, is it really ethical, for you to take such blatant advantage of a company that has done so much for you?

Sure it is—provided you can stand in front of a mirror, look yourself in the eye, and answer yes to the following questions. First, have you served the company long enough for it to have recouped its initial investment in you? There's seldom a precise way to estimate the payback period, so judge this conservatively. More important, how well have you served the company? Have you given your work its full share of time, effort, and commitment?

If your answer to all those questions is yes, the score is even. The company has been loyal to you, and you've been equally loyal to the company. Neither side owes the other side anything, unless their interests continue to coincide.

And that's the real issue. *Loyalty* is a fine old concept whose time has passed. It is a relic of the era when good jobs and benign employers were hard to find, and when the fortunate few who had such jobs were damned glad of it. The real issue in today's world is whether your interests and your company's interests continue to coincide. If they do, you and your company can continue being loyal to each other. If they don't, it's your responsibility to look after your own interests.

You can probably bet your bottom dollar that your company will look after its interests. If it doesn't, it is headed down the tubes, and there is no point in your remaining aboard a leaking ship. If your company is well managed, it does not want to face the cost and inconvenience of replacing you until that is clearly in its own best interests. You must never forget that such a day may come, if you let it.

In defending your interests, you have to play hardball. That is not disloyalty. On the contrary, it's fair play. If your company's management is mature and professional, they expect that of you and would be rather disappointed if you didn't look after yourself. Both you and your company must never forget that employment does not carry the same level of commitment as marriage or parenthood. Employment is really only cohabitation, no matter how long it lasts.

How, then, do you manage your own career? Most careers consist of at least four phases, and the answer varies from phase to phase. Although you may already have passed through one or more of these phases, you should read through all of the following sections. That way, you can check on how well you've handled your responsibility to yourself until now. You'll also find that decisions made in one phase of your career can affect your decisions in later phases.

The four career phases are preparation, ascent, peak, and windup. What do they have to do with motivation? If one of your own principal motives is to gain satisfaction through what you accomplish in your work, the answer is, "Not quite everything, but almost." For winners, one's career is the vehicle through which most of life's victories, and life's disappointments, as well, are encountered.

Preparation

Preparation consists of everything you do before the first job that counts, which is the one that leads you permanently onto the career track you really want to follow. This phase usually includes both your formal education and two kinds of jobs—the moneymaking jobs that did nothing to prepare you for your career, and false-start jobs that ultimately led you nowhere.

Young people who are eager to get off their parents' payrolls, and onto some company's, are usually obsessed with two questions. Which entry-level jobs should they aim for, and which college major will get them that first real job with a real company? Nothing would please them more than having to choose between too many job offers, and nothing haunts them more than graduating with none. But quite often they're asking the wrong questions, and by the time that finally dawns on them they may have committed themselves to the wrong career.

Students often find this hard to believe, but there are worse things than graduating into a weak job market. You could, for example, invest four irreplaceable years and a lot of money preparing for work you won't like.

This point seems awfully abstract to many young people. But they ignore it at their own peril, so I'm going to digress for a few paragraphs to drive home the point as concretely as I can. Preparing yourself for a career that doesn't fit your inclinations is nearly always a mistake, regardless of the supply and demand situation in the job market when you first enter it.

Consider, for example, computer programmers (or for that matter, people in any highly specialized occupation, such as engineers or accountants). Many of them discover, a few years after launching their careers, that bending over flow charts and peering into computer screens leaves them bored, restless, and starved for human contact. Some manage to escape from this kind of career trap, and some don't. That's why it's better not to get caught in it in the first place.

Some are lucky enough to make it into hybrid jobs, like systems analysis, which involve working with clients, and which draw on both their prior schooling and their "people skills." Others manage to move into management jobs, most of which are hybrids that combine specialized knowledge with human contacts. But other, less lucky specialists, remain stuck in jobs that do not offer the kind of stimulation that they need. Many of these unfortunates find the burden of keeping themselves up-to-date technologically just too uninteresting. So they drift, through neglect, into obsolescence within, say, six or seven years. Others have no choice but to resign themselves to work to which they cannot give themselves fully, with results that eventually show up on their performance appraisals.

It's instructive to watch the way in which employers react to this phenomenon. In many cases their attitude is, "We hired an engineer (or a laboratory scientist, or an accountant, or whatever), not a dreamer who still doesn't know what he wants to be when he finally grows up." So they will actively discourage employees from seeking transfers to other divisions, or from going to night school to acquire new qualifications.

Attempts by employers to obstruct the natural evolution of their employees' careers are nearly always a mistake. They merely postpone the inevitable, instead of trying to guide it and make use of it. A company that insists on type-casting you in a job that you've outgrown, or that wasn't right for you in the first place, isn't the right company for you now.

Management would be much wiser to help you become whatever you were meant to be. That way they get a new specialist who is already familiar with the way another part of the company works. That's always a valuable asset. It's even wiser for your company to help you, even if that means finding another company that can make better use of the talents you want to develop. That way, your company can at least spare itself the embarrassment of an involuntarily trapped employee who will probably dwindle slowly into mediocrity. You definitely don't want that to happen to you, and neither should your company.

Enough said? Now, back to the question of which career to prepare for.

The right career for you is the one in which your strongest abilities give you the greatest competitive advantage. If you're planning on an upwardly oriented career, you'd better plan on entering the job market with those abilities fully developed. That way you'll compete for jobs that you enjoy doing. You'll be building motivation into your career instead of shutting it out. Major in whatever you do best, and leave the vagaries of the job market to the economists. No one else is paid to worry about it.

Those economists will tell you that the job market goes through cycles. No matter where it is when you graduate, it will be somewhere else a few years later. It will probably go through a good half-dozen cycles, and maybe more, before you retire. In fact, the chances are pretty good that before you retire, you'll enter at least one line of work that didn't exist when you began your career. (People were writing books when I began my career, but not with lap-top word processors like the one on which I'm writing this one.)

Ascent

Get ready to stare another paradox in the face. *The right company with which to begin your career is probably the wrong one to be with ten years or so down the road.*

Last time I checked the statistics, more than 40 percent of all employed Americans worked for companies with ten thousand or more employees. Thanks to mergers and acquisitions, that percentage is still growing. Those big companies are great places to begin an upwardly mobile career. They are not great places for the rest of your career.

First, let's consider why a big company is an ideal place to launch a career. It's the best place to pick up the four "C factors" that are indispensable for getting your career properly launched: competence, confidence, connections, and credentials.

The First "C Factor": Competence

The biggest advantage of a big company for someone launching an ambitious career is that a big company usually has good training programs. In a rapidly developing professional or technical field, you can usually learn more, and learn it sooner, from a good company training program than at a good university. Those training programs are expensive, which is why only big, well-financed companies can afford to offer them. I might add that they also can't afford *not* to offer them, because otherwise their own growth chokes on a lack of qualified personnel. So at this phase of your career, your own interests and those of a big company probably coincide.

The big company will do more than just teach you. More important, it will put you into the field to start practicing what you've learned, and with real clients who will depend on your expertise. That combination of good classroom instruction with hands-on, real-world practice is the best way to become really good at what you do for a living. That's where you'll build your *competence*.

But knowing what to do is only half of what it takes to become an expert. The other half, which is overlooked in some half-baked training programs, is *knowing that you know*. You have to be confident that what you think should be done is what an expert would do in the same situation.

The Second "C Factor": Confidence

I stumbled across this factor a few years ago in Europe, when a multinational company asked me to explain why its Italian technicians were consistently less productive than their counterparts in other countries. I quickly dispensed with the notion that the Italians might somehow be less qualified than the others. They weren't. Their aptitude test scores were virtually the same, and they received the same number of hours of technical training. They used the same tools, and they looked after the same equipment. But average Italian technicians could just about keep up with a workload that was about 80 percent of what their German or French colleagues carried with ease.

Before hitting on the answer, I followed a lot of blind alleys. I won't bore you with them. The right answer proved to be a subtle difference in their training. We knew that Italians expressed considerably less confidence than their counterparts did in their own ability to deal correctly with complex technical problems. The question was, why?

In taking apart the Italian training program piece by piece, I hit upon what at first looked like a clever way to conserve scarce manpower. The Italian subsidiary was growing so rapidly that it needed every available technician in the field. It really couldn't spare any experienced men to act as instructors for the trainees. But of course, it had to spare some, so they assigned that task to the least-experienced (and sometimes the least-respected) men in the field. That kept their strength on the firing line, where, at least in theory, it belonged. But in this case the theory was wrong. The strategy cost far more than it saved, because the students sensed that their instructors were not sure of themselves. As a result, class after class of technicians were sent into the field, prepared to be overwhelmed by problems they had actually been taught to solve. That's why they spent more time on each problem than their colleagues, with the result that they could not handle as much work.

Persuading Italian management that their solution to one problem had caused another problem is another story. Eventually we did it, and the problem gradually went away. The important point here is that the first "C factor," competence, is useless without the second, which is confidence.

You build your confidence by proving to yourself that you can make the right decisions without anyone else's help. Contrary to what the "inspirational" school of motivation will tell you, you can't talk yourself into that confidence. Instead, you teach yourself into it, by doing the job correctly, again and again, by yourself. The best place to do that is in a company that will give you instructors who know what they are talking about, and plenty of practice in the field. That's probably a big company.

The Third "C Factor": Connections

A big company is also a good place to start your collection of people who are building careers of their own that are related to yours. Some day, some of them will be in a position to be helpful. Of course, you can meet such people in smaller companies too, but a big company will have more of them. Also, in a big company more of them will be outward bound, like you. Eventually, many of them will decide that the time has come to pursue their careers elsewhere. As they disperse, your connections expand with them, into what gradually becomes a network of *connections* in many companies.

Your collection of connections eventually becomes your private employment agency. You'll be sought for jobs, consulting assignments, and speaking engagements by the people who already know you. (Until and unless you acquire a widespread reputation, the *only* invitations you'll get will come from people who already know you. Thus, if you should receive an invitation to speak in public, grab it. Short of appearing on nationwide television, that's the best way to publicize your talents. There is nearly always someone in the audience who will remember your name when an interesting opportunity crops up for you later on.)

Another advantage of connections is that they convert you from an unknown quantity outside your company to someone who is not merely known, but highly regarded by well-positioned people in well-regarded companies. This kind of connection makes your résumé credible and relevant. That's what gives your résumé an edge over all the others, which are probably written with the same glowing adjectives and the same eye-catching appeal as yours.

Everyone reads the same manuals about how to write résumés, but not everyone comes highly recommended by a collection of successful people. Choose your friends carefully, help them unstintingly whenever you can, and build their sense of obligation to you. Most people like to take full credit for their accomplishments, so your friends will probably feel less indebted to you than you might think they should be. Don't hesitate to call on them when you need them, but be careful not to overdo this. Reserve your requests for help strictly for those rare, big, irresistible opportunities. Otherwise, just let those favors done for others pile up, like interest in a bank account.

The Fourth "C Factor": Credentials

This brings us to the last of the four indispensable "C factors": your credentials. It's better to have a well-known company on your résumé for the same reason that it's better to have an Ivy League college there. That's true even if dear old Unknown University has a Department of Whatever that can run rings around Harvard's. As candid Ivy League academicians will concede, there are lots of such departments, but that doesn't matter because no one knows that but a few experts like them.

Résumé readers assume that your first one or two employers performed the same screening function that prestigious colleges are expected to provide. That is, they assume that they had more applicants than they had openings, so they could afford to be choosy. It's that presumption of selectiveness that gives the prestigious schools and the bigger companies their reputations. It's also assumed that such a company would not have hired you, or kept you, if it hadn't been satisfied with both your credentials and your performance. These assumptions are not always correct, but nevertheless they give the ex-employees of big companies a big advantage in the job market. Correct or not, they are a fact of life for anyone seeking an upward-and-outward move. The base from which you make that move matters a lot.

All four "C factors" are more readily acquired in a large company than in a smaller one. That's why a big company is the best place to start your career. But unless you'd be contented with slow progress in your middle years, or even no progress, a large company is *not* the place to be by the time you get into your late thirties or early forties. We've already been through a number of reasons for this, but the most potent reason of all is that the sheer mathematical odds on further advancement tilt badly against you as you rise into middle management.

Every time you're promoted in a large company, the number of jobs above that level, to which you might aspire, shrinks. Further, the competition for those few remaining opportunities heats up. Thus, every time you are promoted, the statistical odds against your winning another promotion get worse.

You can get stalled for any number of reasons that have nothing to do with your abilities or your performance. Management will have a benchful of great talent to choose from, and it may prefer someone with a different profile for those jobs that happen to open up while you're waiting your turn. That's why the higher you go, the more your further upward progress becomes a roll of the dice, and the less influence you can have upon it through your own efforts. The outcome passes out of your hands. It's you versus the laws of chance. If you should ever decide to bet against the laws of chance, you'd better have a damned good reason. The two best reasons for that kind of gamble are knowing that you have the inside of the track and knowing that your opportunities elsewhere are no better than those you have where you are now.

Otherwise, the best place to spend the middle of your career is in a medium-sized company, with between one thousand and ten thousand employees. Your big company experience will be a big advantage here, and you'll have a good shot at jobs that might take years (or forever) to get in your big company.

There's another advantage in moving from a larger to a smaller company. Suppose your secret ambition is to take over a big company someday as chief executive officer, or as chief of your professional specialty. Despite the noises that most companies make about promotion-from-within, your best shot at a top-level job in a big company is to be recruited from an outstanding career in a smaller company. If you don't believe that, ask your friendly local management recruiter, and he will quote the statistics to you.

Peak

Upwardly mobile people usually have at least two companies on their résumés by the time they hit their early forties. One, of course, is the company with which they launched their careers. The second is the one they moved to in order to accelerate their upward growth. The next big career decision usually crops up about seven to ten years later, after they've had a chance to attract a lot of favorable attention as high-level executives in medium-sized companies.

The question is whether to stay put, or risk everything on a bid for the top somewhere else. This is where your personal encounter with Hamlet's dilemma begins. Shakespeare's prince was torn between settling for familiar troubles—the famous "slings and arrows of outrageous fortune"—or gambling, at the risk of making everything much worse, on the hope of making it all better.

Short of deciding whom to marry, you'll never make a more portentous decision in your life. So you'd better make this one right. The best way to make the decision is by using facts, not hopes, to estimate the probabilities. For example, have you been sought out by recruiters? Their most entrancing ploy is to call and say, "Perhaps you can help us find someone with these qualifications." They then proceed to list *your* qualifications. (That's the way I was recruited by IBM. More about that in chapter 18.) But if they haven't sought you out, you have to ask yourself why. If your head isn't attractive to the headhunters, what makes you think that a big company would want to entrust you with a big job? You might be better off staying right where you are.

You might be able to engineer your own entry to another company, without the aid of recruiters. Have you, for example, targeted companies that need, or soon will need, someone like you? Do you know someone influential in that company, or an important outsider (like someone in their law, advertising, or auditing firm) who can help you get an appointment with the right person? Failing all that, can you arrange a meeting yourself with someone that right person will listen to, like an executive assistant?

If you don't have this kind of advantage, you'd be better off waiting until you can somehow get it. What you don't want, with a move of this importance, is to have your résumé get lost in a big pile along with other people's résumés. If you can't have the inside of the track, your chances of landing a job this big are not that good.

Windup

Yogi Berra was right. The game isn't over until it's over. But eventually, it *is* over. For all practical purposes, that day comes long before your first pension check arrives in the mail. It comes when you reconcile yourself to the fact that you've already risen as high as you're going to rise. That's as inevitable as death and taxes, but much preferable to both.

For the rest of your active career, the only way to advance is to keep setting new performance records in the job you've already got. You want to hit the finish line running faster, so to speak, than at any time since you left the starting line. You want to become a problem for your successor, in the sense of becoming one hell of a hard act for him to follow.

This is where, for the first time in a long, active career, a bit of philosophy may be helpful. What, you may ask, does philosophy have to do with motivation? At the end of your career, your attitude toward the past that you have already lived through can have a major effect on what remains of your future. You want to stay motivated all the way to the end, because the alternative is to die on the vine. To avoid that fate, you've got to look at your own past from a realistic perspective.

If you're still young, the end game of your career may seem so remote as to be irrelevant. But if you're lucky, you'll survive to that stage, and when you do, you'll be surprised at how rapidly you got there. The question you'll have to answer then will be: how do you measure the success, or lack of it, in your own career?

Surely not by how much money you made. Where you finish monetarily has a lot to do with when you started. Because of inflation alone, you've probably made more than your father did, and for the same reason, your kids will make more than you did.

Neither does it make much sense to measure a career by how high you managed to climb on the organizational pyramid. Because it narrows so drastically near the top, a lot of outstanding people are caught in a corporate traffic jam just below the summit. Probably most of them are capable of handling the top job, were it to be offered to them. If you were among them, the best explanation for not having made it to the summit may lie in the laws of chance.

The best way to measure a career is not in terms of where you ended it, but in terms of how far you have come. Given the hand you were dealt, so to speak, at the start of your career, how well have you played that hand? Did you take advantage of lucky breaks? Did you manage to avoid the worst consequences of bad luck, or to recover from them quickly? Did you work your advantages for all they were worth, and did you manage to minimize the effects of your disadvantages? Most important of all, can you honestly take credit for what success you've had, or was it largely a matter of being in the right place at the right time? The ultimate question, in other words, is not "How successful were you?" Rather, it is, "Whose success was it?"

Can you stand in front of a mirror, look yourself in the eye, and say, "By God, *you* did it"? If you can, then regardless of where your career may have ended, you can measure it, and yourself as well, as a success. If you want to be able to make that kind of judgment of yourself when your own time comes, the time to get to work on it is now. Get going. And good luck!

CHAPTER
7

HOW TO MANAGE CAREERS

Ambitious people provide their own motivation, as long as they feel that their ambitions have a decent chance of being fulfilled. If they cease to feel that way, they'll either seek another employer or suffer a motivational collapse. To keep their motivation alive you've got to manage their careers. That's what this chapter is all about.

The main problem in managing *other people's* careers is to find ways to make the interests of a company and those of its best people coincide for as long as possible. They almost never coincide forever, but the longer a company's best people feel that they are right where they belong, the greater the return that company will earn from its investment in them.

In well-run companies, maximizing this period of common interest is not left to chance. Instead, it is an assigned responsibility, usually given to a little-known group known as "management development." The task of management development is to make sure that people with the right managerial qualities are right where they are needed, right when they are needed there.

More precisely, their mission is to guarantee that if a key management position becomes vacant, it can be filled by any of several fully qualified candidates. Preferably, these will be home-grown candidates who came up through the company's own ranks. But if necessary, they can also include external candidates who were plucked, so to speak, from other companies.

In other words, the management-development folks manage the company's talent farm. If necessary, they also deal discreetly with certain outsiders called "management recruiters," who rustle talent from other company's farms.

A company's management developers play on behalf of the company, not its managers. Nevertheless, your first two questions in assessing how well your company is managing the most important career in the world should be, "Do we have a management-development function at all?" (You'd be surprised how often the availability of top-level replacements is left virtually to chance.) Second, "If we do have such a function, how well does it do its job?" (There's quite a range, all the way from superb to pitiful.)

Managing the Talent Farm

Your company probably has a manager, or director, or whatever, of management development. That doesn't mean, however, that it has a management-development *function*. Unfortunately, you have to read the fine print. Some management-development departments merely collect seminar catalogs, or contract to bring in packaged courses of one kind or another. In other words, they are really purchasing agents for training programs. Others maintain lists of people who have been nominated as potential replacements for managers in key jobs. In other words, they are trusted clerks who keep the confidential files.

A real management-development function must have its fingers in a lot of pies. That's the only way it can do its job. It has a say in the company's basic *recruitment* strategies, which determine the kinds of talent that flow into a company in the first place. It has a lot to say about the *nomination* process, in which a company seeks out potential managers among its own younger people. It keeps score, in detail, on the *performance* of those candidates who are still in the running for top jobs. It develops *contingency plans,* including the identification of needs that can not be met from within. On short notice, it can put a thin folder on the CEO's desk, summarizing the pros and cons of each available *candidate* for any given managerial job. In brief, a real management-development department has a responsibility that is comparable to that of the corporate treasurer. The treasurer is charged with acquiring and looking after an indispensable resource: money. Management development is charged with acquiring and looking after an equally vital resource: managers.

Note that the management-development function exists for the company's benefit, not for yours or anyone else's. Nevertheless, you still want to be sure that someone, somewhere, is saddled with making sure that plenty of managerial talent is flowing through the pipelines that lead to the top. Otherwise, your own opportunity to get into that pipeline in the first place may be left to chance. And that just won't do for the most important career in the world.

You want to be where they are always hunting systematically for up-and-coming leaders. What's more, you want to be sure that the hunt is intelligently managed, and not left to *anyone's* hunches. To rate your own company's system for managing careers, compare it to the ways in which the best of them do the job. I'll give you some examples in the following sections. Note, however, that it isn't sufficient to handle one of these tasks well. You have to handle *all* of them well.

The Importance of an Unfair Advantage

The right company in which to launch your career is one that has an unfair advantage over all the other companies with which it competes for talent. That's because the process of managing managerial talent effectively is both wasteful and impersonal. You see, it doesn't really matter *which* outstanding person is available when he is needed, as long as *someone* is.

That's why you need to start with copious quantities of talent, more than you would really need just to run the company. You have to anticipate losing lots of good people along the way, simply because they'll happen to become ripe for promotion before a suitable job can open up for them. To pull in so many promising people, you need powerful bait. You need something that will motivate exceptionally capable people to beat a path to your door.

You can't do that with money alone, if only because that would be much too expensive. For baiting purposes, it's really sufficient if the pay is competitive. The best bait is more intangible. It's something that will give ambitious people a competitive edge in the *next* two or three stages of their careers.

Not everyone appreciates the value of that kind of advantage. But people who think ahead appreciate it, the way champion chess players anticipate a whole sequence of moves. And that's exactly the kind of person you want to attract to your company, if you can. What kind of bait will attract them?

Just as your education gets you your first job, but not your second, it's whatever prestige your first job carries that gets you the next one. The bait, in other words, is the ability to put a line on your résumé that tells the world that you were trained by the best in the business. The best bait for luring lots of managerial talent is the reputation of your company's *training program.*

Some companies have become, in effect, "training academies" for their industries. Each year they bring in large numbers of new trainees. But after ten years or so, most will have left to work for other companies. In one sense, that's a wasteful process. But a closer look reveals two huge advantages for the "academy companies" that more than repay their cost.

First, the entry-level and lower-level jobs of those companies are done by outstanding, highly motivated people, most of whom stay long enough to repay the company's training investment. You're not dealing with bored clerks at these levels, but with eager, sharp, helpful people. (Customers usually love having to deal with them.)

The second advantage is even more important. It's the quality of the few people who survive the rigorous culling process. The academy companies almost never have to bring in a key executive from the outside. Instead, they have an internal "embarrassment of riches" from which to choose their top executives. That pays for it all.

How can you tell whether your company has the unfair advantage it needs to out-compete other companies for top talent? First, look at your fellow trainees. Do you expect to easily outdistance them, or will you have to run hard just to keep up with their pace? You're better off with colleagues who push you to your limits, and make you bring out the best in yourself. You'll develop farther and faster under tough competition than you would if winning came too easily for you.

Remember, too, that if you ever leave your company, you're

going to be judged not so much by your record as by your company's reputation. Until you develop a new track record with another employer, you're going to be just another ex-(your company's name) person. Your company's reputation inevitably rubs off on you. So make sure it's a good reputation. Are "alumni" of your company already well placed in respected firms that don't choose to match your company's training program? Are your more senior colleagues wined and dined by recruiters? Is your company well regarded in its industry? These are all good signs.

But if you see none of them, you have to address the question of whether your company is going to be a springboard for your career, or a small pond in which you might someday become a big fish. In the latter case, you have to face the question of whether that is what you really want. This is not the kind of question to which there is a "right" answer that fits everyone. The important issue is not how you answer the question, but whether you ask it at all. If you don't, time and fate are going to answer it for you.

Getting Noticed

People get ahead in companies largely on the basis of other people's recommendations. So the obvious question is, who does the recommending? The answer is that it really doesn't matter, as long as a large enough *number* of informed observers are consulted. We've already been through this point in chapter 2, so I won't belabor it here. The point to remember is that nobody's intuition is better than the combined intuitions of a lot of people, provided they've all looked at pertinent evidence.

A company that wants its most capable leaders to rise to the top is constantly asking questions about them. Anyone who has been in a position to see them in action, up close, is likely to be asked for an opinion. These companies don't wait for the annual performance appraisal ritual, or the annual salary increase exercise, to inquire into how well their best people are doing. They want data while it is still fresh in people's minds, and they want input from as many people as possible.

What the management developers are looking for is the weight of evidence and the trend over time. That's why no single opinion or observation is necessarily more valuable than another, no matter how exalted a particular observer might be.

The management developers are looking for answers to questions like these: Is this person willing to experiment, or does he always play it safe? If this person makes mistakes, does he repeat them or learn from them? Does this person win the confidence of people who have had more direct experience with the problems at hand than he has had? Is he particularly well adapted to certain kinds of challenges, but not as well equipped to handle others?

The purpose of this constant questioning is not to rank the candidates, but to describe and compare them. The moment of truth comes when the management-development team has to come forward with a short list of candidates for a particular opening. What matters then is not who has the most votes, or is the most widely admired. What matters, rather, is who best fits the demands of the particular job at that particular time.

THE BULLDOZER AND THE DIPLOMAT

In one of my client companies, it became necessary to replace the head of a small subsidiary that had drifted from low profitability to a rapidly accelerating loss. The management–development staff produced two candidates, both of whom were available and qualified. One was blunt, assertive, and rather insensitive. He was a bulldozer: the kind of person who could get things done, regardless of the cost. The other candidate was subtle, patient, and shrewd. He was an artful diplomat. Time and again, he had demonstrated his ability to win people over gradually, regardless of their initial opposition.

We all have a natural preference for working with people with whom we can feel comfortable, and whose styles are compatible with our own. For this reason, you may prefer either the first or the second candidate. But the issue is not whom we like best, or who resembles us the most. It is who best fits the current demands of the job.

In this case, either manager could have turned the subsidiary around. The first could have done it rather quickly, at a horrendous cost to morale and customer good will. The second could have done it much more gradually, with very little pain for anyone. So it became a question of how long the parent company could wait for profitability to be restored to its subsidiary.

In this case, the judgment of top management was that things had already deteriorated too far, and that the subsidiary could not survive a lengthy attempt to rescue it. So the first candidate was given the job.

> He performed as predicted. There were howls of pain, many people were fired, and many others elected to leave. Some customers, annoyed at having costly support services taken away, took their business elsewhere. But costs were slashed, efficiencies improved, and profitability was restored. The job was done. Inelegantly, perhaps; but it was done within the time limits set by management.

There are two reasons why you want to be in a company in which anyone who has an opportunity to see you in action is likely to be asked about you. First, that is your best evidence that you are still in the running, and have not been written off as just another manager. Second, when an opening occurs for which your particular strengths and skills may be just what is needed, you definitely want that information to be included in the thin folder that your company's management developers place on the CEO's desk.

Getting Rated

Another point already made in chapter 2 needs to be reiterated here. In the race for top jobs, outstanding job performance is *assumed*. It is nothing more than your entrance ticket to the race, and in itself it won't set you apart from most of your fellow contenders. How, then, can you distinguish yourself? Especially after a few promotions, when the competition heats up, and virtually every one of your fellow contenders is handling his responsibilities superbly?

What the management developers are looking for at this stage is breadth and adaptability, as well as growth. It's not entirely within your power to demonstrate these qualities, because much depends on the kinds of assignments you are given. Therefore you want to be given assignments that test your abilities to handle unfamiliar tasks, or to work effectively with new groups, or in different areas. You want chances to prove that your résumé is nothing more than your history, and is by no means a complete catalog of what you can do well.

How can you influence the kind of challenge you are given? Well, you can *ask* for it. But that is a strategy to be used with great discretion.

Don't make a habit of continually asking for assignments that can stretch your abilities. The danger is that you'll start to sound like a broken record. There is a price that you pay for asking. The first time you ask, you risk being marked as someone who is in too much of a hurry, who doesn't want to *earn* that big upward move. The second time you ask, you risk being marked as a nuisance. Don't take those risks unless the opportunity is clearly worth it. In other words, know when a job is worth asking for.

Keep your eyes, ears, and nose open for assignments that may be just right for you. Never forget Louis Pasteur's brilliant observation that "Chance favors the prepared mind." Don't go after a job just because it's different. Go after it because it can clearly add something exceptional, something distinctive, to your record. Go after it because, even if you're not familiar with much of the job, you won't be going into it naked, either. Go for the jobs to which you can bring some already established strengths that will give you a head start. Until such a job appears on the horizon, bide your time and keep doing outstanding work in your present job.

Knowing Which Opportunity to Seize

I used this strategy once myself, with a spectacular effect on my career. So I can speak from firsthand knowledge. It did not require any particular courage, but it was heavily dependent on timing. You have to be sure that you are really faced with a once-in-a-lifetime opportunity, and not just another attractive job. If you are that sure, go for it.

MY ONCE-IN-A-LIFETIME OPPORTUNITY

In my case, I had been working for one of IBM's domestic divisions for several years, running a program of employee attitude surveys. The idea was to pick up small gripes while they were still relatively easy to fix, before they could fester into serious discontent. We thought of the program as "preventive labor relations," precisely because IBM had no unions and liked it that way. The fact that our customer support services were not subject to interruption by strikes was a huge competitive advantage.

One day I was asked by Harold Christensen, personnel director for IBM's international operations, to come down to New York and describe the attitude survey program to him. At that time it was common knowledge that IBM was about to commit a substantial number of managers and specialists from its domestic divisions to the international side of the business. The idea was to boost the growth rate of the international subsidiaries by providing certain talents that were more abundant, at that time, in the United States than overseas. I put two and two together, and figured that Christensen was toying with the idea of an attitude survey program to minimize his exposure to foreign unions.

So after I presented the program to him, and had answered his questions, I swallowed hard and said, "Mr. Christensen, if you are thinking of starting this kind of program in the international subsidiaries, I'd like you to consider me for the job." Christensen, who was to be my boss for the next four years, was one of the world's great poker players. His face and voice betrayed nothing. All he said was, "Oh?"

I plunged in. I knew that IBM had other people with the same qualifications I had, who ran similar programs in different divisions. I had to distinguish myself from them in Christensen's mind. So I said, "Yes, sir. You see, I've already lived in Europe for a year and a half, while I was in the army. So I have some familiarity with those countries."

Christensen showed the faintest glimmer of interest. "Speak any languages?" he asked. "Yes, sir," I replied. "French and German. Very rusty, but I could shine them up if I had to." "Ah," said Christensen, taking it all in. After a moment's reflection, he said, "Well, it was nice of you to tell me these things. Thanks for coming to visit."

I was unaware of it at the time, but during the next few weeks a great tussle ensued between Christensen and my boss in the domestic division. Christensen wanted me, but my boss claimed that there was no one available to replace me. The upshot was that my domestic boss was told to find a replacement for me, which he did. And I got one of the most exciting, challenging jobs of my life: introducing employee attitude surveys in thirty-five countries.

A Time for Self-Assessment

Of course, there is no guarantee that the strategy will work. I was lucky. The breaks of the game won't always go your way. What if you should ask for a job only to see it given to someone else? You must always be prepared for that possibility. In that case what you should do is to take it like a pro. Congratulate the winner, and make sure that the decision makers know that you're not going to sulk. You're still a player, and the game is by no means over. But beneath those externalities, you've got some serious reappraisal to do.

The two basic questions to ask yourself are, first, did you over-reach yourself by asking, or were you really viewed as a serious contender right down to the final decision? If you overreached, you had better be a lot more selective about asking again. If you had a serious shot at the job, be patient, because you'll have serious shots at other jobs, too—mostly *without* having to ask for them. The second question to ask yourself is whether your path of ad-vancement is blocked in this company. *Blockage* is a relative term. The question is not whether you can ever move forward at all; unless you're well into middle age already, you probably can move ahead somewhat, someday. Rather, the question is whether you can be content with that pace of movement. If not, the time may have come to test the waters outside your company.

The Recruiters' Happy Hunting Ground

Most decisions are about as good as the amount of time that went into making them. That means that really important deci-sions, such as who should be assigned to a major executive post, should never be put off until the necessity for making them is upon us. That's why a good management-development group is always asking "what if" questions about every key job in the company.

What if we needed to replace (name any key executive) tomor-row morning? Who is qualified, ready, and available? And if we promoted any of them, how would we replace *him?* Remember that the higher the level of the opening to be filled, the longer the chain of follow-up promotions that are generated downward through the pipeline.

If you were running the management-development operation yourself, here's where you'd probably encounter the most common problem in executive succession planning. You'll find the same few names showing up as potential replacements for more than one job. There are nearly always more prospective openings than there are candidates to fill them. The potential demand usually exceeds the available supply by a considerable margin. That's one reason why many large companies won't let their top executives travel on the same airplane.

The problem has two causes. First, too many companies simply don't look far enough ahead. They think of their new hires only in terms of their entry-level roles, for example as potential sales representatives or as financial analysts, rather than as potential executives. So not enough high-potential people are hired in the first place. Consequently, the managerial pipeline is underfilled from the start.

Inevitably, ten or fifteen years down the road, a shortage of home-grown managerial talent will show up. You're going to have perhaps five or six people ready and qualified to fill a dozen or fifteen key executive jobs, if they should become open. (*All* key executive jobs become open sooner or later, as regularly as death and taxes.) That's why management developers pray for the good health and good performance of incumbents. They don't want too many key jobs to open up at about the same time.

The second cause of the imbalance between supply and demand is mismanaging an *adequate* supply of managerial talent. As the pyramid narrows near the top of the organization, you face the problem of what to do with those executives for whom the management developers pray. They are the ones who are performing well but have no place to go unless the CEO retires, quits, is fired, or dies.

The velocity of movement through the managerial ranks tends to slow down near the top, which backs up into the level just below (that is, the upper ranges of middle management). That's where you're going to encounter the most restless and frustrated of all the high-potential managers in the organization. Their ability to progress at their own rate is blocked by those top people just above them, who are performing well and are too young to retire.

That's why the upper range of middle management is the happy hunting ground for your friendly local management recruiter, who earns a good living by plucking top talent from one organization and repositioning it at a higher level in another. That's good for the receiving company, the repositioned individual, and even, arguably, for the economy as a whole. It's not so good for the company that loses a high-potential manager, unless it has plenty more where he came from.

A Short List of Names

What you have to do is create movement at the top of the pyramid, so there is always some perceptible upward flow from that critical "upper-middle" level. Some companies have mandatory early retirement for the corporate officers, typically at age sixty. Others approach the problem more creatively, for example, by encouraging "younger senior executives" to plan a new enterprise, which they can launch with financial backing from the company.

One way or another, you have to create approximately the same velocity of movement at the top of the organization that the younger, restless generations of managers demand at their levels. Otherwise, too many good people will leave, and too many others will simply give up and lose their ambition. The result will be the syndrome of a short list of names, matched against a long list of jobs.

There is an interesting conflict of interest here. It calls for *very* astute management. The incumbents of top positions at any given time have a vested interest in staying there as long as they can. That's mainly because top-level jobs are so much fun. They offer more scope and fewer restrictions than most other jobs. For all the stress that goes with top jobs, most executives are having a ball, and they have no interest in seeing the ball come to an end. So the incumbents don't mind that syndrome of too few names for too many jobs. After all, the more irreplaceable you are, the less likely you are to be replaced.

But that motivation to cling to top jobs is in direct conflict with the interests of the eager, impatient managers in the threshold jobs just below the top level. They want to move upward as soon as they are ready, and don't want to wait forever for their superiors to vacate their offices. Of course, as soon as the new generation moves into the executive suite, the tables are turned. Now it's their turn to dig in and prolong their stay as long as possible.

The best way to deal with this touchy problem is to try to create realistic expectations among all concerned. No job, not even the CEO's, belongs to the individual who holds it at any given moment. They all belong to the company. Short-range considerations should generally yield to long-range consideration. In general, you should look forward to a finite tour of duty in your "peak" job, during which you make a maximum effort to leave your mark on the company's fortunes. Then you move on to yet another phase of your career, and give someone else a chance to make a mark of his own.

Managing Ambitions

Once you've begun to advance, you'll have to deal with subordinates who in some cases will be just as ambitious as you are. So you'll face the same problem that all your bosses will have to face with you. How do you motivate people whose primary motive is to use their current job as a springboard to a better one?

There are three points to keep in mind. First, what the ambitious person wants in a boss, above all else, is an active awareness of his ambition. So be prepared to talk about that openly, and without waiting to be asked. Talk about the various options that might open up, about how each individual's chances could be improved, and try to assess the probabilities as realistically as you can.

Your purpose is not to dangle a glittering future in front of your subordinates, but rather to demonstrate that you're actively involved in trying to help them shape their futures. You've got to demonstrate that you're just as concerned with your subordinates' futures as you are with your own.

Second, look for ways to coach them. Look for faults that could undermine their strengths, and try to show them how to correct them. Frequently these are mere mannerisms of which the individual is hardly aware, and are not that difficult to change once attention is drawn to them.

One of my subordinates had such a quick mind that his thoughts tended to race ahead of other people's. Unfortunately, he picked up the habit of finishing other people's sentences for them. He did it mostly out of impatience, to move the conversation along, never quite realizing that the people whom he thought he was "helping" felt that he was patronizing them. When I told him about this he was at first astounded. He felt quite genuinely that I was making a major fuss over a minor matter.

So I asked him to try to keep count of the number of times he did this during the next few meetings that we attended together. I told him that I would keep my own count, and that we would compare notes after each meeting. With his attention focused on the problem in this manner, he virtually eliminated it. But he admitted to me that he had been biting his tongue, fighting back his tendency to interrupt people in mid-sentence. I told him to keep on biting, because with that irritating habit out of the way he should have clear sailing on his way upward.

Third, if you've got a subordinate who appears to have considerable upward potential, make his advancement your top priority. By definition, this kind of person will be hard to replace. Nevertheless, don't stand in his way when a chance to move upward presents itself. Your department's loss will be the company's gain.

That kind of loyalty to your subordinates will be noticed by two sets of people who will have a lot to say about your own future. First, your other subordinates will work as hard as they can to please you, because they'll hope for the same unselfish support from you when their turn comes. That will improve your department's performance record, which will catch the eye of the second group.

Those are the decision makers who will pass judgment on your own promotion prospects. They'll mark you down as someone who can develop managerial talent in others. That's something that you definitely want to have noted on the management developers' summary of your special strengths, especially when it is included in the thin folder on the CEO's desk.

CHAPTER
8

IF NO ONE IS FOLLOWING, YOU'RE NOT LEADING

The most immediate and personal form of motivation is your direct influence on someone else's behavior. If that influence causes the person to act as you want him to, we would call your influence leadership. However, if someone who is expected to lead has no effect on what other people do, he is not leading. We could call his influence an annoyance, or even an irrelevance, but we could not realistically refer to his lack of motivational effect as leadership. That would be true regardless of whether his job title implied that he had leadership responsibilities, or of whether he had formal authority over the people on whom he was having no discernible effect.

Supervisors, sergeants, and for that matter, CEOs and generals, all have to get other people to do what they want them to do. But merely holding such a job does not, in itself, guarantee that you can do it. John W. Gardner, a former marine captain and cabinet secretary who was no mean leader himself, observed, "There are government department heads, bishops, and corporate chief executive officers who could not lead a troop of cub scouts out of their pup tents."

The only people whom we can realistically call leaders are those who can get others to act as they want them to. A real leader is, quite simply, anyone whom others follow. It's the response of the people you are trying to lead, and not your position title or your job description, that determines whether you are a leader.

If someone has been given the authority to lead but is followed only halfheartedly or not at all, he is not really a leader. He is really just an officeholder, or a bureaucrat, or to call him by a more memorable name, a flunky.

Flunkies in Leadership Positions

It is not unusual for flunkies to be nominally in charge of real leaders. If you see someone in authority who considers any clever, influential subordinate to be a trouble maker, that's a sure sign that you're dealing with a flunky. A real leader will regard the same subordinate as someone who is worth developing.

Flunkies are by no means rare. Most organizations have their share, and some (alas!) have more than their share. So we have to ask why so many flunkies have had leadership responsibilities thrust upon them.

If you're expecting a reprise of the "Peter Principle," you're in for a disappointment. Dr. Lawrence Peter was pulling our leg when he published his famous, funny, but fallacious idea that in a hierarchy, everyone inevitably rises to his level of incompetence. That's been good for a lot of laughs, especially for anyone who has ever reported to a flunky. But when you stop laughing and look at facts, it's clear that it just ain't so. Most people never even get close to their level of incompetence. Underused talent is a much larger problem. (More about that in the next chapter.)

However, there is a germ of truth in Peter's idea; otherwise we wouldn't laugh at it. The real problem is that we tend to put people with the *wrong kinds* of competence into leadership jobs. Then, being human, we proceed to insist that our mistakes were non-mistakes.

There are three reasons why there are too many flunkies in jobs that call for leaders:

The first is our fondness for those "wrong kinds of competence." By far the most common of these is skill in doing the work to be supervised. There are, for example, lots of former salespeople who did an outstanding job of selling. On the strength of that they were promoted, only to become (in too many cases) mediocre or worse sales supervisors. The reason is simply that selling and supervising call for very different skills. The same can be said of almost any job. To do a job well is one thing, but to supervise it well is an altogether different job, calling for quite different skills.

Another "wrong competence" arises from resembling the person doing the selecting. For example, if you went to my college, or share some of my social or political ideas, or even look like me, I might conclude that anyone as fortunate as you has got to have potential. I might be tempted to hire you, or to promote you if you had already been hired. This would not necessarily involve any conscious favoritism. Rather, it would be because your similarity to me made me feel more secure about taking a risk with you. No one is really immune to this kind of self-deluding fallacy, unless he works full-time to keep it in check. So reason number one for the flunky glut is that we put people in leadership jobs for reasons that have nothing to do with leadership.

The second reason for our oversupply of flunkies is that many of the people who have to choose leaders are flunkies themselves. While they seldom rise high enough to be involved in the selection of key executives, many of them are in "gatekeeper" positions at lower levels. Just like you and me, they are favorably disposed to people like themselves. No surprise there. So reason number two is that flunkies are to some extent a self-perpetuating breed.

Third, it is by no means clear that the supply of good leaders is equal to the demand. In some organizations, there just may not be enough good leaders to go around. Leaders have to motivate all kinds of people, including some whose own motivation may be rather weak, and others so well motivated that they really don't need to be led at all. Leading such a wide variety of people is not an easy job, and most people just can't do it very well.

Suppose you've got some leadership jobs to fill, and there's no one in sight who clearly has the qualities you're looking for. What do you do? You take a deep breath, pick the least unlikely candidates, mutter a silent prayer, and then tell them to get out there and lead. If some of them turn out to be flunkies, that isn't necessarily your fault. Your company may not have hired enough potential leaders in the first place. Or perhaps most of your company's potential leaders left, long ago, in search of more appreciative employers.

So reason number three for our abundance of flunkies is that we sometimes have no real choice but to appoint them, and then pray for a miracle.

For all of these reasons, the lower ranks of management, and even the middle ranks, are often cluttered with flunkies. This is a major reason for the prosperity of the executive recruiting industry. Too many companies that search among their own managers for executive talent find that the pickings are too lean. That leaves them no choice but to extend their search to other companies.

Mass Leaders and Personal Leaders

Having distinguished between real leaders and those who are expected to lead, but can't, we now have to make yet another distinction. There's a big difference between motivating small groups of two or three or even a dozen people and motivating large groups of hundreds or even thousands of people. You motivate a small group through your personal relationship with each member of the group. You motivate large groups by projecting a charismatic image with which masses of people will want to identify. Those are quite different leadership tasks.

Forgive me, but I'm going to have to invent some terminology to keep these two kinds of leaders properly sorted out. Let's call someone who can successfully influence the actions of a small group a personal leader, and let's call someone who can get large numbers of people to do what he wants them to do a mass leader. The distinction is important, because what works for one isn't likely to work for the other. The lieutenant faces an altogether different leadership challenge than the general does, and so do the first-level supervisor and the CEO. But where do you draw the line between a large and a small group? And how does leading a mass of people differ from leading a few?

For our purposes, a group is "large" once it becomes too big for you to communicate effectively with each of its members. You're always limited by the dynamics of communication. Usually, the largest number of people that you could lead effectively, solely through your personal influence on each of them, is somewhere around fifteen or sixteen. Beyond that, you start running into the physical limits of how many people you can meet for those all-important frequent face-to-face dialogues.

Leading a small group effectively is largely a matter of maintaining close contact with each of its members, demonstrating your responsiveness to each of them, and making sure that they know what you expect of them. The messages that you exchange with your followers are mostly clarifications of facts and ideas, so that the communication is essentially from one brain to another. But to lead a large group effectively, the communication has to be mostly the gut level. You have to stir deeply felt needs that have more to do with emotions than with logic. Not many people can do that, which is why mass leaders are so scarce. Fortunately, we don't need that many.

Mass leaders are only useful at the top of big organizations. Their gift for generating excitement, and even hysteria, would be wasted on a small group. Most people don't mind acting like fools when they are inconspicuously lost in a crowd, as (for example) at a football game. But most would prefer to be calm, cool, and collected in front of their boss.

Mass leadership is largely a matter of playing on emotions. Alas, the darker instincts are there to be played upon. But so are the finer ones. Not all mass leaders are demagogues, although obviously some are. I have never had the misfortune of seeing a demagogue in action. (Bad bosses, yes. I'll tell you about them in chapter 14. But demagogues, no.) So the case that I will share with you now is a demonstration of mass leadership at its best. It involved an executive who had to appeal to the finest instincts in literally thousands of people in order to turn around a disastrously declining company.

BRINGING OUT THE BEST IN MANY, MANY PEOPLE

An executive was promoted to the presidency of his company at a time when it was beset by scandals. There were charges of bribery, kickbacks, falsified reports, and inflated invoices. Before the charges were filed, the company had enjoyed a pristine reputation. But the charges were mostly true, and they shattered the morale of the employees. Events had seemed to make a mockery of the company's informal slogan, which had been "We fight fair to win."

It was clear to the new president that he could not restore his company's reputation without first restoring its employees' pride. But he also had a reputation of his own to contend with. Although no one questioned his integrity, he had many well-known shortcomings as a personal leader. His hair-trigger temper was famous, as was his tendency to publicly denounce anyone whose work displeased him. Fortunately, he usually apologized as soon as his temper had cooled. Nevertheless, he created a pressure-cooker atmosphere for his immediate lieutenants. In at least some of his relationships, he probably qualified as a bad boss.

For these reasons, a major organizational shake-up was expected when he took over. But that did not happen, because there were other sides to the new president's character. Although he was certainly hotheaded, he was no fool. He had learned to seek good advice and to take it seriously, even when that advice conflicted with his instincts. Also, having spent his entire career in this company, he had a deep appreciation for its traditions.

He was, in brief, a complex mixture of good and bad qualities. In that respect, he was not very different from you and me and a lot of other people. However, he also had a latent quality which no one had ever seen, because until he rose to the presidency he had not had an occasion to display it. He was a superb mass leader, with an intuitive grasp of what thousands of his company's employees wanted to hear.

The new president spent several weeks traveling to virtually all of the company's installations, speaking to as many of its managers and employees as he could reach. He made a point of visiting remote locations as well as those that were easily accessible, and of showing up on the night shift to address workers who were usually overlooked. He was astute enough to make sure that these "inconvenient" visits were well publicized.

In each of his talks he hammered away at the same message. He was a dramatic speaker and knew when to whisper and when to roar. To seize and hold the attention of his audience, he did a lot of both:

Our principles did not fail us [he thundered]. We failed our principles! Now we have to win back the respect of our customers. To do that, we are going to return to the ideas that made this company great in the first place. So let me remind you of what they are.

We make fine products, and only fine products. We sell those products at fair prices. We won't do anything that has to be covered up, or for which we would ever have to apologize. We are honest with our customers and suppliers, and we expect them to be honest with us. We will walk away from any deals that would require us to compromise those principles. And regardless of what the cynics say, we expect to make money this way, because most people want to do business with an honest company.

Some say that this is an outdated attitude, that it's a bad world out there, and that our job is just to survive in it, and not to make it better. I've heard that kind of cynical garbage before. But my entire business experience tells me that it isn't true. And even if that is the way the tide is running, I hope we'll swim against it. We can do the right thing, and prosper at the same time. In fact, that's the only way we can prosper. We did it before. And by God, we are going to do it again!

In one sense, it was a message that his audience wanted to hear. But they were understandably skeptical. The new president knew that he needed a dramatic way to prove that he meant what he said.

Reasoning that the prosecutors might not have uncovered every shady deal in the company, he launched a quiet investigation of his own. Sure enough, he came upon an incident in which subcontractors had paid "consulting fees" to some of his lower-level managers. He promptly fired them. It was unnecessary to publicize what he had done, or why he did it. The grapevine took care of that for him quite efficiently.

It took almost two years before he was satisfied that morale had been restored to its former levels and that the company's ethics were demonstrably clean. Customers were reassured, and the company's sales eventually set new records. Individual managers and employees cleaned up their methods, because they felt that it was once again safe to do their jobs the way they had always wanted to do them. For the hot-tempered president, it was a virtuoso performance.

The Prevailing Mythology

At this point I should say a few words about the prevailing American mythology on business, because the example I have just given may strike you as naive or as too good to be true. Aside from a few details that were altered to mask the identity of the company, the story is true. However, the prevailing mythology is that there's at least a little bit of larceny in every executive's heart, and that if it were not for competition and the Department of Justice, most companies would wallow in orgies of lying, cheating, and stealing.

The surest sign that you're dealing with someone who is genuinely naive, who really doesn't know what he is talking about, is an affectation of cynicism in an attempt to seem sophisticated. Some people go through life that way, trying to demonstrate their "worldliness" by asserting that nobody is going to fool *them*, because they *know* that neither you nor I nor anyone else is up to any good.

There are three signs by which you can tell that you are dealing with people who are genuinely worldly. First, they have no need to advertise their sophistication; you'll get no knowing winks from them, no conspicuous displays of disbelief. Second, they are neither cockeyed optimists nor sour cynics. They are simply open-minded. They know that some people are always crooks, and that a few more are sometimes crooks, and that many, many more are never crooks. They are willing to judge each person solely by his conduct, and never prejudge anyone. Third, they are not incredulous when they hear of people who did the right thing solely because it was right, any more than they are shocked when they hear of self-serving or of bad faith. They know that human nature is not simple, and that it includes both altruism and selfishness, sometimes in the same individual.

Bringing Out the Best in a Few People

Most of the leading that gets done in this world is done by personal leaders, working with small groups. The basic function of personal leaders is to provide whatever their followers lack to do their jobs effectively. They may lack information, or training, or the courage to do what must be done, and the leader's job in such cases would be to inform, or to teach, or to encourage.

Because the range of followers' needs is almost infinite, the key requirements of personal leaders are *adaptability* and *responsiveness*. Effective leaders do not try to lead everyone in the same way. Instead, they are constantly adjusting their tactics to meet the varied and changing needs of everyone with whom they have to deal. Now, that happens to be an extraordinarily difficult thing to do. Here's why. Most people who find themselves in leadership positions will do whatever makes them feel the *least uncomfort-*

able. They will respond to their own needs, rather than to those of the people they are supposed to lead. That's why insecure supervisors tend to reject suggestions from their subordinates. They feel more secure if they can stay in control of their subordinates than they can by improving the methods that those subordinates use.

The critical leadership skill of responding to other people's needs, rather than to your own, can be learned. But most people never learn it. That, in brief, is why highly effective leaders are so scarce. (How do you learn to respond to other people's needs? Simply by trying to do it, again and again, preferably with the help of someone who can observe both you and your followers as you interact with each other.)

Leadership, like love, is a complex relationship between people that we don't understand very well, but which virtually everyone recognizes when they see it. Both are real, both are extremely important, and both are elusive. That's why it's easier to illustrate them with case histories than to generalize about them. But there is one safe generalization about both leadership and love. The key phrase in both cases is "between people." Leadership is not a quality that some people possess and others don't. It is an effect that people sometimes have on each other, when they happen to fill each other's needs. (The same is true of love, but that belongs in another book.)

The leadership influence flows both ways, from the leader to the followers, but also vice versa. That is why the most skillful leaders study the conduct and attitudes of those whom they would lead. A wise leader gets to know the motives of his followers and can call on those motives when the need arises.

The most severe test of personal leadership occurs when the group runs into adverse circumstances. The next two cases, both of which are drawn from my consulting files, illustrate personal leadership at its best.

GETTING OUT OF TROUBLE

Several years ago I had an opportunity to observe several factory foremen as they carried out their duties in one of my client companies. The following example, with a supervisor named David, shows how an effective leader can rally a group that is faced with seemingly insuperable problems:*

I met David in the supervisor's lounge at 6:45 A.M. On the way to his department, he expounded his philosophy of managing the packaging department. He stressed the importance of getting off to a good start: "The first couple of hours pretty much set you up for the rest of the shift," he said. "You get a good start, everybody's feeling good about it, and that will carry you right to three o'clock. But you get a bad start, people start getting mad at the machines, then they get mad at each other, and then you know nothing's going to go right. You're just going to have 'one of those days,' and you'll be fighting it all the way."

When we arrived at David's department, the first thing he did was talk to the preceding shift supervisor. The poor fellow looked worn out and said he had been having trouble with the machines and the pneumatic feeds. "Well," David sighed, after his predecessor left, "things are going to be a little tough this morning. When they get a lot of mechanical trouble on the second or third shift, they leave most of it with us, because we have more maintenance people."

He moved quickly into the line, watching each machine in operation. Two or three were shut down because the operators on the preceding shift had told David's operators that they weren't running right. David asked them to start up anyway, so he could judge for himself how bad the machines were and whether they could be run for a while at slower speeds or had to be shut down altogether.

Some workers who were operating had problems that would simply have to wait until the maintenance crews could get to them. David spent much of his time with these people, helping in small ways by rolling a stack of containers a short distance to where it would be needed, or picking up debris. One operator seemed quite agitated, and he engaged her in a fairly lengthy discussion, out of earshot. As I watched from a distance, another operator looked up at me, smiled a bit sadly, and said, "We're all running bad today." I tried to be encouraging. "Don't worry, we'll get it fixed pretty soon," I said, knowing full well I hadn't any clear notion of how long it would take. I guess she knew it, too, because her only reply to me was another sad smile.

But I could see David's point about the psychological reaction to

---

*Excerpted and adapted from the author's article, "Supervision: Substance and Style," *Harvard Business Review*, March–April 1976.

a bad start-up. These people were facing the possibility of eight hours of unavailing effort to overcome problems they had not created. Some were depressed, some were angry, and some were grim. David was concerned that some of his people might just give up and try to get lost in the restrooms. Others might sit sullenly at their machines, paying no attention to the dials and indicators, but ready to snarl at anyone who criticized them.

David returned from his lengthy discussion with the subordinate, and I asked him what the trouble had been. Evidently the operator did not get along with one of her helpers, and had given David an earful of her troubles. "That's always just below the surface with her," David said. "Just takes a day like this, and it all boils over. I had to hear her out, and then I jollied her along like I always do. She'll be all right for now."

I asked why he hadn't transferred one of the two women, ending the problem that way. "I could," he said, "but then I'd have to transfer anyone else who got sore at somebody, and there'd be no end to it."

Slowly, David's department began to pull out of its slump. By working on the more easily repaired machines first, the maintenance crews began to restore some measure of productivity fairly quickly. Of course, recovery slowed as they moved on to more serious problems, but David finally had some momentum and he wanted to take advantage of it. "We're moving again," he announced cheerily to those workers whose machines were still limping along. "Look at old number eight over there! Just hang in there, we'll get to you, too."

No one was euphoric, but at least the gloom had started to lift. David continued to spend most of his time with the operators who needed help, leaving those whose machines were already repaired to their own devices, and looking in on the maintenance crew only often enough to be sure that they were proceeding more or less according to his expectations.

By lunchtime the line was running fairly well. David's manner of supervision reflected the change. "When we're running right," he said, "I just leave them alone." He was still very visible, moving about the floor, but with very little contact now. He spoke mainly when he was spoken to. He noted with satisfaction that some of his operators had begun to help each other in small ways, something they were not required to do.

"We could go down again at any minute," he said. "But I've got a different job now. The first four hours, I was just trying to hold everything together until we could get fixed up. Now I have to start checking all the little things to make sure we don't start sliding backward."

I asked David about his belief that a bad start meant bad running for the entire shift. "We've pulled out of the worst part," he answered. "But don't forget, we don't have any chance at all of a good run, because we've lost too much production in those first few hours. You ought to be here some day when there's a real good run. That's when you'll see them all happy."

PULLING CHESTNUTS OUT OF THE FIRE

The most dramatic example of personal leadership that I ever witnessed occurred in one of my client companies during the last two months of a particularly difficult year. Sales had consistently lagged behind forecasts, and as October approached it was clear that a financial disaster was in the making.

The vice-president for sales had been appointed earlier that year, and had the misfortune of presiding over one of the worst sales debacles in the company's history. He argued in vain that the sales forecast he had inherited was unrealistic from the start and that sales results were actually about as good as could be expected. But the president was not impressed. "I don't know if the forecast was realistic or not," he said, "and I don't care. All that matters is that we're stuck with it. Our hiring plans, our manufacturing plans, even our borrowing plans were all based on this forecast. So the only question that matters is, how are we going to make our numbers? Because we have to."

"But we've done everything," said the vice-president. "We've brought in all the sales that are out there."

"Then try something else," said the president. "I know you didn't create this mess, but only you can get us out of it. I'm not going to go to the bankers and tell them that we don't know how to forecast. If I did, our interest rates would go out of sight from now until the next century. So get out there and sell as if both your job and my job depended on it, because maybe they do."

The vice-president had been promoted rather late in life, after a long career as a highly respected regional manager. He had personally trained many of the company's district managers. They regarded him fondly, and in some cases with adulation. As he reflected on what to do, the vice-president realized that the time had come to draw on the vast inventory of good will that he had accumulated. So he called a meeting of his regional and district managers, of whom there were perhaps twenty or so in all.

"You all know me," he said. "Never mind this vice-president stuff. That's just to impress headwaiters. You all knew me in the old days.

We've been through the wars together. We've checked into hick town motels at two in the morning, and met each other for breakfast five hours later.

"In those days you needed me. My job was to teach you how to earn the respect of the customer. If you ran into a problem, I was there. That was my job. But now the tables are turned. Now I need you.

"We're way behind quota. We've got November and December left, and that's it. There's only one way that I'm going to get out of this alive. I'm being very frank with you. What I need is a superhuman effort from every man and woman in the field.

"I know that's asking a lot, but that's what I need. I want you to go out into your districts, and tell your people that now is the time to start their day a little earlier, and keep making sales calls until the last customer has gone home. There's no extra reward for this. Just the usual commissions. But what I'm asking you is, will you do this for me?"

The managers' response was unusual. They didn't cheer and whistle, as they did at most sales meetings. Seriously, almost somberly, each of them walked up to the vice-president and shook his hand. They said things like "You can count on me, boss," and "Don't worry, we'll get it for you." Some of the women in the group hugged him.

And perform they did. For the next two months, they spent virtually all of their own time in the field, exhorting the sales force. The number of sales calls multiplied, and so did their intensity. The volume of orders began to increase. By late December, the sales quota had been reached. Barely, but it was reached.

In this instance, the managers wanted to protect their vice-president, and also wanted to show him their gratitude. Not many managers acquire that much good will in the first place, or could evoke it as skillfully as he did. The real leadership in this case took place in the years before the vice-president took office, while he was still in the field with his protégés. That is where he earned the loyalty that he called upon so effectively only once, when he needed it the most.

Back in chapter 6 we spoke of "choosing your friends carefully, helping them unstintingly, and letting those favors pile up, like interest in a bank account." By building a sense of indebtedness, you'll be in a position to call in those obligations if you should ever need them. That's long-range leadership. Even if you never need to ask for anything in return, it's the kind of leadership that makes you invaluable to your company and to your colleagues.

On Leading

Except for chief executive officers, every manager is simultaneously somebody's leader and somebody else's subordinate. The two roles are related. As a leader, you are there to guarantee that your subordinates accomplish what they're supposed to accomplish. As a subordinate, you are a link in a communications chain. Your job is to know what your boss expects of your department and to make sure your boss knows whether those expectations are going to turn into results and what you need to make those results happen.

Let's deal with your leadership role first. To be an effective leader, you have to pass several tests. I'll list four of the most important ones.

The most important test of all is that you must *handle other people's egos with care.* Any adult leader of adult subordinates is in a super-delicate position, chiefly because of the power difference between them. Unless you're a lot more experienced than any of your subordinates, there's no avoiding the question that every subordinate asks, at least implicitly, about every leader.

Bluntly stated, that question is, "Who the hell are *you* to tell *me* what to do?" To put that somewhat more elegantly, they could ask, "What qualities in you justify your having authority over me?"

That attitude is perfectly normal. After all, bosses can affect your income, your career, and even your job security. If someone is going to have that much power over you, you'll want to be sure that he or she is going to exercise it responsibly. The greatest danger, however, is that *you,* as a boss, might become defensive about this. You might decide that in order to stay in control, you have to put people in their place by threatening to use your authority. But that would miss the point. The question is not whether you know how to use your power, or would dare to, but whether you deserve to be entrusted with it.

If you use your power to intimidate someone, you create an enemy. That's worth avoiding if you can, because a manager has enough problems without needing enemies. Besides, the only effective way to lead an adversary is by the nose. Unless you have that kind of total control of someone, you'd be well advised to minimize the number of your followers who really don't want to follow you at all.

The best way to take good care of an adult's ego is to ask for his opinion, especially on matters with which he has had even a little experience, or on matters in which he has some kind of stake, whether it's large or small. If you hear some opinions that sound ridiculous, you can bet that they're not ridiculous to whoever has them. Ask for a restatement. Seemingly absurd statements by mature adults are often good ideas that have been poorly expressed. Another advantage of continual opinion seeking is that it keeps your finger on the pulse, so to speak, of group morale.

A second requirement of effective leadership is *responding to the competence and maturity levels of each subordinate*. You don't want to oversupervise people who know perfectly well how to do their jobs, even if you can do their work better than they can. A good leader never forgets where his job ends and his subordinates' jobs begin. On the other hand, you don't want to leave people to their own devices if they have no devices that matter. If your subordinates are less than fully competent, it's your job to get them to that level. But you do that by training and coaching them, not by doing their work for them.

In an ideal world, leaders would gradually make themselves unnecessary by making each follower self-sufficient. In the real world, leaders are always necessary. That's because self-sufficiency is a distant goal for most people, and even the self-sufficient must be pointed in the direction that the organization wants them to follow. The important point is to respond to each person's behavior every day, giving guidance where it is needed and approval whenever it is deserved.

Good work is too precious to let it go unrecognized, even for a day. The same is true of work that is getting better, even if it is not yet good. In whatever way comes naturally to you, show every person whom you are leading that you are aware of good work, that you don't take it for granted, and that you appreciate it. I know that sounds elementary. Maybe that's why it is the most frequently overlooked principle of good leadership. But if you overlook it too often, you risk motivational disaster.

Some people find that praising other people is awkward and uncomfortable. If you're one of those, try pointing to a specific example of work well done, and tell the individual who is responsible for it what you especially like about it. Then tell that person, in your own way, that work like that makes you proud of him, and ask him to try to continue doing that well. Better still, ask if he'd mind if you showed that example of his work to his colleagues, as a model of how it should be done. As long as he won't be embarrassed, public recognition is usually more effective than praise in private.

A third requirement of leadership is your *management of your own time*. Most of it should be spent with your followers at their workplaces. Your office should be where you hang your hat, receive your mail, discuss matters that can only be discussed privately, and do whatever can only be done by telephone. Otherwise, you have no good reason to be there. Leaders should spend as much time as possible where their followers are, rather than behind their desks.

Fourth, your *example* accounts for much of whatever leadership effect you will have on others. It goes without saying that you should never ask others to do anything that you would not join them in doing. The more onerous the task, the more your presence is required. When there is difficult work to be done, or when work must be done at inconvenient times or in inconvenient places, simply being there with your followers, sharing their difficulties and their inconveniences, matters a lot. It demonstrates, better than any words can, your concern for them and your respect for the importance of what they do.

On Being Led

Finally, some advice on how to be a good follower. The most important rule is "Thou shalt not surprise thy boss." You should keep your own leader informed of anything that could result in unintended consequences, or of any possible need for a change in plans. Well-informed bosses can work out contingency plans that cope with the unexpected. Uninformed bosses can't.

Surprised bosses have to explain those consequences to their own bosses, and that annoyance can make them quite unpleasant. That is why it is better to go to your boss now with potentially bad news, even if it never actually materializes, than to bring him bad news later which you had hoped would eventually go away.

What leaves you vulnerable to criticism, or worse, is not the bad news itself, but your answer to your boss's key question, which will be, "How long have you known about this?" If your answer is anything longer than a few hours, you will be in well-deserved trouble. A surprised boss is likely to remember the surprise when the time rolls around to review your performance, and to determine what your next salary increase, if any, will be.

CHAPTER
9

HOW TO FIX
A BAD JOB

If you've ever had a job that you couldn't wait to get to in the morning and hated to leave at the end of the day, you already know that jobs can be motivating. And if you've ever had a job that made you reluctant to get out of bed in the morning, you know that jobs can also be demotivating.

From a motivational point of view, a bad job is one you wouldn't do unless you had to. It makes you do things that you find repugnant, or unrewarding, or (most commonly) just plain boring. Just doing a bad job day after day is quite enough to make you want to flee from it, if you could.

There are three ways to get away from a bad job. You can escape from it temporarily, just by taking the day off, and thereby contributing your share to your company's absence rate. I doubt if you do that very much, because it's more typical of blue-collar and clerical workers than of managers.

When professionals like you find themselves in a job so bad that they want to avoid it, they are more likely to avoid it permanently. They will quit the job altogether and seek more attractive work elsewhere. Of course, that would contribute to their company's turnover rate.

The third way to flee a bad job is probably the most common way for people wearing collars of all colors, and for employees at every

■ 133

level of an organization. You just flee the job mentally, by thinking about something else. You could do your work unthinkingly, in a state of mental detachment. Or perhaps you could just sit there, lost in your own thoughts, not doing your work at all. That would contribute to your company's error rate, and possibly to its accident rate, as well.

Consequently, you're unlikely to do a bad job well, even if you've got more than enough ability, training, and experience to do it without much effort. In fact, *especially* if you've got more than enough ability, etc., to do it that easily.

High absence rates, turnover rates, error rates, and accident rates are obviously bad. But many managers don't realize *how* bad they are for a company's bottom line. Precise measurements are difficult. However, the accountants, who are usually fussier about documenting their numbers than anyone else, have recently taken an interest in the question.

At Motorola, for example, their best guess is that costs of this kind add up to about 8 percent of sales. That's a cool $800 million *per year*, right down the tubes. And Motorola is a well-managed company. The thought of how much money must be wasted in the economy as a whole boggles the mind.

The point is that bad jobs are bad for companies, as well as for the poor devils who have to do them. But are bad jobs really all that common? And what makes a bad job bad? And most important of all, how can you fix a bad job?

How Many Jobs Are Bad?

That's a hard question to answer, because when you set out to count bad jobs you find that you're chasing a moving target. First, no job is intrinsically bad. Even if you or I or a great many other people would recoil from doing a particular job, there are some people who would tolerate it and possibly others who would even profess to like it. Professional trash collectors, for example, will tell you that their job has its compensations. If you like outdoor work, dislike being told what to do, and have a lively curiosity about the amazing things that people throw away, perhaps you too could learn to love the job. Professional cookie packers, who spend their working lives stuffing endless rows of cookies into plastic trays and then stuffing those trays into cartons, take considerable pleasure in anticipating the delight of the little kids who will soon be tearing those packages apart to get at their contents. Besides, your fingers learn to do the packing with minimal guidance from your brain, which leaves you free to engage in eight hours of friendly gossip each day with your fellow cookie packers. What could be better, they'd ask you, than making all those kids happy, while getting paid for chatting all day with people whose interests are similar to yours?*

The point is that human minds have ingenious ways of making peace with circumstances that cannot be escaped. You just learn to make the best of it, to think positively about it, and not to dwell on things you dislike but cannot change. But that adaptive process takes a while, perhaps a few months or even a few years.

Suppose you asked people, while that process was still incomplete for them, whether their job was good or bad. Some would probably tell you that the damned job was just bad, period. Others would express varying degrees of acceptance. Then you could add up all of their answers and report the percentages of those who liked their jobs, those who could tolerate them, and those who actively disliked them. But your numbers wouldn't mean much. That's because if you waited a year or so, and then sought out the same individuals who had told you that they had bad jobs, you would find that relatively few still felt that way. The rest will have coped with their problem, either by learning to live with it or by leaving the job altogether. Meantime, a fresh crop of people will have been assigned to the job, mostly to replace those who couldn't stand it, and many of those new folks will tell you that, sure enough, it's a bad job.

That's why the number of bad jobs in a given company, or the entire economy, is a moving target. The answers you will get to a survey depend on whom you ask, on how carefully both you and they define a "bad job," and perhaps most of all on *when* you ask your question. Your attitude toward a job has a lot to do with how long you've held it. Probably the best way to count the number of

---

*I am indebted to my colleague, David Sirota, for these examples, which he encountered in the course of his consulting work.

bad jobs is to list all jobs that have *ever* caused complaints, regardless of whether those who currently hold those jobs like them or not.

If you made such a list of bad jobs, and then dug into them to see what they might have had in common with each other, you'd be closing in on a working definition of what makes a bad job bad.

What Makes a Bad Job Bad?

What makes a job "bad," in the sense of motivating you to leave it if you can, is a bad fit between what it requires you to do and your abilities and interests at the time we ask the question. The best fit, for motivational purposes, is a job you can handle *if* you give it all of the time, attention, wisdom, and ingenuity that you've got. The motivation comes from learning how to master a challenge.

If the job does not present a challenge to your abilities, your employer is going to have to think of some other way to motivate you. The job itself is not going to do that job for him. And that's a pity, because *nothing* motivates dedicated, concentrated effort like a job that's fun to do.

A good job stretches your mind and massages your ego. It gives you knowledge, mastery, and success, all in one intoxicating dose. A good job is the cerebral equivalent of an aphrodisiac. Only those who have not had that heady experience themselves feel pity for the so-called workaholic. A *lot* of people have never had that experience, however. That's why so many look at retirement as a kind of deliverance, and watch the clock and the calendar impatiently as their long, dreary workdays drag on and on. Why do people have such a variety of experience with their work? Why do some people love their jobs, while others hate theirs?

It's because the ideal balance between the demands of a job and the abilities of an individual is very delicate. If the work requires more skill or more know-how than you've got, you're definitely going to fumble and you're probably going to fail. It is precisely to avoid that kind of fiasco that management bends over backward and puts entirely too many people into jobs that are simply too easy for them.

What Happens to Unused Ability?

When a job does not use all the brainpower you've got, that unused ability creates a problem for you. You've got to do *something* with it. You can't just switch it off, or store it away in some mental closet. On the contrary, it will go looking for something to do, something that can give it a workout. So it finds a worry, or a speculation, or a daydream, and preoccupies itself with that, while the rest of your mind is monitoring, or rather, sort of monitoring, that overly easy job.

In other words, the natural result of work that does not demand enough of your attention is divided attention. But divided attention is seldom divided evenly. The lion's share goes to what interests you the most. Whatever attention may be left goes to what interests you least. In this case, that would be your job.

In all probability, most of the world's jobs are done with less than half the brains of those who do them. That, and not "levels of incompetence," is why idiotic errors are almost impossible to erase from computer records, why receptionists put your telephone calls on "hold" and leave them there forever, and why what one reservation clerk will tell you is unavailable or even forbidden is cheerfully arranged for you by the clerk at the next desk. It is not that these people are necessarily stupid. They are simply acting stupidly because their attention is divided. And that is probably because they have bad jobs, although I will admit that it could also be because they are poorly trained or even, in a few cases, genuinely stupid.

What makes a bad job bad for you is its failure to demand the use of your best talents, its failure to require you to learn, its failure to provide the thrill that only comes when you accomplish something that you consider both important to do and hard to do right. A good job, on the other hand, is one that starts you out at the upper limits of your talents, and then demands that you expand those talents.

THE CASE OF THE VANISHING MBAs

Several years ago, one of the nation's largest bakery companies invited me to analyze the disastrous turnover rate among its executive trainees.

The company had been phenomenally successful, expanding from a relatively small midwestern base to regional and then national distribution. Eventually it had several thousand employees, and it was clear that it would need a team of sophisticated executives to run such a large, continually expanding business. So the company hired twenty young MBA graduates from several of the leading business schools. They were told that they would be groomed for top-level responsibilities, and they were paid what it took to hire graduates from those schools at that time. However, attrition began rather quickly, and after somewhat more than a year *every last* one of the executive trainees had left.

I was called in to conduct a post-mortem examination of the failed project. Management told me candidly that they expected recommendations on how to do a better job of selecting its next crop of executive trainees. They attributed the failure to their own inexperience in evaluating individuals of this caliber.

However, when I looked at the procedures they had used, I could not fault them. On paper, at least, the twenty young graduates looked about as qualified and as promising as those of other companies I had studied. So I began to look for other possible explanations of what had happened. That's when I asked about the kinds of jobs to which the trainees had been assigned.

The company was convinced that its main competitive advantage was the twice-daily delivery of freshly baked products to supermarkets and other retail outlets, and the carefully arranged display of those products on the store's shelves. Delivery and display were the responsibility of the company's driver-salesmen. Management was convinced that the effectiveness of their driver-salesmen was the key to the company's success and growth. I agreed.

But management was also convinced that in order to guide a company that depended so heavily on its driver-salesmen, its future executives would have to completely master the details of operating a driver-salesman's territory. That took the typical driver-salesman about two years. That was why every executive trainee began his career with the bakery company as a rather overpaid driver-salesman. It was also why the company planned their first upward move, to district sales manager, to be made about two years after they were hired. I disagreed on both counts.

With the trainees already gone, there was no feasible way to interview them, and as a rule, one speculation is as good as another. But in this case, some additional evidence supported my speculation that the MBAs had simply gotten fed up with being driver-salesmen, no matter how well they were paid to endure those jobs.

After some debate, management accepted my suggestion that the driver-salesman phase of on-the-job-training for executive trainees be cut from two years to two weeks. After all, the MBAs did not need to know every last nuance of any particular territory. What they did need to know was the major problems faced by driver-salesmen *in general,* and they were clever enough to develop those insights quickly. The next crop of new MBAs moved upward into management jobs much more rapidly, and more than 90 percent of them were still with the company two years later.

Fixing Bad Jobs

There are four ways to fix a bad job. All of them involve finding a better fit between what you can do and what you are asked to do. The target is to use all of the brains, skill, and wisdom that you've got, and perhaps even a little more than that. We want you to have to reach a little bit in order to do what is asked of you. That bit of stretch that we're going to demand from your learning muscles is our secret weapon. It's where the motivation is going to come from. That's because certain kinds of people get an unmatched thrill out of learning how to master something new.

You're probably one of them yourself. You're probably hooked on personal growth. If you weren't, you probably would not have been interested in this book. And there are enough people like you out there to make an enormous difference, if we could give all of them jobs that were worthy of their talents.

Give Them More to Think About

One way to fix a bad job is to deliberately reverse about eighty years of industrial engineering. Early in this century, most production workers were barely literate. Yet that's the labor force that handled the transition from relatively simple, handmade products to more complex, mass-produced products. They did it by following a strategy that was both brilliant and simple. The engineers of that era broke each complicated production process down into a very large number of very small jobs. The idea was to use as little of the workers' brains as possible. It was an enormously successful strategy that still affects the way in which jobs are designed.

The problem today is that we are dealing with an enormously

changed labor force. For all our complaints about the educational system, it still produces tens of millions of people who can think for themselves, and whose minds go searching for something to do when their work demands too little thought. So you can fix a bad job by giving each individual more of the segments into which the total process has been broken. You enlarge the fraction of the total process for which he is responsible. Hence the name by which this method is commonly known: "job enlargement."

There is a legend, which may be true, about an industrial tycoon who was visiting one of his factories all the way back in the 1930s. He came upon a worker who was standing idly by his machine, which was shut down. "Is something wrong, my good man?" asked the paternalistic tycoon. "No, sir," replied the worker. "I need a new cutting head in this machine, and I'm waiting for the maintenance man to come and install it."

"Well, do you know how to install that cutting head yourself?" asked the tycoon. "Yes, sir," replied the worker. "But that's the maintenance man's job, not mine." The tycoon, who was noted for his courtesy with production workers, thanked the worker politely and walked without undue haste to the plant manager's office. Once the door was closed, he proceeded to raise hell. What bothered him, of course, was the inefficiency. The legend has it that job enlargement was born then and there.

The ideal way to enlarge a job is to give someone a start-to-finish responsibility for doing a task in its entirety. That maximizes the challenge, and also adds a motivational bonus, which is the "signature" effect that comes from being solely responsible for a product or a service.

But start-to-finish responsibility isn't always feasible. So job enlargement frequently gives you just a bigger piece, but still only a piece, of the whole job. That's the source of complaints that job enlargement doesn't necessarily "work." That is, attaching tasks that formerly preceded your job or followed it doesn't automatically make the job more interesting. That would only happen if the revised job added enough challenge to give you that thrill of accomplishment when you did it well.

So job enlargement is an iffy way to motivate someone. If you're going to use this method, it would be better to use it in a big way than in small experimental doses. In general, small motivational experiments don't work, but big changes in the motivators have a fighting chance of success. Some product development teams, for example, have a start-to-finish responsibility for a product throughout its life cycle. They design it, sell it, produce it, install it, service it, and they eventually even shepherd it into the market for used products. Then they start all over again with a new product. Life on such a team is seldom humdrum, because there's always a new challenge waiting for you.

Of course, that kind of job isn't for everyone. For example, there are those who find constant change upsetting. But for those who enjoy learning, life on a product development team is one long, exhilarating joy ride. Such people are living examples of the fact that under the right circumstances, jobs can be motivators.

Self-Supervision

Bosses are sometimes unnecessary. For example, if the subordinates are well-trained and reliable. It is also true if the boss's contribution to their work consists largely of decisions that the subordinates could make, or learn to make, for themselves.

Superfluous bossing isn't merely inefficient: it demotivates the workers. No matter how genial and inoffensive the superfluous supervisor might be, the very existence of his job carries an onerous implication. It suggests that the workers aren't bright enough, or mature enough, to do their work without someone to tell them what to do.

This is why you can sometimes change a bad job into a motivating job just by cutting back drastically on the amount of supervision, or even by eliminating it altogether. You can achieve major motivational gains this way—but only if you can handle the backlash from an unexpected source.

Simply fixing a bad job in this way is relatively easy. The really tough part is dealing with the political effect of lots of switched-on, highly motivated people. Fixing bad jobs raises the question of whether we really want motivation as much as we claim we do. That's because motivation, like everything else that's worthwhile in this life, comes with a price tag attached to it. And that price is something that we're much more sensitive about than mere money. It's the comfort and peace of mind that comes with knowing that you're in control and that nothing is going to happen unless you make it happen.

Mass motivation happens to be a little bit chaotic. It requires managers to master the art of managing the unpredictable. Some managers enjoy that, while others find it terribly unsettling. They are paid to see to it that what is intended happens, and that what is unintended doesn't happen. So it should not be surprising that high levels of motivation are not always welcomed enthusiastically and are sometimes actively resisted. One person's motivation can easily be another person's headache.

THE CASE OF THE DESKILLED MACHINISTS

A company that made machine tools had a long history of almost continual conflict with its unions. When the company began to introduce highly automated equipment, it was obliged by the union to preserve the jobs of workers whom the equipment had actually replaced.

One group of highly skilled machinists was kept on the payroll even when their work was taken over by machines that were controlled by magnetic tapes. The machinists now had only four functions. They pressed the "start" button, they pressed the "stop" button, they called their foreman when signal lights indicated a malfunction, and they kept the area around the machines clean. They had been "deskilled," reduced to performing menial tasks that were well below their true abilities. On the other hand, they were still employed and had suffered no loss of pay.

Management expected the new machines to be so productive that they would more than offset the cost of the highly paid, no-longer-necessary machinists. However, much of the work was done in small batches, which required frequent revisions to the control tapes. The foremen made the revisions, and errors were so frequent that the hoped-for savings did not materialize. So everyone was tense. The foremen were upset because they could not handle the tapes properly, and because management was upset with them. The workers were upset because they were skilled men doing unskilled work. To them, that meant a loss of status, even though they retained their jobs and their wages. The workers and the foremen were upset with each other, partly because of long-standing animosities, and partly because both were irritable to begin with.

One day, a machinist noticed yet another malfunction signal. So he pressed the "stop" button and called his foreman. The foreman was already angry and frustrated, and as he approached the machine he muttered, "I'd like to see you guys handle these damned things!" The machinist replied, "Are you serious?"

Then both of them became suddenly, awkwardly silent, because they realized that they had been overheard. They also knew that they had violated some of the informal taboos that governed the relationships between management and labor at their level: they were talking about matters that were the province of people at a much higher level in both the union and the company.

Rumors then began to race through both the union's and the company's grapevines. The upshot was an unusual agreement. For the next three months, these machinists would operate their machines *without supervision*. They would handle their own control tapes. Each of them would have the full authority of a supervisor, but only over himself. None could give orders to anyone else. They reported, collectively, to a second-level supervisor. At the end of the period, a joint decision would be reached to extend the experiment or discontinue it.

It was, of course, a highly controversial decision. The plant manager who approved it was newly appointed and felt that he had to do something dramatic to break the pattern of constant antagonism between the union and the company. Those who favored his decision said it would lead to improved production and enable the company to get the full benefit of its investment in new equipment. Those who opposed it predicted that the machinists would undermine discipline by refusing to show proper respect to supervisors.

Both predictions were correct. The new machines were soon operating at, or even above, their rated capacity. But the machinists also took every opportunity to heap conspicuous abuse on supervisors from other departments. They took special delight in flouting certain rules, such as prohibitions on bringing coffee to their workstations.

As the experimental period drew to a close, the pressure on the new plant manager became enormous. On the one hand, he had released powerful, pent-up motivation by changing a bad job into a good one. But he had also antagonized and demoralized his managers and foremen. After listening to all of the arguments on both sides, and several long, agonizing debates with himself, he made his decision. The experiment was discontinued.

Was his decision wise? We have the luxury of second-guessing him without having to endure the pressures under which he made it. If productivity were the only issue, I would say that he should have extended the experiment.

But the whole point of this case is that productivity is *not* the only issue. Managers need each other's support. When they are criticized, as they often are, they tend to become mutually protective. The plant manager reasoned that his management team could not stand the pressure of a continued experiment, and that it was more important to hold them together than to find out where an unconventional path might lead.

Involvement in Management

A third way to fix a bad job is to give people a voice in decisions that affect them. This is sometimes referred to as "participation." Although we tend to think of this as a typically Japanese approach to motivation, in fact, as we will see in a moment, it is actually as American as apple pie.

Participation is quite possibly the smartest managerial decision-making technique that we have. Nevertheless, it is often mistaken for "industrial democracy." Let's get that misconception out of the way first. Managers who use participative decision making do not simply count the votes of their subordinates and then do whatever the majority wants. But they do consult with those subordinates before making a decision, partly to enlarge their information base, but also to take advantage of a common quirk of human nature.

Here's that quirk. Most people will work harder to carry out a decision that they have helped to influence than they will work to carry out a decision that is imposed on them. That sentence is a bit of a mouthful, so you may want to read it again.

It's mostly a question of dignity. One of the best ways to recognize someone's abilities is to ask for his opinion. And one of the most effective ways to demonstrate contempt for someone, even if you don't intend to, is to act as if they had no opinions worth asking for. Participation is a good way to make sure that those who have to implement a decision will feel reasonably good about it.

Participation has an interesting, and revealing, history. It dates back to some pioneering experiments in the 1930s by a psychologist named Kurt Lewin. Working in a pajama factory in Virginia, Lewin proved that American workers were most productive when they helped to design the methods they used. They were least productive when those methods were designed for them by experts. But the participation effect simply went into the textbooks, and was largely ignored by American managers. Then the Japanese picked up the idea and made it the cornerstone of their famous "quality circles." It turned out that Japanese workers also got more done when they had some say about the methods they used. Soon, the quality of Japanese products so exceeded that of their American competitors that the balance of world trade began to shift.

At that point, alarmed American companies sent delegations to Japan to see what they could learn about their quality-control techniques. They discovered quality circles and brought them back to their original home as the latest Japanese business fad. After a long detour, participation had come full circle, back to the country that had not recognized its merits during the decades when it had a monopoly on it.

Contrary to popular mythology, a manager's primary responsibility is not to make decisions. A decision is nothing more than your choice of a method that you hope will produce some preferred outcome. Making that preferred outcome actually happen *is* the manager's primary responsibility. Managers are paid for results, not decisions. And those results are nearly always accomplished, or botched, as the case may be, solely by the manager's subordinates.

Therefore, the best decision is the one that gets the most whole-hearted support from the people who have to carry it out. Brilliant decisions that are badly implemented are no better, in the final analysis, than idiotic decisions. You can, for example, fill a shop with delectable merchandise, price it quite reasonably, and advertise it brilliantly. But if you staff that shop with uninterested, dispirited, lackadaisical salespeople, your sale will probably fall flat. Customers will walk out almost as fast as they walk in.

Implementation is everything. And that is why we can say that participative decision making is quite possibly the smartest managerial decision-making method that we have. It is also a pretty good antidote for an otherwise bad job.

Go for the Goal

Who would work if someone was not there to make him work? The answer seems to be that most people would. Not only that, but their work will be done quite well. But as you probably suspect, you need certain conditions to get this utopian result.

First, you need mature, well-trained people. Second, you need supervisors who know where their jobs end and where their subordinates' jobs begin, and who have the restraint to avoid crossing that line. Third, everyone needs a precise understanding of what he is expected to accomplish.

That's why the fourth way to fix a bad job is to set specific performance targets for everyone. You give each of your people a list of perhaps five or six outcomes you want them to produce and define each of them as objectively as you can. The idea is to avoid debates over whether the results they produce actually fit your specifications. You commit yourself in advance to approving each person's work if it meets the standards that you set.

This method is commonly known as "goal setting." It works because it makes the outcome of your work entirely your own. It has the added advantage of getting your boss off your back. Thus at one stroke it eliminates oversupervision, which is one of the main reasons why bad jobs are bad, and gives you a good dose of one of the strongest motivators of them all, which is knowing that you've done something important and done it well.

Those All-Important "It Depends" Factors

Nothing always works. That's also true of the four methods for fixing a bad job. But when certain conditions are met, they work well enough so that it would be to your advantage to try to create those conditions. You need the right people, the right jobs, and a system that can be changed.

Every one of our four fixes involves giving someone's brain a good workout. That means that you have to be dealing with someone who likes to think. But some people don't. How can you tell whether a particular person is going to have fun figuring out how to handle a tricky job, or hate it?

It's not just a simple matter of finding a match between the job to be done and that person's ability, although that is part of the solution. And you can't simply ask people if they'd like work that is mentally demanding, because most people simply don't know how they'd react to an unfamiliar experience.

There are only two ways to find out if someone will blossom in a job that puts his or her brain to work. One is to put him in such a job and see what happens. The other is to watch the way he does his present job. Is he annoyed, or merely indifferent, when the work doesn't flow along as it should? Does she keep track of how much she's done, and how well she's done it, or simply forget what she's done as soon as she's done it? Does he try to fix what needs fixing, or does he simply limp along with defective tools until somebody notices? Is her output just as high when her supervisor is away, or does she slack off when no one is watching?

To each of these questions, the first answer would be more promising than the second. It would also be more common. That's why effective motivation isn't nearly as hard to achieve as you might think. The odds are usually in your favor. But they are not *always* in your favor. That's why, if you happen to be dealing with someone who is accustomed to thinking of work as a curse rather than as an opportunity to do something that matters, it would be better to try to motivate him some other way than with a well-fixed job.

Some jobs don't lend themselves to fixing. It may be too costly, or just impractical, to make the necessary changes. For example, you need a way to inform the people who do the work about the results of their work. But if those results occur miles away, or weeks afterward, they may just have to get along without that information. That would dilute the motivational effect, because they wouldn't really know whether they had done the job well.

Sometimes a job is one of many that contributes to a particular result. Responsibility for those results is shared with a lot of other people. That makes it hard to demonstrate that any individual's efforts really matter.

You also have to reckon with the fact that some results don't matter very much to those who have labored to produce them. When I see enormous piles of cheap souvenirs in "tourist trap" shops, I shudder to think of the poor souls who put so many of their hours into making them. Those who devote their lives to making junk that will mostly be thrown away have to be motivated by something other than their jobs. Subsistence wages are the probable answer, but that is a topic for the next chapter.

Some jobs can't be fixed because capital has been invested, concrete has been poured, and steel has been bolted into place. In other words, the system of which the job is a part may be too rigid to change. That's why the best time to fix a job is when it is being designed. It's much easier to design a motivating job into a new system than to try to retrofit that job into an established system.

Having conceded all of those limitations to fixing bad jobs, a final word is in order. Bad jobs *should* be fixed, whenever it's feasible to fix them. That isn't merely because of the productivity payoff, although that's real enough. It's also because bad jobs are a terrible insult to the human spirit. And life is too short to be wasted doing dumb work.

CHAPTER
— 10 —
THE MOST
COMPLICATED
MOTIVATOR

An old joke says that money may not be everything, but it's still way ahead of whatever is in second place. It would be more accurate to say that money isn't everything, but almost all other motivators would be nothing without it. Money is really more of a catalyst for other motivators, either magnifying or diminishing their effects, than a motivator in its own right.

That is only one of several paradoxes about money. Back in chapter 1 we noted that money is not only the most expensive motivator but also the least efficient. Money is, in brief, the most complicated motivator of them all. Whatever is the second most complicated motivator really *is* way behind.

Still, if you understand what money can and can't do, it can be a highly cost-effective tool for getting people to do what you want them to do. There are ways to get a pretty good motivational bang for a wisely spent buck. Unfortunately, much of the money spent on motivation is wasted because there is so little understanding of what it can and can't do.

Back in chapter 4, we looked at the "fairness equation" that determines whether any given person will feel that his or her pay is justifiable. The fairness issue is a major part of the psychology of pay. But there's more to it than that. So we'll begin this chapter by looking at the *inefficiency* of money as a motivator. Then we'll examine the effects of *fixed pay*, which is the form in which most people get their money. After that, we'll consider *variable pay*, which is the kind that can produce spectacular motivational effects, but only under the right conditions. Last, on the assumption that your interest in this subject isn't altogether academic, we'll also look at how you can *maximize your own income*, and at the interesting question of whether that is what you really want.

Big Bucks, Bad Bargains

For most people, money is an inefficient motivator. Note that I said "inefficient," not "ineffective." If you've got enough money to throw at people, you can usually induce them to do whatever it takes to keep your money flowing in their direction. But that takes *a lot* of money. Most people "have their price," but very few of them are cheap. Also, the changes that money can induce in their behavior are likely to be short-lived. So you *can* buy motivation, but the price is likely to be exorbitant.

You've also got to cope with the "ingrate" effect. Most people get used to higher pay rather quickly. Today's big raise becomes tomorrow's big yawn. So even that little bulge of extra effort is likely to disappear unless you pump in even more money to keep it bulging.

If you add up the gains of money motivation and balance them against the costs, you'll usually find it's no bargain. There are a few important exceptions, which we'll come to later. For the moment, note that most people are already working as hard as they care to work for money, at least in the amounts you can usually afford to pay. The almighty dollar is not a motivational panacea, simply because it costs far too much to use it as a motivator, and because it buys far too little motivation.

Of course, there are exceptions to every motivational rule. In this case, the exception would be your ability to recruit a genius. Money can do that for you. It won't necessarily motivate the genius to work any harder. But it can motivate the genius to do his or her inventing or creating on your payroll rather than on someone else's. A resident genius can be a distinct advantage for any employer.

My favorite example of using very high pay to reward a genius concerns Charles Proteus Steinmetz, the great electrical engineer who made alternating current possible. Steinmetz was employed by General Electric, for whom he constituted a unique pay problem. How, after all, do you compensate someone who creates an industry for your company to enter and to dominate?

The solution that GE hit upon was to give Steinmetz a checkbook. "If you want anything, anything at all," they told him, "just pay for it with one of these checks. The company will see to it that each of your checks is good."* Both Steinmetz and GE were happy with the arrangement. I imagine that you would be happy with it too, and so would I. But alas, neither of us is a Steinmetz.

And that brings us back to the basic inefficiency of money as a motivator. Only rarely can we justify using it in amounts that are large enough to motivate major increases in effort. For most of us, all any employer can afford is to attract us, make us indifferent to the possibility of leaving, and minimize the risk that we might decide that our pay is intolerably low. It takes a great deal of money to do even that, and all that it really buys is an opportunity to expose us to nonfinancial motivators.

The Inefficiency of Motivating with Money

Most of us earn our livings by selling our time and our effort. But not all of our time and effort are for sale, because we need to reserve some of them for our own purposes. While you would probably welcome more money if it simply fell on you, you aren't likely to expend much of your scarce *unsold* time and effort trying to make that happen. Unless, of course, someone made you that proverbial offer you couldn't refuse.

So if I want to buy some additional time and effort from you, it's going to come down to a question of price. The time and effort that you have not already sold will cost a lot more than the time and effort you have sold. That's because of supply and demand, and also because of competition. Your unsold time and effort are both

---

*The checkbook story is a persistent legend. There is at least this much truth to it: GE told Steinmetz that he could build a house to his own specifications, for which the company would pay. He built an impressively large home. Whether GE paid his other expenses as well is unverifiable. He was in any case extraordinarily well paid by the standards of the times.

scarce commodities. In fact, your supply of unsold time could be effectively zero, especially if you're starting out in a demanding profession such as law, where you'll scarcely have the time to spend what you earn.

So the supply of time and effort that are, so to speak, "for sale" can be very tight. And at the same time, the demand for them can be very strong. Some tough competitors could be bidding up the price. They would include your family and friends, as well as your recreational interests, and even, perhaps, a second job.

You might be willing to exhaust yourself, and to sacrifice all of your free time and most of your sleep time, for *enough* money. But unless you're a fool, which I seriously doubt, that sum would have to be enormous. No amount of money, be it a fortune or a pittance, is going to do you much good if you haven't the time or the strength to enjoy it.

So if I use nothing but money in my attempt to buy your unsold time and effort, the arrangement will quickly become so expensive that I could not afford to continue. Neither I nor anyone else can make a lot of offers that you can't refuse, because the bidding war would bankrupt us all. Sorry about that.

But money is not only inefficient as a motivator: at times it's also close to being unnecessary. There are certain occupations to which eager young recruits are drawn the way flies are drawn to honey. Some examples are publishing, the theater, and jobs in and around filmmaking. The supply of would-be editors, actors, and scriptwriters usually exceeds the demand by a considerable margin. Employers in these industries are able to hold their wage costs way down because their employees not only love their work but are entranced by the lure of getting that "one big break" that they think is all they need. They may grouse about low pay, but are usually reluctant to take the one step that could put them firmly on the path to better incomes. That would be to enter a profession in which the odds are not so long against them.

Fixed Pay

From a motivational point of view, there are two kinds of money. We have to distinguish between fixed pay and variable pay, because the way in which money is paid out produces quite different effects on behavior.

Fixed pay gets its name because it seldom changes more than once a year and because those changes are relatively small. Most wages and salaries are examples of fixed pay, and so are most benefit programs. Variable pay, on the other hand, is paid out in varying amounts and can be quite substantial relative to fixed pay. Bonuses and commissions are examples. For simplicity's sake, we'll just ignore cost-of-living increases. They merely recognize changes in the purchasing power of money and have little or no motivating power of their own.

Most of us, most of the time, are paid with fixed pay. Its effect on job *performance* is somewhere between marginal and nonexistent. Hardly anyone pumps extra time, effort, or imagination into his work just to get the same check every payday.

Although we have glorified money into a kind of cultural icon, for most people it is only one of many motivators. The truth is that most people, most of the time, have something other than money on their minds. The amount of effort that they put into their work depends on the importance of those *other* needs, and on the extent to which they expect to satisfy those needs through work.

Suppose your main purpose in life is to enjoy wine, the opposite sex, and song. In that case, you'll pour enough time and effort into your work to be able to afford them, but not so much as to interfere with your enjoyment of them. If, on the other hand, your main passion in life is to solve the fundamental equations of the universe, you'll be interested in money only to the extent that it provides you with a few necessities and creature comforts.

This brings me to my favorite story about the effects of high pay on someone who was relatively indifferent to money, namely Albert Einstein. Back in the 1930s, Einstein was visited by a delegation that invited him to join the Institute for Advanced Study. They offered him a salary of fifteen thousand dollars a year. Of course, that was a much more substantial amount then than it is now. But the committee was apologetic.

"We realize that your services would be extremely valuable, Dr. Einstein," the chairman said. "But fifteen thousand dollars is all that we can afford, and we hope that you can accept our offer." Einstein rolled his eyes upward toward heaven. "Fifteen thousand dollars!" he exclaimed. *"Gott in Himmel!* What will I ever do with so much money?"*

Einstein was in a class by himself intellectually. Motivationally, however, he was not so unusual. Many people spend much of their lives in sublime indifference to their pay. The exception, of course, is when their pay falls far short of their expectations. That converts indifference into irritation, and then into agitation. But not into motivation. People who are walking the picket lines are not producing goods and services. The motivational difference between indifference to pay and agitation over pay was beautifully summed up by the late Douglas McGregor. He wrote, "Man does not live by bread alone, except when there is little bread."

When purchasing power sinks too low—because of inflation, for example—most people will exert whatever pressure they can to increase their pay. But exerting pressure should not be confused with working harder. Also, when pay seems to be unfairly distributed, most people will try to correct that. But as we noted back in chapter 4, the easiest way to soothe your outraged sense of fairness is by deliberately letting your effort deteriorate. So most of the time the effects of fixed pay on most people's *output* are indifference, agitation, or less work.

Those are not very impressive results. But you can't look at output alone, because fixed pay has two other major effects, both of which are indispensable. The primary functions of fixed pay are to attract the necessary talent to a company and to keep it there. It does both jobs extraordinarily well.

Motivating Membership

Your fixed pay is what you live on. It pays the bills. It's hard to get more fundamental than that. That's why the amount of fixed pay is usually the most important of all the factors that enter into your decision whether to accept a job offer. And the same can be said of your decision on whether to go looking for another job elsewhere or to stay put.

So while fixed pay is not much of a motivator in the sense of

---

*I am indebted to the late Albert L. Williams, the former president of IBM, for this story. As a young accountant, he was a member of the committee that recruited Einstein to the Institute.

influencing job performance, it is one hell of a recruiting tool. It is rather like a magnet, except that it attracts people instead of iron filings. Nothing attracts or holds talent nearly as powerfully as a regular paycheck with the right numbers written on it. In that restricted sense, money really is "way ahead of whatever is in second place." It is the principal reason why people will tolerate dull jobs or bad bosses. But don't confuse job retention with motivation. People who can't get a better-paying job will endure a bad job, but they will work no harder at it than they must.

It's competition between packages of fixed pay that creates the labor market. No wonder economists are so impressed with its effects. Psychologists are not, however: there's a big difference between, on the one hand, shuttling people from one employer to another and, on the other hand, getting some work out of them. That's what most people have in mind when they speak of a "motivator": something that extracts extra effort, something that lifts job performance above its ordinary levels. There are ways of doing that, but simply providing fixed pay isn't one of them.

When you stop to think about it, that's a rather shocking thing to say, because fixed pay is a very big chunk of our gross national product. We're talking about *trillions* of dollars, all for attracting people to their present employers and, ideally, keeping them there. Is it worth it?

The answer, as always, is that it depends. In this case, it depends on how wisely each employer uses the opportunity his money has so dearly bought, which is to motivate people through mostly *non-financial* means. You can do that, for example, with smart supervision, challenging goals, and jobs that are worth doing. Of course, you can also use your hard-bought opportunity to motivate people by throwing even more money at them. But it takes another kind of money to do that trick. That's variable pay, which we haven't discussed yet.

However, all of those nonfinancial motivators, and variable pay as well, share the same fatal flaw. *They can't motivate anyone unless he or she is on the payroll.* And that's why fixed pay, costly and unrelated to effort as it may be, is indispensable. You can't motivate someone who won't join your organization, and you can't motivate someone who has left it. Membership has to precede any attempt to motivate effort, and nothing motivates membership like fixed pay.

The various packages of fixed pay that are on offer when you go job hunting will largely determine *where* you will go to work. But fixed pay won't determine how *hard* you work, unless you think it's too low, in which case its effect can be catastrophic. Fixed pay almost never improves effort, simply because effort seldom has any discernible effect on fixed pay. The check comes in because it's payday, not because of what you've done, if anything, since the last payday. Fixed pay pays you to be there, but not to reach for the stars.

Variable Pay

If our discussion of what money can and can't do has disappointed you so far, take heart. Remember that we've been looking only at *fixed* pay. Now we're ready to look at the effects of *variable* pay. That's where the motivational action is.

You can motivate extra effort with variable pay, but only under certain conditions. First, you have to pick the right people to motivate, because some are more susceptible to the lure of money than others. Second, those people have to consider that extra effort reasonable. Most people are not about to risk life and limb, or for that matter, much inconvenience, merely to get their hands on a bit of extra cash. Third, you've got to offer enough of that extra cash.

Who Works Hardest for Money?

You can get to three kinds of people better with monetary incentives than with any other motivator. The first of these might be described as the "temporarily poor." That's really a stage of life, not an income level. You are temporarily poor if your income has not yet risen to a level where further effort starts to yield diminishing returns. This is typically a ten- to fifteen-year waiting period at the start of a middle-class career, during which you consciously make do with less than you really want. You're busy paying off your college loans, or saving up that down payment on your first house, or furnishing it. The effect of variable income is to ratchet up your income, which pays those bills sooner and terminates that waiting period faster.

Eventually, the income of the temporarily poor rises to comfortable levels. Of course, they would still *like* to receive additional income. But they are unlikely to sacrifice much time, effort, or convenience to get it. Further, the bonus that would get their attention at this stage of their lives would have to be much, much fatter than the ones that got them excited when their incomes were thinner. So in time, the temporarily poor work their way up to incomes at which they join the permanently complacent. Until that happens, you can motivate them with variable pay, depending on the two other "it depends" factors on our list.

There are two other groups you can motivate with variable pay. One might be described as "just barely poor." These are people whose incomes have to be stretched to cover their needs. Nevertheless, their incomes rise faster than the increase in their expenses. As the gap between expense and income starts to narrow, they can see an end to a way of life they never really liked. They can see an end to constantly going into debt, to deciding which creditors to pay and which to avoid, and to just plain doing without things that they need.

They are on the verge of entering the great American middle class, with a few extra bucks left over every month to do with as they please. The closer they get to having some discretionary income, the more attractive it becomes. During the few years that it takes to close the gap, they will work diligently, even furiously, to close it faster. They will leap at opportunities to earn variable income. But this is also a temporary condition. Sooner or later, the just barely poor become complacent and contented.

The third group that will respond to variable income might be called the "psychologically poor." This is the only group that is permanently money-motivated. These people will sacrifice time and effort to increase their incomes regardless of how high those incomes have become and regardless of how much wealth they have accumulated.

These people tend to be obsessed with, and driven by, money. They usually make a lot of it, and even their money makes a lot of money. But it brings them no joy. For them, the wolf is always at the door, and making money is a kind of ritual for staving off disaster. Offer them some variable income and they will work like beavers to earn it.

I can see your eyes lighting up right now. "Bring me enough people like that," you may be thinking, "and let me dangle some nice fat commissions in front of their greedy little eyes, and they will set performance records for me that the world has never seen!" Nice try. But it probably won't work. Here's why. The psychologically poor are *very* focused on making money, so much so that they quickly figure out that they'll never get rich on someone else's payroll. So they quickly gravitate into self-employment, where they can keep all of the profits for themselves, or they start their own companies. Either way, they seldom give other people an opportunity to motivate them. They do that for themselves.

Now, if you add together all of the temporarily poor and the just barely poor and the psychologically poor people in the world, the sum will be considerably less than 50 percent of the labor force. If you happen to be dealing with people from one of those groups, your variable pay system should work just fine. That would depend, of course, on the two other "it depends" factors that we haven't looked at yet.

But if you're dealing with people who are not susceptible to variable pay, your system would only work if you offered them a very good deal. In other words, lots of money for only marginal increases in effort. You could only make the deal attractive to them by making it less attractive to yourself. And there you have the basic irony, and the basic inefficiency, of trying to motivate most people with money. It usually doesn't pay.

But there are some important exceptions, and that brings us back to the three "it depends" factors that determine the effects of variable pay. The first, as we have seen, is picking the right people to motivate. Now we are ready to consider the second factor, which is the amount of extra effort required to earn the extra pay.

Reachable Targets

Variable pay is usually tied to the accomplishment of certain specific goals, such as a sales or profit target, or the attainment of certain quality standards. Setting those goals correctly is probably more important than the amount of money to be paid if they are reached. A goal is correctly set if it seems attainable to those who are asked to attain it. That is, of course, a subjective perception on their part. But we know a lot about how these perceptions are formed. Briefly, what makes a target seem attainable is not its size but how much say you had in setting it.

If you impose a goal on others, they will probably see it as difficult if not impossible to reach, even if it has already been reached in the past. The task will seem hopeless rather than challenging, and only token efforts will be made to reach it. But if you take their opinions into account, the goal will seem more reasonable to them, and therefore more deserving of a good, hard try.

A big reward will not make a goal seem attainable, and it won't motivate effort if the goal seems out of reach. But a big reward will make the effort required to reach an *attainable* goal seem worthwhile and will have the added benefit of making the pursuit exciting.

A simple example will illustrate the relationship between goals and rewards. Suppose I were to place a bar across the seats of two chairs so that it formed a barrier about eighteen inches high. Then I would offer you a reward of five dollars if you could run up to that bar and successfully jump over it. You would probably consider that a sporting proposition. You would probably think, "I can probably do it, so let's give it the old college try." You will be motivated by the attraction of success in achieving an attainable goal, not by the five dollars. The proof of that would come if I changed both the goal and the reward. Suppose I offered you a Steinmetz reward, everything that money can buy for the rest of your life. To win it, all you'd have to do is jump over a tall building in a single bound, Superman-style. Although the reward is as attractive as monetary rewards can get, you'd only laugh at it. The reward would not motivate you, because the goal would be too difficult.

The Reward Is in the Ratio

This leads us to the third of the "it depends" factors for variable pay, which is the size of the reward. What makes a big reward big enough?

You can't really measure variable pay in dollars. A bonus or a salary increase that would seem quite substantial to a junior employee would be sniffed at by a senior executive. In both cases, the motivational effect, or the lack of it, comes from the *ratio*, or proportion, of the pay increment to the previous pay.

If that ratio is too low, the reward will be seen as trivial and possibly as insulting. If it is more or less equal to the inflation rate, it will be seen as minimal and barely decent. If it is about at the average of certain comparison groups, it will be perceived as decent but not exceptional. If the ratio is well above that of the comparison groups, it will be seen as meeting proper expectations. If it is so far above the comparison groups as to be in a class by itself, it may attract some favorable comments.

You can draw three conclusions from these perceptions. First, it's ratios and not dollars that make people mad at, indifferent to, or delighted with their pay, as the case may be. Second, don't expect applause or even gratitude from the people to whom you grant pay raises or bonuses. Third, if you want to use pay for motivating extra effort, rather than merely making people happy with it, you have to combine the right pay ratios with the right performance goals with the right people. And if you can't combine all three of those factors, you can't use money to motivate extra effort.

How to Make a Bundle

I assume that the lesson learned by the psychologically poor was not wasted on you. There's no way to get rich on somebody else's payroll. If really big bucks really matter more to you than anything else, you will have to cast aside the security of corporate employment and launch your own business.

Perhaps you'll defer that big move until you've acquired the four "C factors" that are best found with big employers: competence, confidence, connections, and credentials. But once you've got them, a corporate job simply holds your income down. Even if your company has a profit-sharing plan, you'd be sharing those profits with too many fellow employees and too many shareholders. Why share when you could have it all?

But before you leap at those juicy rewards, consider an old French proverb: "Be sure that you want the effects of what you want." Being solely responsible for your income is like walking a tightrope without a safety net. If you can handle that exposure, farewell and Godspeed. You're on your own, by choice.

If you're not the entrepreneurial type, and still want to milk the corporate payroll for all it's worth, stick around. You probably won't become obscenely rich that way, but you can become very, very comfortable, if you know how. As always, there's a caveat.

You can maximize your corporate income, but only if you really want to. There are some prices you'll have to pay.

To maximize your corporate income, you'll first have to go to where the big salaries are. With only a few exceptions, that means the big coastal cities. If you don't think you'd like the lifestyle in such places, you'd better do some serious soul-searching about how badly you want those big bucks.

Next, you'll want to work for a company that offers lots of variable income. Salaries alone, even when they are competitive and buttressed with lots of nice benefits, will never make you wealthy. You'd be best off in a company that offers you plenty of opportunity to lever your income upward with commissions and bonuses. The great advantage of both is that they depend entirely on your own efforts. Your achievements can't be canceled out by someone else's non-achievement.

You have relatively little control over the results of profit-sharing plans, stock options, or Employee Stock Ownership Plans (ESOPs). You might get lucky with one of them, if the company as a whole happens to do very well. But then again, you might not be so lucky. Plans that tie your income to corporate performance are really a kind of lottery. You're more of a spectator than an active participant. And while lotteries are interesting, they are not motivating.

If a company has such a plan in its compensation package, that is probably a net motivational advantage for you. But it can't compete with employee-controlled forms of variable pay for tying your effort to your income. And the two stock plans would only be advantageous if the company's stock price did at least as well as the well-known averages, such as the Dow-Jones or Standard & Poor's, over a period of several years. Otherwise you'd be better off investing the money in any good mutual fund.

Another form of variable income worth hunting for is a partnership interest in your firm. This typically divides a company's profits into far fewer pieces than is the case with corporate stock. Therefore each piece is more valuable. A partnership gives you a significant piece of the action. Some firms attract large numbers of eager young recruits each year with the lure of eventual partnerships, even though it's common knowledge that only a few will actually win them.

These recruits, most of whom would meet the criteria for being "temporarily poor," proceed to work like fury for a few years. They know that the odds against winning one of those partnerships are formidable. But there's a *quid pro quo*. Yes, most leave the firm after a few years—but with a highly marketable résumé that's enhanced by the training and experience they've had. Real estate developers such as Trammel Crow, home builders such as U.S. Home, and big accounting firms such as Arthur Andersen, all use this strategy. So do many law firms.

Once you've identified the companies with the most advantageous pay plans and managed to get yourself hired, your next step is to maneuver your way into jobs that offer lots of variable income. Usually this involves an "apprenticeship," during which you prove your worth to the firm by laboring, so to speak, in its vineyards. Your problem is to distinguish yourself from a lot of equally eager, equally hopeful young people.

Your best strategy for doing that was outlined in chapter 1. You want to demonstrate that you can multiply your own effectiveness many times over. You do that by motivating those around you and those who report to you to get more good work done than they ordinarily would.

But don't forget the price. You're in an exposed position if you're eligible for variable income, because you're expected to earn it. If for some reason you can't produce consistently favorable results, you could be in jeopardy. Before you get yourself into a position to earn big bucks, be sure that you can take the pressure. You might sleep better and live longer with a less volatile income.

If you succeed in approaching the apex of the corporation, you ought to see if you can cut your own deal. An employment contract should, at a minimum, include a sliding scale that increases your profit participation as profits themselves rise, and should also cover you with prearranged severance terms in case your job is eliminated. There has been much debate about whether these preferential arrangements unfairly benefit a few executives at the expense of the shareholders. In practice, it really comes down to a question of whether that's what it takes to attract or hold the particular executive the company wants. If you have proven yourself to be that valuable to the firm, my advice would be to go for it. But first be sure that your perception of your value is shared by those who will decide whether to grant you such special treatment.

The End Game

No matter how high you may rise in the hierarchy, you will ultimately face the prospect of retirement. I might add, "if you are lucky." Some people never make it to that stage. But if you are lucky enough to make it to retirement, you'll find that your opportunities to lever your income upward are drastically reduced. There are no merit raises in retirement, no bonuses, and no promotions. There may be cost-of-living increases, but they are seldom guaranteed. How can you deal with that?

There are two ways. My own preferred alternative is not to retire at all. Of course, you will want to collect the pension for which you've been saving and the social security payments for which you've been taxed. But even as you collect them, you can aim to go right on working, albeit for a new employer, as long as that's practical. That will keep your income fairly high. More important, it will give you something to do.

There are four ways to remain gainfully employed even after the retirement dinner at which they give you your gold watch. Three of them are varieties of self-employment. If you can write well, you'll find that publishers don't care how old you are. If you're skilled enough at your professional specialty to be able to sell your advice, you'll find that clients don't ask how old their consultants are. And if you start your own business, you can enforce your own policy against age discrimination.

The fourth way to continue working past normal retirement age is to launch a second career as a teacher. As a practical matter, you had better do this well before you reach your mid-sixties. Don't expect to be hired solely because you would love to teach; experience as a part-time teacher would help your cause. So would lots of practical experience in applying the subject you propose to teach.

Making Money Make Money

If you really want to retire, in the sense of no longer being employed, how can you compensate for your lost leverage on your income? The answer is disarmingly simple, but devilishly hard to do. You just make it a rule to keep your discretionary spending well within your income. You also keep investing your surplus conservatively, and you pray that when the end comes it will be quick and inexpensive. It's a sobering thought that most people pile up 90 percent of all the medical bills they ever incur during the last six months of their lives.

So if you manage to avoid medical catastrophe, you can build a retirement nest egg that you literally can never outlive. A good financial planner can show you how to do this. But let me warn you. It's going to take financial discipline, all the way to the finish line. And the best time to start was probably yesterday.

CHAPTER
——— 11 ———

THE GREAT
MOTIVATIONAL
MINEFIELD

If you're a manager in an organization of any size, you will probably have to find your way through a first-class motivational hazard called performance appraisal. It's a danger to both your own motivation and to that of everyone you supervise. The good news about performance appraisal is that under certain conditions, it can actually help to motivate people. The bad news, alas, is that those conditions are quite rare.

Performance appraisal works just fine when there is no bad news to convey, when bosses and subordinates have no secrets from each other, when there are lots of rewards to be handed out, and when you can take all the time you need to prepare for a nice, relaxed discussion. But if you're lacking even one of those lovely conditions, you're likely to be in trouble the moment you sit down for that interlude of mandatory candor with your boss, or with someone who reports to you. Performance appraisal, in brief, works best when it isn't really needed, but can be very cantankerous when it is badly needed.

This chapter will begin with a look at what performance appraisal is and why it is so widely used despite its well-known shortcomings. Next, we'll look at why it is such a minefield for managers. Then we'll consider ways in which the mines can be defused. Unfortunately, you may not be able to do that defusing yourself until you reach the executive level. So we'll follow with a section on how to lead your own troops through the minefield with the fewest possible casualties. Finally, a section on how to make the performance appraisal system work to your own advantage, so you collect whatever rewards your company gives for top-rated performance.

Why It's a Required Ritual

Performance appraisal in one form or another has become a fixed feature of corporate life. In most companies, it is an entrenched annual ritual. Everyone does it, if only because personnel departments insist on it. Since they are the folks who tell the payroll department how much to pay us, they generally get their way.

The process usually has three parts. First, your boss rates you on how well you've done your job. Then, in one manner or another, that rating is made known to you. Ultimately, those ratings could trigger various actions that could motivate you, such as a nice big promotion, or at the other extreme, a pink slip.

On the surface, it seems terribly straightforward. The company periodically checks up on whether you've been earning your salary, lets you know where you stand, and uses that rating to determine the size of your next salary increase. If it were really that simple, managers would be spared a lot of bother. So would you and I, because if performance appraisal really worked the way it is supposed to work, this chapter would be unnecessary.

Performance appraisal could be compared to a medication that doesn't work very well, and has lots of terrible side effects, but which we continue to use because we have nothing better, and because the disease it is supposed to cure is so awful. We cling to performance appraisal because we prize its purposes, despite abundant evidence that what it actually accomplishes is something altogether different. Our persistence is mostly a testimonial to the passion with which we pursue those purposes. Otherwise, our continued dedication to such a cumbersome, controversial ritual would be irrational.

And it *is* cumbersome. In some companies, for example, managers spend, on average, about six hours getting ready for each of those awkward interviews. It's also controversial, because most line managers would cheerfully dump it overboard if you let them. On the other hand, human resource managers and their learned consultants are likely to think of it as almost, but not quite, a panacea. Performance appraisal is a bureaucrat's way of trying to impose objectivity on the inherently subjective task of evaluating other people's work. If that could really be done, it would eliminate a lot of debates, complaints, and challenges to managerial judgment. That's why the personnel experts tinker with performance appraisal so much, hoping to find just the right set of adjectives with which to describe performance, or just the right training method for making managers into mentors, as if nothing was wrong with it but a few technical details.

What's wrong with performance appraisal is that it rests on naive assumptions about human nature. It overlooks the nearly universal human instinct to defend one's pride and self-esteem against criticism. Any performance appraisal that could make you think less of yourself, if you were to take it seriously, is probably going to be rejected out of hand.

Human defense mechanisms have a very high kill rate for incoming criticisms. Most of them are simply dismissed as being either biased or misinformed. The same fate probably awaits your criticisms of your subordinates. Performance appraisal is, in brief, a game without winners when it requires the manager to dwell on "weaknesses," or "areas needing improvement," in an employee's work.

Performance appraisal has plenty of defenders, however, and many of them would rate that last statement as unduly pessimistic. They prefer to think positively. So they urge managers to continually try to improve both their own results and those of their subordinates. Continual improvement is, of course, an absurdity. Sooner or later, you're going to reach the limits of your ability, or of your willingness to sacrifice any more of your time and energy. "Thinking positively" is fine when there is something real to think positively about. Otherwise it is a sure-fire formula for either frustration or self-deception.

What *are* those lofty, irresistible goals of performance appraisal, the ones we want so badly that we choose to ignore its many faults? Performance appraisal persists because we hope it will respond to the security motive and the fairness motive, both of which are very powerful. The goals are to reassure people who have nothing to worry about that they are really safe, and that they can count on a fair day's pay for a fair day's work.

The goals themselves are admirable. The nagging question, however, is whether performance appraisal, however we might tinker with it, can actually achieve them.

Falling Short of Glorious Goals

We have already taken a long look at the security motive, back in chapter 3. All we need to say about it here is that it can have a powerful influence on anyone whose income is derived primarily from selling his work to an employer. That's roughly 95 percent of the labor force. The rest are unemployed, and most of them depend on checks from a different paymaster, the government. So it comes as no surprise that a secure income is of intense interest to just about everyone.

Performance appraisal is meant to be an annual reassurance that your income is not in jeopardy and that you can sleep peacefully as far as those all-important paychecks are concerned. Without that reassurance, some people will start feeling vulnerable, especially as their own marketability declines with age. Can performance appraisal provide that reassurance? Yes. In fact, a bit too well at times.

Managers usually tolerate any work that is not grossly unacceptable. Consequently, people whose work is actually marginal receive the same more-or-less satisfactory appraisals that nearly everyone else also gets. So they understandably conclude that all is well. The system feeds them slightly inaccurate signals. Managers consider the resulting slight delusions to be inconsequential, and not worth the fuss that accurate signals would create.

Here's where we reach one of those points on which experts disagree, and where honesty compels me to acknowledge that some respected colleagues differ with the conclusion I am about to reach. My own view is that the managers who tolerate marginally acceptable work and give slightly inaccurate performance appraisals are more likely to be right than wrong. They are usually wiser managers than those who demand more of their subordinates than they can comfortably deliver. The real question, most of the time, is not whether work can be improved but whether the improvement that can be gotten is worth the cost of getting it. That cost can easily include suspicion, resentment, and animosity, any of which can make your task that much harder next time you have to motivate someone. The real art in performance appraisal is not to demand more constantly but to know when you can push for better results, when to settle for what you've got, and when to get rid of someone whose work is hopeless.

For all of these reasons, managers who bend the rules of performance appraisal are more likely to achieve its aims than those who follow them blindly. It's the zealots that you really have to worry about, not the pragmatists.

I remember one personnel manager in a company that had an elaborate ten-point rating scale for job performance. He was assigned to a division that had a high percentage of older employees, most of whom did their jobs in a competent if lackluster way. On the ten-point scale, most of them received ratings of six or seven, which would translate to "slightly above average," although arguably a more accurate rating would have been five, or even four.

That subtle difference infuriated the personnel manager. He was determined to correct what he regarded as a glaring abuse of the system. So he decreed a "forced distribution" system, which would have required the division's managers to assign a predetermined number of employees to each of the ten ratings. "You can't tell me," he thundered at a management meeting, "that a four should get the same raise as a six!"

He was an angry, hotheaded man. But he did not get his way, because one of the division's managers stood up at the meeting and said, "Look, somebody's got to say this to you, so I'm going to say it. You're talking nonsense. We know these people better than you do. If we did what you want, we'd ruin morale. The people who we pushed down would be mad at us, and the ones we pushed up would be embarrassed. And what for? What would that accomplish? If we have to make anyone unhappy in this division, I would rather make you unhappy than do that to my people."

The personnel manager had clearly lost his credibility with the division's managers. A few weeks later, he was asked to resign.

A Crossfire of Egos

So much for the effect of performance appraisal on security. Now let's consider its effect on the fairness motive. There's not much point in trying to excel in your work if you're convinced that the deck is stacked against you, because you're not your boss's pet. Even the possibility of favoritism can be a potent demotivator. To counteract it, performance appraisal prescribes a system for using the same standards to evaluate everyone.

In theory, at least, how well you do your work should matter more than who you know, or even who you are. At one stroke, that should relieve you of the fear that you can't possibly win whatever rewards are given for doing your job well. The greatest rewards would then go to the greatest contributors, and the competition for those rewards would be fair and open to everyone. That would fit the definition of justice under a free enterprise system, which is "from each according to his abilities, to each according to his results."

So much for the theory. In practice, performance appraisal runs headlong into the fact that it is unavoidably based on perception. That means that your rating of someone else's performance is always exposed to charges that you are biased, or that you overstated the negatives and overlooked the positives, or (the unkindest cut of all) that you wouldn't know good performance if you fell over it, because you're not an expert yourself in doing the job you're rating. So performance appraisal, despite its idealistic purposes, gets caught in a crossfire it creates between the egos of the appraiser and the appraisee.

As for your own performance rating, it is exposed to all of the vagaries of human nature, including bad bosses (see chapter 14), who might be more interested in asserting their power over you than in rating you fairly.

If the Facts Don't Fit the Theory

Performance appraisal is also supposed to be the linchpin of the merit pay system, through which rewards are matched to results. But that seldom actually happens. The main problem is that there usually isn't much difference between the results that various people produce on the same job. Neither is there much difference in the size of available rewards. So in real life, there isn't much to match.

If you compare the work of the best worker in a group with that of the worst one, you'll usually find there isn't that much difference between them. That's because the truly outstanding people get promoted (or pirated away), and the really incompetent ones get demoted or fired. So the distribution of work performance is constantly being pruned at both ends, leaving a tightly bunched mass in the middle who do their work at more or less the same level of effectiveness. The reason most people's performance ratings are pretty much the same is that most of the differences in their work are subtle, or subjective, or just plain unimportant.

Incidentally, the most common performance rating, by far, is "above average." Of course, that's a statistical absurdity. But what those figures really tell us is that most managers are not terribly displeased with the work of most of their people. That news should produce at least as much rejoicing as a year without accidents or a year without defective work. Actually, it gives some personnel departments fits, because the lumping together of most people's job performance makes a mockery of the merit pay process. If you're going to treat people differently, you need a way to sort their achievements into distinct categories. But if their results are so similar that the sorting has to be arbitrary, the system won't work, because it's based on a false premise.

This is where some personnel departments lose their grip on reality. They take the position that "if the facts don't fit the theory, so much the worse for the facts!" Like the unfortunate manager in the preceding case, they try to impose the theory on the facts by insisting on a predetermined distribution of ratings. But line managers are usually ingenious enough to defeat that system, too. They simply rotate individuals into the "above average" category, so that over a period of years everyone gets his turn at winning the rating they deserve.

In real life, most people's job performance ratings are bunched together. The same bunching can be seen in their pay. What constrains you from handing out widely different pay increases is the budget. You usually can't afford to give many big pay increases because that would just reduce the smaller increases to the point of absurdity. So in practice you tend to have most people receiving both "performance ratings" and "merit pay awards" that are not quite identical, but not all that different from each other, either. Thus the performance appraisal system doesn't really link pay to job performance at all, except in a few extreme cases.

Into the Minefield We Go

Performance appraisal systems are supposed to encourage candor and to let people "know where they stand." Those are worthwhile goals. But that does not make them reachable. In fact, both are extraordinarily difficult. The proof of that is that they are only rarely achieved.

The problem with candor is that we seldom know how much of it another person can take without becoming defensive. There is not much point in your telling someone the unvarnished truth if most of it will be rejected, or distorted in his or her mind into what you did not say. Nor is there anything to be gained by visiting so much unmitigated candor on a sensitive and marginal worker that we reduce him to a submarginal basket case.

Perhaps we err too readily on the side of caution. Perhaps most of us could handle, and even benefit from, a straight dose of someone else's opinion of us. But why take the risk of finding out how far the other fellow can be pushed, when there is so little to gain, and so much to lose?

Most managers, contemplating the gain-to-pain ratio in performance appraisal, conclude that it's a fool's bargain. That's why they abstain from it, or modify it as much as they can. The last thing in the world that they want to risk is making an adversary out of a subordinate.

As for "letting people know where they stand," very few people actually have a need to know, or for that matter, want to know, exactly where they stand in someone else's esteem. If your job is in jeopardy, you certainly need to know *that*, so you can do whatever you can either to save it or find another. But most people's jobs, most of the time, are not in danger. For them, to be told periodically that all is well is really quite sufficient.

But that won't do for the would-be motivators who design performance appraisal programs. They want you to fix what ain't broke, on the theory that everyone's performance can be improved. If you fall for that common oversimplification, you will have wandered into the minefield. The fact that the people who lured you there were well intentioned will not make your situation any less perilous.

The Art of Rating Results

There are really only three kinds of job performance. At any given time, we could fairly describe the work done by about 85 percent to 95 percent of the people in any given group as "good enough for that group's purposes." The fact that some or all of that work might conceivably have been done better has little practical importance, because the risk of making matters worse by seeking those improvements usually exceeds the likelihood of getting them.

Most managers have nothing to gain, and a lot to lose, by trying to make fine distinctions between work that is "barely good enough," "more than good enough," and something in between. If work is anywhere within the broad range of "good enough," then it's good enough, and the wise manager will usually let it go at that.

Occasionally, but not inevitably, someone's work will be atrocious. That's unacceptable, and the problem must either be fixed or eliminated. So you call the person in, sit him down, and tell him what's wrong, and what must be done to make it right, all in no uncertain terms. Unless you're dealing with large numbers of entry-level people, however, you're unlikely to face that problem very often.

Don't make the mistake of confusing a ranking with a rating. In any group, there's someone who brings up the rear in any measurement, including measurements of work output. But that doesn't make that person's work unsatisfactory, any more than the shortest person in a working group is necessarily too short for the job. Every championship basketball team has a shortest player, usually well over six feet tall, who wouldn't be on the team in the first place if he did not play superbly.

The same is true of workers who have the lowest production record in their department, or students with the lowest test scores in their class, or the low man on any other totem pole. If you're smart, you won't measure people against their peers. You'll measure them only against an absolute standard of acceptable work. If they all exceed it, you ought to take all of them, including the least of them, out for a drink or a dinner, and tell them that they're *all* wonderful.

Then there's the other extreme of job performance. Occasionally, but also not inevitably, someone's work excels. But you'd better watch your semantics here. Don't get carried away with superlatives. If someone is merely the best of an ordinary lot, no special recognition is called for. But if someone's work clearly exceeds normal expectations and reaches rare levels of excellence, that does call for special treatment. But by definition, you won't run into that situation very often, either, because "normal expectations" nearly always include some instances of work that is very good indeed.

So except for the rare exceptions, it is neither necessary nor desirable to go to elaborate lengths to "let people know where they stand." All you really have to do is mark your calendar to remind yourself that three or four times a year you're going to tell each of your subordinates who has nothing to worry about that they needn't worry. Telling them that in a few simple words (like "I want you to know that I really like your work," or "You're doing a nice job. Keep it up.") provides a graceful way to end one of those many routine conversations that you've got to hold anyway. To emphasize the point, some simple body language (looking them straight in the eye, and shaking their hand) would help.

That simple gesture will be at least three or four times as effective as most performance appraisals and will cost you a lot less in time and agony. It will also virtually eliminate the risks that conventional performance appraisals unintentionally, but almost unavoidably, create.

Defusing the Mines

Performance appraisal is a "noble experiment," like Prohibition. Each attempted to mandate a virtue. In the case of Prohibition, that virtue was abstinence. In the case of performance appraisal, the virtue is candor. The lesson we learned in our experiment with Prohibition was that human nature can be stubbornly, even ingeniously, unvirtuous. The captains of industry are still learning that lesson with performance appraisal.

You may be lucky. Perhaps you work for a company that has already learned to live within the limits of what performance appraisal can do, and does not attempt to make it do what it can't do. In that case, your company has already defused the mines, and you can lead your people safely through performance appraisal. If you're not so lucky, you may have to wait until you get up around the vice-presidential level, so you can do the defusing yourself.

Workable Performance Appraisal

In the next few paragraphs, I'll summarize the features of a workable performance appraisal program. You can rate your company's program against it and decide for yourself whether what you've got is practical and safe, or unrealistic and explosive.

The most important characteristic of a workable performance appraisal program is *simplicity*. It should not assume that managers can acquire the skills of a Park Avenue psychiatrist. It should not require managers to discuss delicate subjects with their subordinates, or to say things that could threaten the subordinates' self-esteem, or to attempt to change fixed characteristics in the subordinates' personalities.

It should be based on the belief that most employees are fine just as they are and need no tinkering or manipulating to make them better. The only people who need to be improved are those who could not be permitted to keep their jobs without a dramatic, clear-cut upgrading of their results. For everyone else, the purpose of performance appraisal is reassurance and recognition, not rehabilitation and repair. If someone isn't sick, don't try to cure him.

A workable performance appraisal system requires no subtle distinctions between different "degrees" of satisfactory work. Everyone who gets through the Pearly Gates is equally welcome in heaven, and everyone whose work exceeds the minimum standard is equally welcome in the company. So you only need three rating categories for job performance. One of them will be broad enough to encompass nearly everyone's work nearly all of the time. The adjective that you pin on that category can be plain (like "good enough") or fancy (like "usually meets commonly accepted standards of adequate performance"). All that really matters is that the category be understood to mean that everyone who is assigned to it is in good standing with the company.

A second, rarely used category will take care of those occasional instances of superb work that clearly deserve some kind of extra reward. A third category, also rare, will deal with those whose work is intolerably deficient, by giving them both a last chance to save themselves and a fair warning of impending dismissal. Anyone whose work is not clearly in the second or third category belongs in the first. It's that simple.

But what about merit pay? How do you reward people according to their job performance, when nearly everyone gets the same rating? The answer, of course, is that merit pay systems can't do that anyway, regardless of the number of categories you provide for rating performance. As we saw in chapter 10, that's because most merit increases are too small, in proportion to total pay, to have a motivational effect.

If you want to give rewards that are large enough to matter to the people who unquestionably deserve them, there's only one way to do that. You would have to give big bonuses, but only to those few who qualify for that second category. For the rest, modest and rather similar increases will do. Some of them will find that not to their liking. The best thing for them to do is to check the job market to see if they can make better arrangements elsewhere. If they can't, perhaps they will come to realize that the privilege of keeping a competitively paid job is also a reward, and should not be taken lightly.

Using a Bad System Safely

What if your company is still trying to use a performance appraisal system that you think is unworkable? In that case I have two words of advice for you. First, don't lead the palace revolution yourself. The other side in this conflict may be foolish, but it is probably stronger than your side. You'll just have to wait until enough people who share your ideas get into positions of power.

Second, you work with a bad system the same way you drive an old, dilapidated car across the desert. You do that *very* carefully, with ample allowances for its infirmities, and you use lots of ingenuity to keep it from falling apart. Don't regard performance appraisal as a routine nuisance that you can just dispense with as quickly as possible. On the contrary, it's an exceptionally tricky nuisance that has to be handled with great care to be sure it doesn't explode right in your face. You're going to have to invest more time in it than its benefits are worth, simply to avoid the damage it can do when it's handled carelessly.

The first thing you should do is to make sure that each employee understands what you're trying to accomplish with performance appraisal. It has two purposes. One is administrative, and the other is motivational. These purposes tend to conflict, so if you want to get a motivational effect you're going to have to deemphasize the administrative aspects.

Administratively, performance appraisal is a formal way to put one more year on the record books. It's also an annual report card that tells each individual what has been entered in his work record for the year. Motivationally, however, performance appraisal has altogether different purposes. One is to show appreciation for what someone did well last year. Another is to highlight those things that might be done better next year. But its most important motivational purpose is to give you an opportunity to sit down with your subordinates to discuss some highly charged motivational matters, such as promotion or training prospects, or the prospects for keeping one's job.

To make the process as motivational as possible, you make it as unadministrative as possible. Try to dedramatize it. You don't want your subordinates to walk into your office with a sense of impending doom. The best way to take the tension out of performance appraisal is to make sure that nothing you say to your subordinate will come as a surprise. To do that, you'll have to hold lots of informal "mini-appraisals" throughout the year, every time an opportune moment presents itself. That will make the formal appraisal interview a very ho-hum nonevent, which is exactly what you want it to be. The nice thing about nonevents is that they don't come back to bite you.

Try to make the interview more of a planning session for the coming year than a post mortem of last year. Regardless of whether last year was great, dismal, or so-so, it's over. The only aspects of last year that are worth dwelling on are those that have direct implications for this year. Otherwise, try to focus on ways in which your subordinates can measure their own performance. That's their key to winning a better performance appraisal for themselves next time.

Since you've got to sit down with your subordinate anyway, you might as well make a virtue out of necessity. Try to convert the appraisal interview from a courtroom scene in which verdicts are handed down to a classroom scene in which people learn how to manage their own work. That way you can make your own job easier, while simultaneously teaching your people to get more done with less wasted effort.

You can use the time set aside for the interview as an opportunity to do some coaching. For example, if you're managing salespeople, you can teach them to divide the number of dollars generated during each call by the length of the call. The result is an index of their productivity per minute. If that figure rises, they're using selling time, which is their most precious resource, more effectively. If the index drops, they're wasting it. If they watch that kind of index day by day, or even hour by hour, their results over longer periods are likely to show steady gains.

If the rules require you to tell people how they were rated, or to show them the forms you've had to fill out, do that toward the middle of the interview, and do it as briefly as possible. Most people remember the end of a discussion best, the beginning second best, and the middle part is remembered least of all. So consign the potentially harmful stuff to where it will do the least damage. Don't dwell on it.

What really matters is the next performance rating, because that's the one that you can still influence. The performance appraisal should give no more than a nod to the past, and instead take a long, searching look at the future.

How to Make the System Work for You

The trick to making a poorly thought-out performance appraisal system work to your advantage, when you are trying to motivate someone else, is to convert it quietly to a system that is motivationally effective. This means subtly avoiding what the bureaucrats in the personnel department want you to do, while making a discreet switch to some high-potency motivators.

The bureaucrats will eventually find you out. But they will probably think of you as just another thick-headed manager who doesn't understand their system. On the other hand, your boss, and the chain or command above your boss, will probably want to pin a medal on you. Not because you've evaded the performance appraisal system, which they may not even notice, but because your job performance is probably going to be brilliant.

Remember that second, rarely needed performance category? That's your target. You have to think hard about exactly what kinds of results would be literally *superb* for anyone doing your job. Not just good, not just better than most, but rare, unexpected, exceptional. You want to set a standard that no informed person could reasonably consider just ordinary. Still, you can't set it unreachably high, because you're going to reach for it yourself.

The trick is to set certain specific performance targets, and then convince your boss that anyone who could reach all of them, or even most of them, would clearly have given the company more than it could reasonably expect from someone in your position. You want to pin a precise definition on what is sometimes referred to as the "extra mile," or as "110 percent effort," or as results that are "above and beyond the call of duty."

Then we get to the heart of the matter. You're going to negotiate a deal with your boss. Your part of the bargain is to devote yourself entirely to putting those extraordinary results right on his desk by an agreed-upon date. You'll agree to give all you've got to that effort. Your boss's part of the bargain is to agree in advance that if you can do that, you will have earned the highest performance rating your company can bestow. Your boss agrees that there will be no quibbling, no second thoughts, and no ifs, ands, or buts. A deal is a deal, and both sides must agree to be bound by it.

It won't be easy, but it won't be impossible, either. Here's why. You can focus your efforts entirely on a limited number of narrowly defined goals. Everything else is either secondary or unimportant, and you won't allow yourself to be distracted by them. You're going to perform the mental equivalent of a karate chop: an intense concentration on what must be done to make certain sharply defined results happen.

This is where the inspirational type of writer or speaker will tell you that you can do literally anything if you "really" believe in yourself. If you still can't do it, well, obviously, you didn't "really" think you could. Their prescription is for you to do a selling job on yourself, banishing doubt and talking yourself into a fervent belief in your own omnipotence.

That actually works for some people. It doesn't for me, and I doubt if you would have read your way through the ten preceding chapters if it worked for you. Fortunately, you don't need to pump yourself full of imaginary confidence to accomplish some very ambitious goals. But you do need to be smart.

That means thinking long and hard about those goals before you sit down with your boss to negotiate your performance appraisal deal. You've got to know, in some detail, just how you're going to get to them before you commit yourself to making the effort. You've got to plan the practical steps that will be needed to get you there *before* the promised date. You'll need to build that much slack into the plan to allow for the unforeseeable.

Your boss will consider your plan superambitious, because not many people could do what you propose. Obviously, you want your boss to think that way, because the object of the entire exercise is to present him with an overwhelming case for giving you the highest performance appraisal (and the biggest bonus) your company has to give. But by the time you get to the negotiating table, you'll consider it feasible, because you will have thought through what you have to do every day, even every minute, in order to get that job done.

Let's turn the tables for a moment. What should you do, as a boss, when one of your subordinates marches up to you and asks for the kind of deal I recommended that you make with your boss? My answer is, bargain hard to make sure that what he's offering is both realistic for him and a good deal for the company, and then pin a medal on him for showing so much initiative.

On Setting Ambitious Goals

The people I've known who accomplished the most did not walk around trying to convince themselves that they were confident. They were careful planners who knew that what they were attempting wasn't really as ambitious as it looked, because they had thought it through and were following a step-by-step plan. Others considered them to be bold risk takers. They considered themselves pragmatists.

I remember interviewing an executive who had served, during the war, as a commando officer operating behind enemy lines. I asked him why he had volunteered for such a risky assignment. "Well, you see," he said, "it wasn't really as risky as you may think. There was a war on, and I figured that we were all going to get shot at anyway. Under those circumstances, I felt I would be safer with a bunch of chaps who really knew what they were doing, rather than with some blokes who were mainly trying to save their own skins." Since he lived to tell the tale, I have to conclude that he was not a swashbuckler, but a hardheaded realist.

And that's what you'll have to be if you want to make your company's performance appraisal system play into your hands.

PART
III

THE HARDEST
PEOPLE TO
MOTIVATE

CHAPTER
12

MOTIVATING
MINORITIES

Nowadays, to speak of a "minority group" is to use a dated phrase. The term originated in the not-so-distant days when white English-speaking males outnumbered everyone else in the labor force. In those days, to refer to someone as a "minority" was a polite if slightly ungrammatical way to say that he, or more likely she, was probably relegated to one of the low-paying jobs that most white males didn't want to do.

However, the old "minorities" have become, at least in a statistical sense, a majority of the labor force. So we no longer define minorities by merely counting them. What defines a minority today is not their headcount, but their lack of influence and affluence.

The main problem for minorities and majorities alike is that it's difficult for them to think straight about each other. Motivating minorities is not so much a matter of the tactics you use as of the *attitude* with which you use them. What you do and what you say in your dealings with minorities are not nearly as important as the subtle messages you convey about what you really think of them. You do that with facial expressions, tones of voice, choice of words, body language, and many other ways as well.

Rather than try to control all the ways in which your attitudes can express themselves, which is close to impossible, it's better to clean up your attitudes themselves. That way, what your tone of voice expresses will enhance your motivational efforts, rather than interfere with them. What all those subtle expressions of attitude have to convey, if you're going to do an effective job of motivating minorities, can be summed up in one word. That word is "respect."

To be "a minority" in an economy dominated by people unlike you is to have a severe case of the Rodney Dangerfield problem, except that it isn't funny. You can start with the assumption that most of those different-looking people out there will take one look at you and conclude that you can't possibly amount to much. And, I regret to say, your assumption won't be too wide of the mark, most of the time.

When two groups have very unequal power and prestige, the minority person's self-esteem is at risk in every contact with a majority person. The inequality of power causes relationships to begin with the minority person feeling threatened. Unless you can avoid making that minority person feel bad about himself, or her-self, you're going to have to contend with resentment and various forms of subtle and not-so-subtle retaliation. That's why, to moti-vate minorities effectively, you have to take a candid look at how you feel about them. Then you have to engage in what amounts to a mental housecleaning until you no longer harbor any attitudes that you could not proclaim proudly in public.

Three Motivation Killers

Three common assumptions affect the attitudes of white males and the various minority groups toward each other. Each of them can have very nasty effects. If you're a white male, and you want to motivate minorities effectively, you're going to have to learn to control all three of these assumptions. Better still, just get rid of them. If you're part of a minority group, you face the same need to control, or better yet, clean out your assumptions about white males, as well as about minorities other than your own.

The first assumption is that there are no real individuals in groups other than your own, and that everyone in such a group is just a cookie-cutter copy of everyone else. Call that *stereotyping*. The second assumption is that you can't expect much from anyone in that group, because they are all inferior. Call that *low expecta-*

tions. The third assumption is common within minority groups themselves. It's that their misfortunes are mainly the fault of bigots, rather than of their own shortcomings or even plain bad luck. Call that *defensiveness.*

Let's get one thing straight from the start. You'll find these demonstrably dumb ideas inside the heads of both minority group members *and* majority group members. It's true that the white male majority inflicts these assumptions on minorities, but it's equally true that minorities inflict them on white males, and on themselves. No one has a monopoly on foolishness, and no one is immune.

People on each side of the minority/majority divide expect the other side to be unfairly critical of them, to say disparaging things behind their backs, and to play dirty tricks on them if their own side lets its guard down for an instant. As a result, civilized discourse with or about minority groups is often difficult, and sometimes impossible. However, within a business organization there is at least this advantage: people have an incentive to cooperate, because the work must be done. So there is usually a kind of watchful, restless truce between the various groups, with occasional outbreaks of conflict. The challenge to the motivator is to convert the truce into active collaboration and teamwork.

But that isn't easy, to say the least. When you talk with someone of another race or sex, you may be suspected of deliberately concealing your disdain, perhaps because you know that overt racism and sexism are no longer fashionable among the educated. Or you may be suspected of hypocritically hiding the hatred in your heart, only because you fear that you could wind up in big legal trouble if you were to display your racism, or your sexism, too blatantly.

What is the sane thing to do amid all this rampant suspicion and prejudgment? About all you can do is to recognize that it exists, try to rise above it, and try to help others to do the same. Kipling had it right. What you have to do is "keep your head when all about you are losing theirs, and blaming it on you."

Now let's take a closer look at those three nasty assumptions. Each of them makes it close to impossible for you to deal with individuals one at a time, on their own merits or demerits. If you allow that to happen, your ability to do any serious motivating is going to shrink drastically. So if motivation is your goal, those assumptions are your enemies. You're going to have to learn how to shove them unceremoniously out of your mind, and keep them out.

Stereotypes

A *stereotype* is an assumption that all members of a given group share the same (usually unattractive) qualities. The usual stereotype goes something like this: "All (name the minority group) are (some uncomplimentary adjectives), and this one (who could even be *you*, dear reader) is obviously no better than the rest."

If anyone thinks of you in terms of a stereotype, you're going to find it awfully difficult to get him to credit you with any qualities that don't fit the stereotype. And if you've ever held a stereotype about someone else, your chances of getting that person to exert himself or herself on your behalf are close to nil, because you have given them an incentive to displease you.

If a stereotype is directed at you, it's someone else's blatant denial of what you probably regard as the central fact of your life, which is your own uniqueness. You go through life telling the world, "Here I am, a person in my own right with accomplishments and qualities of my own." But a stereotype inside someone else's head could be murmuring, "Oh, no you're not. You're not a real individual at all. You're just another (insert the uncomplimentary slang term for your group)." Of course, anyone who demeans you in that way is much more likely to antagonize you than motivate you.

So stereotypes are really wicked, harmful things. Nevertheless, they are a great convenience for the mentally lazy. Just latch on to a stereotype, and you don't have to do any more thinking. Not only that, but your stereotype will also tickle your ego. It will give you a pleasant, but phony, sense of superiority to millions of other people. That's a great comfort to those whose self-respect is a little shaky to start with. The fact that stereotypes are oversimplified, damaging, and even reprehensible is, alas, no match for the fact that they are convenient and comforting.

What can you do about stereotypes? Don't let yourself get away with them. And don't let anyone you can influence get away with them, either. The way to judge other people is the way you would want to be judged, which is by your deeds alone, and not by your demographics.

When I moved to Texas, I became mildly annoyed with some Eastern friends who continually expected me to wear cowboy boots and a cowboy hat whenever I visited them. Of course, they were stereotyping me, and Texans in general (most of whom do *not* wear cowboy regalia). In my case, my friends' reaction was harmless, but nevertheless it taught me a lesson: the best way to get out of the habit of stereotyping is to be on the receiving end of it yourself. I realized that my own complaint of "Damn it, I'm not a cowboy" must have been pretty mild next to the black man's complaint of "Damn it, I'm not a welfare client or a mugger," or the woman's complaint of "Damn it, I wasn't put on this earth to satisfy your sexual fantasies, or to bring you your coffee."

The best way to teach people how misleading and unfair most stereotypes are is to expose them to some popular stereotypes about *them* and ask them if that's how they think of themselves. How would *you*, for example, like to be thought of as: a hick, a snob, a street brawler, an ignoramus, or a clever cheat? These are all popular stereotypes for various groups, and I dare say you wouldn't like any of them. Neither do the people in those groups.

Low Expectations

Low expectations are a direct consequence of stereotypes. People in advantaged groups usually don't expect much of people in minority groups. We tell ethnic, racist, and sexist jokes as a way to reinforce our shared illusion that people who are different from us are, *because of those differences,* ludicrously incompetent. But an ethnic joke is a cheap shot. It's an attempt to make yourself look smart by making someone else look dumb. Ditto for racist and sexist jokes.

The worst effect of low expectations is that many people in minority groups swallow them. They don't expect much of themselves, and the result of low aspiration is low achievement. Very few people ever exceed their own, or anyone else's, expectations of them. While some people in minority groups outsmart their detractors, many others simply choose not to risk more frustration than they already have to endure. Their attitude is, "Why add disappointment, or even humiliation, to a life that is already hard enough? To hell with it. I give up." The effect of low expectations is to thoroughly undercut their motivation.

Perhaps you'd like to change all that. I'd like to help you do it. But don't underestimate what you're up against. Minority group members have already had to deal with other people who look a lot like you. So you can assume that they already assume the worst about you. They may expect you to have a low opinion of them, to feel that their only talent is for evading work, and that the only motivator that works with them is fear.

If there's any truth to any of those assumptions, your ability to bring out the best in them is going to be very, very limited. They'll get even with you by using the age-old weapons of the powerless: foot dragging, time wasting, and managing to "misunderstand" even simple instructions. Their revenge will consist of giving you no more than you expect, and possibly less. And if those assumptions about you are not true, you're going to have to *prove* that, convincingly, before you can hope to motivate those people effectively.

Defensiveness

Defensiveness is the tendency to see ourselves and people like us in an unfailingly flattering light, and to ignore or reject criticism. It's hard to get through life without *some* defenses to protect your self-esteem. But it's entirely too easy to let your defenses run wild, in which case they can blind you to your own faults.

Defensiveness is like a misshapen mirror. It distorts your perception. Thus, a white person, on meeting a black for the first time, may assume that the black might be a pretty good athlete, but can't be much of an intellectual. The black in the same situation may assume that the white may be well-dressed and well-mannered, but at heart is really a redneck who would rather wear a white sheet than a white shirt. In both cases, reality is distorted to make the other party look contemptible, and to make oneself look innocent or even marvelous.

Some minority group members blame almost any failure or criticism on discrimination. For example, relatively few of them occupy professional or managerial positions. They may cite those figures as "proof" of bias against them. But white males may cite the same statistics as proof that not many minority people are qualified for those jobs. Statistics, of course, don't "prove" anything. But the charges and countercharges are not really meant to provide scientific answers. They are intended to score debating points, and to sway decision makers.

Many white males are reluctant to expose themselves to accusations of being racist, or sexist. That's enough to dissuade some of them from openly criticizing the work of members of minority groups. Saying that in print may very well bring down both of those epithets, and some less printable ones as well, on me. So be it. You can't solve problems until you face them.

Given all the charges and countercharges that fly back and forth between the groups, what is the intelligent thing to do? First, stop generalizing, and deal with individuals one at a time, on the basis of their accomplishments and not their ancestry. Second, don't let the hotheads provoke you into joining the shouting match. Just smile at them. As Mark Twain said, in another context, that will impress your friends and confuse your enemies.

Clannish Thinking

If I remember my anthropology correctly, a clan is a collection of families that intermarry mostly with each other, while a tribe is a collection of clans that unite to fight with other tribes.

Here, however, I'm going to use a clan as a metaphor for thinking that is narrow, inward-looking, and parochial, because that's the perspective from which minorities and majorities tend to think about each other. And I'm going to use tribe as a metaphor for the melding together of narrow interests in order to pursue larger interests, because that's what you have to do to motivate members of minority groups who work in large organizations. In fact, that's what a manager has to do to motivate *any* group of people, whether they're minorities or not.

The biggest problem in motivating minorities, or in being part of one, is clannish thinking. The clannish thinker divides the world into everyone who is like him, and everyone who is not. His mind then gets stuck on those distinctions, rather like a ship that has run aground and just sits there, high and dry, unable to refloat itself so it can go anywhere else. However, the clannish thinker doesn't think of himself as being stranded. On the contrary, he thinks of himself as pretty smart. He thinks he's got the world all figured out, and not only that, but it didn't take much thought for him to do it.

Of course, it doesn't take much brainpower to recognize that people are different, especially in the superficial ways that jump right out at you the minute someone walks through the door. Any idiot can tell a man from a woman, a black from a white, a Hispanic from an Anglo, or a youngster from an oldster.

You can tell a clannish thinker by the fact that he is content with finding differences and does not go on to search for similarities. Yet it is the similarities that make motivation possible. You can't motivate minorities if your thinking is going to stay stuck at the clan level. The same principle would apply if you're part of a minority yourself. You can't work constructively with someone in the majority group if you persist in thinking about the world in clannish terms.

The choice is up to each of us, and it's a classical trade-off. Clannish thinking has its pluses and its minuses, as does tribal thinking. Clannish thinking is so easy that it's effortless. On the other hand, it doesn't buy you very much, because it leaves you isolated in a world that grows more interlocked and interdependent every day. And if you've got to get work done by people who are not like you, your clannish thinking simply gives them an incentive to frustrate you.

You *can* go beyond clannish thinking and try to bring people together into tribes. That would require you to search for common goals that cut across the distinctions that divide people from each other. The best way to find those common goals is to accept at face value what each group says it wants from life. Then look for ways to create alliances between them, so they can each help the others to gain what they want. That gives them an incentive to work together. In the process of doing that, each side is likely to learn that the other side is not, in reality, nearly as terrible as advertised.

But of course, there is also a cost to tribal thinking. It's not easy, and you have to work at it, constantly.

Tribal Thinking

The trick to turning adversaries into allies is to submerge their differences beneath a common cause that can inspire them all. To find that common cause, you have to look for compelling needs that are shared by all the groups you're trying to unite and can override their more parochial needs.

One way to do this is to give people a more attractive group to belong to than the one with which they originally identified themselves. In other words, a tribe instead of a clan. For example, becoming part of a group that is known for its excellent service, or for turning out a superior product, can override the need to be identified with one's race, sex, or ethnicity. That's why the employees of some companies wear caps or T-shirts emblazoned with the name or logo of their employer. They are telling you how they want you to think of them.

Now, here comes one of those statements that will have to be qualified almost as soon as it is made. Nevertheless, as generalizations go, this one stands up pretty well: most people have enough pride in themselves *as individuals* to want to be known as more than just another (whatever demographic group they belong to). They would rather be known as a (name their profession or occupation) who is good enough at his or her work to have won a place in an elite organization, and who also happens, but only incidentally, to be (one of that demographic group). The motivational trick for leaders is to awaken desires to be recognized for qualities that distinguish one, such as abilities and accomplishments, rather than for qualities that one shares with many others, such as race or sex.

Now for that qualification. The preceding paragraph refers chiefly to people with certain psychological features. Specifically, it applies to those who want to be the masters of their own fate and who regard life as something that can be managed, or at least steered. It would not apply nearly as well to people who regard life as one long game of chance, at which they are merely helpless spectators.

You can find lots of people who are convinced that life is manageable, but you will also find many others who feel that life manages them. I have seen no good figures on just how many people have settled into either of these outlooks. Neither have I seen any reliable data on whether certain minority groups have more or less than their share of people with either disposition. Perhaps some of them do, but until I see some good numbers I would prefer not to speculate. So whether the motivation formula I have just given actually applies to "most" people or merely to a lot of them remains to be seen.

If you are dealing with individuals who, *regardless of their demographics*, want to take charge of their own life, at least to the extent that circumstances permit them to do that, you can motivate them. What that kind of person needs is plenty of opportunity for achievement and recognition. But if you are dealing with people, also regardless of demographics, who simply await their fate and see no point in trying to influence it, your motivational task is much, much harder. You're going to have to rely primarily on being courteous and friendly and on reminding them that steady work and a good benefits package are a pretty good reward for doing their work well.

Tribal thinking requires you to look for overarching, unifying concepts and to find them in each group's views of itself. The most important thing to be said about this strategy is that it works; the second-most important thing is that it isn't easy. You have to work at tribe building to get it right. But there's a payoff. You'll be more than halfway to solving the problem of motivating people whom the good Lord chose to make a bit different than you. You'll also be making this dear old world of ours a little bit saner and safer, and that much more civilized.

Clannish thinking is easy because it's based on instinct. Tribal thinking, on the other hand, is an acquired skill. As my tennis instructor keeps telling me, a good player doesn't just swat at the ball, even though swatting is easy and natural and makes you feel good. There's only one way to make the ball go where you want it to go, and that is to hit it the right way. To do that, you've got to suppress your swatting instinct and concentrate on doing what will get you the result you want. Swatting, for all its momentary pleasures, simply puts the ball into the net or over into the next court. Clannish thinking is the intellectual equivalent of swatting a tennis ball.

The Major Minorities

To illustrate both clan and tribal thinking with respect to minorities, we'll take a brief look at four of the most important minorities in the labor force. The minorities we'll consider here are women, blacks, Hispanics, and the elderly.

All minorities are exposed to prejudice, which is a failure to think straight about people who are different than you are. However, some minorities are also subject to harassment, which is a failure to act decently toward people whom you think are in no position to defend themselves. There is probably more harassment of women than of any other group. That is not only because there are more of them, but also because a black or hispanic male, or even an older white male, may be too formidable an adversary to tempt the kind of person who takes pleasure in teasing or taunting. So, following the section on clan and tribal thinking by and about women, I will discuss some of the motivational aspects of sexual harassment.

Women

The clannish way to think about *women*, if you are a man, is that they are fascinating but impossible to understand. The tribe-building way to think about women is that some of them are content with traditional roles and others are not. Those who want to combine motherhood with careers have taken on a much tougher challenge than a man following the same career path. Simply by making that choice they demonstrate a level of personal motivation in excess of what most men need to succeed. The practical problem with such women is to keep that extraordinary level of motivation from being worn down by sheer fatigue, or by the frustration of very high, and therefore improbable, ambitions.

Men

The clannish way to think about men, if you're a woman, is that they are sexists who regard all women as brainless sex objects, or as a caste of menial servants. Also, that males have fragile egos that would shrivel without constant flattery. And that the worst of them are chauvinists or wimps, and the best of them are already married—although not so happily married that they are incapable of dalliance.

The tribe-building way to think about men is to accept that there are all kinds of them. Some have so little to be proud of as males that they can only survive by putting women down. That kind is probably hopeless as far as mature relationships are concerned. However, there are also men who are grown up, who deal with each woman they meet according to her conduct and not according to her looks, who satisfy their sexual needs off the job, and would not stoop to treating a female co-worker as a mere sex object. But mostly, men are just innocently ignorant of the similarities between themselves and women with regard to career aspirations and desire for accomplishment. That's a problem that can be fixed, but it has to be fixed the hard way, one man at a time.

Sexual Harassment

There is probably no hotter topic in employer-employee relations today than sexual harassment, which can be anything from conversation laden with sexual innuendo to an unmistakeable grab in an elevator.

But what's very clear is that if you subject any female employee to persistent, unwelcome attention of any kind, you have broken the law and you and your employer may have to answer in court. You might find yourself explaining to a judge that your colleague can't seem to take a joke, or that she misinterpreted your innocent attempts to be friendly, or that you didn't mean what you said the way she thought you did. But even if the judge gives you the benefit of the doubt, that will cost you time and money. It may even raise the question in your employer's mind of whether you're worth all that bother.

Legalities aside, there's also the question of productivity. The effect of unwanted advances on an employee's performance is going to be negative. She might lodge a complaint, which would certainly be costly in time, money, and publicity. More likely she will suffer in silence—but in that case, so will her work.

She may quit in order to escape her unwelcome pursuer, which will then cost the employer money in order to hire and train a successor.

But even if you think there's ambiguity involved in a particular situation, and even if the employee doesn't take the legal route, your role as a manager is clear. As with any difficult situation regarding "minorities," your wisest course of action is to look to your own attitudes—the hard way, which is one at a time, based on experience rather than preconceptions. If you think it's sophisticated to make remarks suggesting that a woman be judged more by her sexuality than her professional performance, dump that misconception immediately. It will only convey your lack of respect toward women to everyone who reports to you. And it will distract you from your goal: putting together a winning group.

You'll also want to make sure that your company keeps its sexual harassment policy posted prominently, and that it's *always* followed, no matter who's involved. To help everyone remain sensitive to the issue of sexual harassment, put the topic on your agenda for frequent discussion, especially in those face-to-face dialogues you'll be holding with each of your subordinates and peers.

How can you discuss such a delicate subject with the people with whom you work every day? Some managers consider sexual harassment just too hot a topic to handle, and would rather deal with it indirectly, if they have to deal with it at all. But since the object is to make a point to people who have something else on their minds, a subtle approach is probably not going to do the trick. The best approach is a straightforward one. I know one manager who puts it this way: "What you do off the job is your business. What you do on the job is *my* business. The company is not paying you to be entertained at work, and it certainly is not paying you to interfere with anyone else's work. The rule is very simple: you don't play where you work. I hope that's clear to everyone."

What about genuine "office romances"? Nothing will stop them—chemistry is chemistry. But the rules are straightforward: interest must be reciprocal and unequivocal. If you're unsure what kind of response you're getting to your expression of interest, *stop right there*. If you don't, the woman, your manager, and even that judge would have every right to interpret your next advance as your first harassment.

What about the vindictive woman who would ruin a man's reputation with false or exaggerated accusations, in revenge for some private quarrel? The best evidence we have so far is that while that *can* happen, it does not happen very often. AT&T, which has one of the strongest anti-harassment policies in corporate America, reports that nineteen out of twenty complaints from female employees turn out to be justified. That doesn't mean that vicious accusations can be discounted. It means that the more forcefully you prohibit harassment, the more valid will be the complaints that your policy flushes out. More women will be willing to risk blowing the whistle on tormenting fellow employees.

The responsibility for stamping out sexual harassment doesn't rest solely with management. Women can at least warn each other of on-the-job harassers. Better still, they can complain to the harassers' superiors. Some women protest that this is very difficult to do. But they must either do what they find difficult in order to end the problem or resign themselves to being harassed.

The most effective thing that everyone, male or female, can do about the dirty little secret of sexual harassment is to get it out into the open. Bothering female employees who are not interested in becoming playmates is not a fringe benefit for male employees— and that includes male managers of female employees. On the contrary, it is a distracting, disruptive, and thoroughly despicable thing to do. If enough people in an organization made that point often enough, at least some of the would-be harassers would get the message.

Blacks

Now back to our discussion of clannish and tribal thinking about minorities. The clannish way to think about *blacks*, if you're white, is that they are all lazy, ignorant, undisciplined, and dangerous. The tribe-creating way to think about blacks is that some of them are middle-class and some of them are world-class. However, too many of them go through life with lower-class disadvantages that most whites are mercifully spared. What matters is not which label you can pin on blacks in general (there isn't any), but what this black man or woman standing right in front of you is like, has done, and can do.

Whites

The clannish way to think about whites, if you're black, is that some are redneck racists and the rest are closet racists, and that any criticisms whites have of individual blacks are either trumped up or grossly unfair. The tribe-creating way to think about whites is to recognize that most know very little about blacks at first hand, because they shun the ghettos. They do that for the same reason that blacks move away from ghettos if they can: because they are dangerous.

So, if you are black, your problem in dealing with whites is not so much that they are vicious and narrow-minded (although some are), as that they are ignorant, *by choice*, of people like you. That problem is bad enough, but it's not nearly as bad as it would be if whites rejected blacks solely, or even primarily, because they *are* black. It would be more accurate to say that whites don't want to get involved in the problems that they expect blacks to have, and that they don't distinguish between those who have them and those who don't. That doesn't mean that whites can't learn. But the learning that counts with respect to race relations comes from experience, and not from sermons or from books, including this one. Whites and blacks will remain ignorant of each other as long as they remain isolated from each other. Meantime, ignorance and prejudice are chipped away each time individual whites and blacks discover that the other person is not so bad after all.

The easiest place to do that is on the job, since the workplace is usually, for better or worse, the most integrated place in America. It is the one place where whites and blacks find themselves in close physical proximity for eight hours every day. Most of whatever breaking down of stereotypes is going to happen between blacks and whites will happen on the job.

Hispanics

The clannish way to think about *Hispanics*, if you're not one of them, is that they resist integration into the cultural mainstream of America. Also, that they refuse to learn to speak English, or deliberately speak Spanish to conceal their true thoughts from nearby Anglos. And that they have a peon mentality that leaves them open to exploitation, and (in the case of Mexicans) are mostly wetbacks anyway.

The tribe-building way to think about Hispanics is that many of them are already as integrated as any other immigrant group after the same number of generations, and that more than a few have been spectacularly successful. The idea that they are determined to be perpetual aliens is at best an exaggeration and at worst just plain untrue. Within the memory of those who are old enough, there were similar perceptions of groups that have long since joined the great American middle class, such as Greeks and Jews and non-Europeans like the Chinese and Japanese.

Anglos

The clannish way for Hispanics to think about Anglos (their term for any white who is not hispanic) is that they are loud and pushy and think they are superior when actually they are just uncouth. Also, despite their ignorance, they have a monopoly on power. Therefore the best way to treat them is humor them when you can't avoid them, but otherwise to stay away from them as much as possible.

The tribe-building way to think about Anglos is that most of them have lived their entire lives awash in the American consumer culture and are only dimly aware of other ways of life. For the most part they are not arrogant, but merely naive. Their minds are not closed, but the only practical way to get access to most of those minds is via the English language.

"Survivors"

At this point I must ask you to forgive me, because I'm going to yield to temptation and invent some jargon of my own. I need a term to describe people who are in their mid-fifties or older and are either retired or will soon be eligible for retirement. However, I'm going to balk at the common term "senior citizens," or "the elderly," because to me those have connotations of rocking chairs, social security checks, and rapidly approaching senility. I prefer to think of this stage of life as extended middle age, but to use a more concise term I'm going to refer to these people as "survivors." That's because there's only one way to get to that stage of life, and that is to successfully dodge fifty-something (or more) years' worth of slings and arrows.

The clannish way to think about survivors is as friendly but ineffectual old codgers who have lots of time on their hands and are therefore perfectly willing to waste yours. They are full of obsolete, irrelevant reminiscences that they think of as valuable experience. In their innocence, they simply don't realize that today's world is much more competitive, complex, and faster-paced than anything they ever had to cope with, back in the Dark Ages when they were young.

The tribe-building way to think about survivors is that some of them are escapees from careers that they hated, and some of them are on a perpetual vacation, but that many of them are just plain bored. They find that work gave them a purpose in life that recreation and travel do not replace. Some of them want to work to supplement pensions that have been eroded by inflation, and some of them have no pensions to supplement. But most of them want to work because they can only tolerate so much recreation, and simply need something meaningful and constructive to do.

The need to be active turns out to be a powerful motivator. Survivors usually make good employees. They work because they want to, which is the best of all possible motives. However, although they supply their own motivation, survivors should not be taken for granted. They need to be treated with respect, to be given responsibility that is worthy of their experience, and, above all, they need to be recognized. You have to *tell* them, in person, both publicly and privately, how much their work is appreciated. Too much recognition is better than too little. If you can provide those things, they will supply the effort and dedication themselves.

Younger Supervisors

The clannish way to think about younger supervisors, if you're a survivor, is that they don't know how little they know and are busily and naively congratulating themselves for reinventing the wheel. They blithely assume that anyone in their parents' generation is over the hill and that anyone old enough to be their grandparent should have the good sense to stay well clear of places where serious work is done.

The tribal way to think about younger supervisors is that they are mostly well intentioned and are at least as teachable as you were at their age, if not more so. That's because they've had more experience with older people than you did, because there are more older people now, and more of them want to work. Most younger managers are willing to let people of your age prove that you can still earn your keep. But you should not expect to be kept on a payroll merely because you want to keep busy. That is only realistic if you can do a job at least as well as it needs to be done. The only survivors who do not have to compete with younger workers are those who work as volunteers in nonprofit organizations.

Attitudes and Motivation

You can't communicate, and therefore you can't motivate, without revealing at least something of your underlying attitudes. They are too much a part of you, and therefore of anything you have to say, to be concealed.

If you are responsible for motivating minorities, your attitudes toward them are going to show. You can count on that. So your wisest course of action is to clean up your attitudes. You can no longer afford to deal with minorities in any way but one at a time, and based on results rather than preconceptions.

Suppose you do all of that. Suppose you make up your mind to clean up your habitual thinking about minorities and then discipline yourself to teach, encourage, and reward each of them. Are there no special tactics to be used, no tricks that work particularly well with minorities, no phrases that will disarm them and make them want to please you?

No, there aren't. There are some phrases to be avoided, because they imply condescension. But the best way to sensitize yourself to those phrases is to get rid of any condescending attitudes.

Other than their sensitivity to put-downs and prejudice, minorities respond to the same motivators, and in about the same way, as everyone else. But positive motivators won't work when they are applied with a negative attitude. That's why the real key to motivating minorities is to examine your own attitudes and dump the ones that interfere with your purposes.

Minorities as Motivators

It should go without saying that the same considerations apply to minorities who would deal with white males constructively, whether as peers, subordinates, or superiors. But to be on the safe side, I've just said it. Contrary to the stereotypes about white males, most of them are sensitive to the attitudes of the people with whom they deal and would rather earn their own reputations than be lumped together with the worst of their kind. So if you're in a minority group, and are in the habit of mentally lumping all white males together, you'd be well advised to clean up *your* attitudes too.

If you're both a member of a minority group and a supervisor, you face some unique problems. The first will arise with your fellow (name your own minority group). You may find yourself facing subtle, or not-so-subtle, pressure for leniency or favoritism. They'll ask you to put your race or your sex or your ethnicity ahead of your professionalism. They'll appeal to your "group loyalty."

But it's a phony appeal. Any supervisor who permits people from *any* group to contribute less than they could to the enterprise that feeds them all is profoundly *disloyal* to that group, because that only feeds the popular prejudices against that group. You express a much higher form of loyalty to your group by making it prove that it's as competent, trustworthy, and respectable as any other group.

If you, as a minority supervisor, find yourself supervising white males, you'll have to deal with the competence issue. You can assume that until you prove otherwise, they'll assume that you got your job solely because management needs a few token people like you to show that it isn't biased. The best way to counteract that is to be strictly professional in all of your dealings. In fact, you'll have to be super-professional, conspicuously preoccupied with getting the job done right.

Many minority supervisors before you have used this tactic. It's a taxing, unrelenting way to do a job, and it has given rise to the common belief that a minority person has to be much more effective than a white male to earn any respect in a managerial role. There is probably some truth to that. It was just your luck to be born into the generation that was given more of a chance to prove itself than its predecessors ever had. No one blazed a trail for you to follow. Yet there you are, on your own, blazing trails for the next generation of people like you to follow. That's a heavy responsibility, because a lot more is at stake than just your own success. It would be better for everyone, especially yourself, if you regarded that responsibility as a privilege rather than a burden. For better or worse, *you* are making history. Good luck.

CHAPTER
13

PROBLEM PEOPLE

Back in chapter 1, we cited the "classic question" that you'll be asked if you should dare to present yourself as an "expert" on motivation. Someone will ask you, "How do you motivate somebody who . . . ," and will go on to describe someone he obviously considers unmotivatable. Well, in this chapter we'll ask that classic question with a vengeance. There are certain groups of people whose own motives drive them away from being productive and useful. How do you motivate them?

These groups produce more managerial headaches per person than just about all other groups combined. Back in the days when firing someone was a simple matter, that was the treatment of choice for most of them. Today the question is not how to get rid of them, but how to make them useful. The answer to that question, in all of these cases, is that it isn't easy, but it can be done—*sometimes.*

Here's our rogue's gallery. First, we're going to look at alcoholics and addicts—the substance abusers. Next, people who are emotionally disturbed. After them, we'll look at the people who stay away from work—the absentees. Finally, we'll look at defectors—the people who decide to leave your company altogether and go to work somewhere else.

You may wonder why we're suddenly descending down to the

dark, dank underside of organizational life. Why the short course in abnormal psychology? There are two answers. First, don't kid yourself. Every one of these problems is so common that you can ignore them only by shutting your eyes. But you'd better not do that. An effective motivator's eyes are wide open, all the time.

Second, let's focus on that word *abnormal*. (Here comes another of our unavoidable detours into semantics.) The word is ambiguous. It can mean "rare, unusual, or uncommon." It can also mean "unhealthy or sick." The problem is that it's not rare to be a little bit sick in the head. To put that a bit more academically, people who are *functionally* abnormal may very well be *statistically* normal. (A psychiatrist friend of mine once defined the psychologically "normal" person as "someone who hasn't been caught yet.") In any case, there are lots of people out there with severe motivational problems, and you are responsible for motivating all of them.

There are three reasons why these problems are likely to be more widespread, and a lot closer to home, than you may think. First, people who have these problems are often very clever at concealing them, especially the alcoholics and addicts. Second, no single manager gets to see a lot of them, because they are seldom concentrated in any one part of the organization. That's why the full dimensions of a problem may not be clear until you look at the overall figures.

Third, and probably most important, these are not pleasant things to think about. Life is much more enjoyable when we just pretend that the seamy things are not really there. Most of us prefer not to confront the unpleasant, unless and until we must. But for a manager, who is paid to solve problems or better still to prevent them, ignoring the nasty side of the job is irresponsible. Don't let yourself get away with that.

Alcoholics and Addicts

We're going to deal with two issues here. First, why do you have to get involved? Second, how can you handle the problem?

When we speak of alcoholics, we usually conjure up images of Skid Row derelicts who have hit bottom. Since most of us never actually have to deal with such people, we comfort ourselves with the thought that "we don't have that kind of problem here." Actually, an alcoholic is anyone whose drinking interferes with his functioning, and who can't stop. By that definition, alcoholics make up at least 2 percent of the population. Some estimates run as high as 10 percent. Figures on drug abusers are harder to pin down, but the best available guess is that they probably run a close second to the alcoholics. So unless you work in a tiny organization of abstemious people, I have an uncomfortable reply to your comforting thought: "Sorry, but you probably *do* have that kind of problem here."

Back in the days when I did a lot of speaking before large audiences, I would occasionally offer an off-the-cuff estimate that there were probably two or three recovered alcoholics in the audience. I based my guess solely on the number of people in the room. Sure enough, after I completed my talk, two or three people would usually come up to me quietly, and each of them would say, "I'm the guy you were talking about." Those were the *recovered* alcoholics. What about those who were still in the grip of their compulsion to drink? They probably outnumber, by a considerable margin, those who have gotten a grip on theirs.

So one reason why managers have to be concerned about alcoholism and drug abuse is that there's so much of it around. If you don't have to deal with it directly yourself, you're probably not very far removed from someone who does. What's more, these problems are not going to go away. Even if you don't have to deal with them today, sooner or later you probably will.

You have probably encountered the idea that a little booze or a little cocaine does no harm, and that people who choose these forms of recreation should be left to enjoy them in peace. That can be a very seductive argument to someone whose real preference is not to "get involved" in the first place. Still, it's a slippery argument that deserves a closer look.

First of all, alcoholics drink and addicts take drugs precisely in order to impair the functioning of their brains, because that's what causes the subjective feeling of being "high." And if someone's brain is impaired, he can't do his work as well as when his brain is clear. One of the legends among addicts is that they actually work better when they are under the influence, but the evidence indicates otherwise. So a drunken alcoholic or a stoned drug addict may be physically present in the workplace, but is at least partially absent mentally. That frequently means that other employees have to take up the slack in the workload that alcoholics and addicts can't handle themselves.

There's also the question of exactly how much drinking, or drug taking, is "a little." As far as the employer is concerned, any amount that impairs someone's ability to do what he is paid to do is more than "a little." That's why we don't measure "a little" in grams or ounces. We measure it in terms of work performance.

If you're holding your subordinates to high performance standards and you're as acutely aware of what they're doing as you ought to be, and one of them has had a drink or a snort but you did not detect any effect, then that was "a little." But if you feel that someone's work has slipped below the level you consider acceptable, then whatever amount of whatever that person took wasn't just "a little." It did do harm. And if you leave that person in peace, his work will only deteriorate further.

The physical aspect of alcoholism and drug abuse is fairly straightforward. Somebody gets something into his bloodstream that makes him feel good, but which can harm his work performance if the concentration exceeds a certain level. If he is not prevented from continuing, he continues. Eventually, assuming no interruption of the process, he will probably deteriorate and die a nasty, premature death.

The Games Addicts Play

It's the psychological aspect that makes these problems so much more complicated. *Two* sets of motives are involved. First, we have to deal with the games that alcoholics and drug abusers play in order to preserve their habits. Then we also have to deal with the games that *we*—yes, you and I—play to avoid having to come to grips with the alcoholic's game, and with the drug abuser's game.

In both cases the games are based on pretense. One can pretend that the problem doesn't exist, or that it isn't bad enough to worry about, or that there's more to be lost than gained by trying to change it, or that it's somebody else's responsibility. The list goes on and on. The important point to remember is that if you're not part of the solution, you're probably part of the problem.

The two most common games played by people with alcohol and drug problems are *concealment* and *disarming*. The motive in both cases is to protect and preserve the habit.

Concealment is often very clever. You seldom catch an alcoholic or a drug addict in the act. That in itself is enough to deter many managers from intervening. Their excuse is that if they can't prove it, they shouldn't get involved, a rationalization that plays into the hands of the alcoholic and the addict. The purpose of their concealment ploy is to be left alone to continue their habit, and the ploy usually works. Unfortunately, it's usually the prelude to a tragedy.

The technique of *disarming* is more subtle. The alcoholic ingratiates himself, appeals to sympathy, goes out of his way to be likable. He makes you feel guilty for even thinking of taking a tough stand with such a nice guy. The purpose of disarming is to get you to look the other way—and it usually works, too.

The Games Managers Play

The two most common games played by the managers of alcoholics and addicts—in this case, you and I—are choosing not to notice, and the "disqualification" gambit.

A busy manager has lots of things to worry about and is constantly prioritizing. You have to be sure that what must be done is done. That provides you with a handy excuse for postponing anything that could turn out to be time-consuming or frustrating. It's easier just to *choose not to notice* the problem while you busy yourself with other, presumably more important, things. However, if you're dealing with an alcoholic or an addict, the problem will eventually explode in your face. While you still have a choice, it's better that you choose to notice.

To determine whether someone really can't abstain from alcohol or from drugs, even if he wanted to, calls for expert judgment. That makes it easy to say that "I'm not a doctor, so I'm not qualified to make that judgment. That's why I'm just going to stay out of this." That's the *disqualification* gambit, and it's true enough. But it also misses the point.

The judgment you are asked to make as a manager is not whether someone is an alcoholic or an addict, but whether his job performance is still as good as ever, or has declined. If you deserve your job, you should be the most qualified expert in the world to make that judgment. And if it's your judgment that his work has suffered, you have a right to demand that the individual submit himself to experts for *their* diagnosis.

Actually, you have more than a right. You have a moral obligation. Here's why. The first signs of deterioration are likely to show up in work performance before they affect the other aspects of an alcoholic's or addict's life. The quality of someone's work can be a very sensitive indicator of how well his brain is functioning. So the supervisor gets an early warning signal of impending disaster, well before most other people would suspect that everything is about to go drastically wrong.

If no one intervenes, an alcoholic will proceed to destroy himself. Unless something else kills him first, alcohol will. By the time the problem is unmistakable and disabling, it is also likely to be incurable. Until then, while it is still concealed and denied, it can still be cured. That is why time is of the essence, and why it is irresponsible for supervisors to look the other way when one of their subordinates drinks too much.

What's more, supervisors have enormous motivational power over employees who are alcoholics or addicts—*if* they choose to wield it. That's because they control access to the paycheck, which in turn provides the access to alcohol or drugs. That's why *no one* is in a better position to save the alcoholic or the addict than the supervisor, and that includes wives, husbands, lovers, relatives, everyone. If the supervisor doesn't step in, the next person who has a chance to help may very well be too late.

Your purpose with the alcoholic and the addict is to get them to stop, because that's the only way to preserve their employability. The way to do that is straightforward. You insist that they seek treatment, either from an Employee Assistance Program, if your company has one, or from a nearby medical facility. You demand that as an absolute condition of continued employment. Tell them that if they won't cooperate, they'll be fired, and that there will be no ifs, ands, or buts. You motivate alcoholics and addicts with a direct, completely sincere threat to their livelihoods. That's strong medicine. But nothing weaker is known to work.

You have to "get involved" with the alcoholic and the addict, painful as that may be. The alternative is to watch passively as a useful employee gradually deteriorates, right before your eyes, into a useless one. Alcoholics and addicts can be saved, but only if the rescue effort begins soon enough. Beyond a certain point, the craving gets such a grip on their bodies that no one knows how to save them. Therefore, the sooner you get involved, the better. Delay only increases the risk.

The Emotionally Disturbed

A lot of alcoholics and drug abusers are emotionally disturbed, and vice versa, but for simplicity's sake we'll concentrate here on people who are very upset but do not resort to alcohol or drugs. Our definition of *very upset* is "enough to interfere with their work performance."

By that definition, just about everyone is emotionally disturbed at some time in their lives. Nearly all of us go through occasional unhappy periods that last a few weeks or so and nearly always clear up by themselves. It's usually just a temporary reaction to a painful event, like a death or the end of a relationship. Eventually we shake it off. No particular managerial response is required.

But there are other emotional problems that can continue for months or even years and can seriously affect the quality of someone's work. These definitely call for managerial action, both because they can be fixed and because it costs too much to leave them unfixed. The most common emotional disorders that managers are likely to encounter are psychosomatic illnesses and depression.

Psychosomatic Illness

We humans have a remarkable way of dealing with fears that might otherwise overwhelm us. We simply shove them out of our minds. That's what "displacement" means. It's a handy little device that enables us to go about our business, blissfully free of fear. Unfortunately, it's really an instrument of self-deception. It only appears to eliminate our fears. What it really does is to hide them, and anything that is hidden must be hidden *somewhere.*

It turns out that the two easiest places to hide our fears are in our heads and in our stomachs. Fears can cause blood vessels to dilate, gastric juices to be secreted, muscles to tense up, not to mention turning on the endocrine glands, and other bodily reactions. All that dilating and secreting turns into headaches and bellyaches.

So our "handy little device" merely trades off one form of paralysis for another. It spares us from being scared out of our wits, but instead makes us so sick that we can hardly do our work. The emotion is displaced from the mind to the body. That's why psychiatrists had to invent a two-dollar word to describe it. They call these illnesses "psychosomatic." The word combines *psyche*, meaning "mind," with *soma*, meaning "body."

Interestingly, we seldom see the connection ourselves. We head for the medicine cabinet, or for our doctors' offices, convinced that there is something wrong with our bodies and unaware that fear or anger had anything to do with it. But most general practitioners estimate that at least half, if not more, of the complaints they treat are really psychosomatic. GPs have to look at a lot of patients to find the ones who are really sick. (As an old joke put it, "That headache isn't in your head; it's in your mind.")

Managers have to get involved with psychosomatic conditions because an employee who has one is just as disabled as an employee with a broken leg. But there is this difference: the broken leg will heal itself in its own good time. The psychosomatic condition won't. It can only get better if a skilled professional helps the individual to confront the displaced feelings that caused the condition in the first place. Your job as a manager is to bring the employee and the skilled professional together.

This is where Employee Assistance Programs can be helpful. During the 1980s, many companies found that it was more cost-effective to provide employees with treatment for psychological complaints than to pay for the consequences of leaving them untreated. Those consequences consisted chiefly of poor performance, absenteeism, and turnover. In a typical company, between 5 and 10 percent of the employees will use this service in a given year. But the return on the investment (mostly in reduced medical and prescription costs) is usually about 500 percent. That's enough to catch the eye of any chief financial officer.

An Employee Assistance Program is basically a free, confidential counseling service, often on company time. An employee whose work is affected by a chronic physical complaint should be encouraged to talk to the counselors to see if they can help. Resistance is much less likely than in the case of the alcoholic or the addict. Gentle but persistent pressure will usually do the trick. Avoid getting tied up in debates as to whether the symptoms are "real" or "imaginary." They are real enough, but to get rid of them the individual has to face another reality: his fears.

Depression

Depression is about as common as the common cold. Sooner or later nearly everyone runs into it. People who are depressed have little energy and respond slowly to what other people may say or do. They are lethargic and moody. Inwardly, they feel miserable, and outwardly, they barely manage to drag themselves through their daily routines.

Most depressions are temporary and clear up by themselves. They are simply reactions to the inevitable disappointments of life. However, some depressions continue indefinitely, and managers have to be concerned with these, because they are a permanent drag on productivity.

People in long-term depression are usually stuck in circumstances they can neither tolerate nor escape, like an unhappy marriage or an unfulfilling job. They tend to blame themselves for their predicaments, which they regard as permanent and unchangeable. They work slowly, listlessly, and without interest or enthusiasm. Pressure is more likely to shatter them than to improve their work pace.

Without treatment, depression just drags on and on. With treatment, it is fairly easy to fix. Once they stop blaming themselves for everything, depressed people can also start to deal constructively with the predicaments that caused their depressions in the first place. So once again, the task of the manager is to motivate the individual to seek treatment.

A depressed person has already given up, so the manager must display a persistent, believable optimism. But there really is a good reason for that, because if a depressed person can be persuaded to talk to the right people, the chances of shaking off the depression are pretty good. Gentle but relentless encouragement is the key.

Absentees

Absenteeism is the oldest management problem in the history of civilization, and it will undoubtedly outlive us all. People have been staying home from work since work began. Some of them are too sick to work, but most of them are not sick at all, and would simply rather do something else. There are obviously no miracle cures for the problem, because if there were, someone would already have claimed the fortune that awaits whoever can make absenteeism go away.

Of all the problem people that we're considering here, absentees probably draw the biggest yawn. Management puts less imagination into dealing with them than with any of the others. Absenteeism is regarded as an intractable nuisance, something you just have to live with, like flies in the summer or frozen pipes in the winter. That's a pity, because absenteeism is a lot worse than just a nuisance. It's actually a severe drain on productivity. The real cost of absenteeism is much more than wages paid for work not done, or people hired solely to be available as substitutes for absent workers. The biggest cost is the effect on quality, because of the interruption of steady work habits. What's more, there are effective ways to minimize absenteeism, and the payoff from doing that is substantial.

None of the commonly used methods for controlling absenteeism work very well, mostly because they are based on unrealistic premises. One is called "progressive discipline." It's a negative approach, based on the idea that if you punish absentees sufficiently, they'll come to work to avoid further punishment. The other common method is "attendance bonuses." This is a positive approach, based on the notion that if people are given enough extra rewards for coming to work, they will come to work more often. One is negative and the other is positive, but both are naive.

If you were using progressive discipline, you'd turn up the heat a little bit more each time someone stayed away from work. You'd start with a mild word or two, then progress to a slap on the wrist, then to some serious words, eventually to suspension without pay, and if all else failed, you'd lower the boom and fire the unfortunate fellow. Your company is now rid of one of its most flagrant absentees. So how can we say that the method doesn't work very well?

There are two reasons. First, all of your warnings and slaps and suspensions failed to deter the fellow you fired. In his case, the system merely acknowledged, after a lot of time and money had been spent, that it couldn't deal with his problem. On any given day, his desire to go fishing or hunting or shopping or visiting or to stay home and watch television was greater than his desire to avoid whatever punishment you could mete out, and that included the loss of his job.

But here's the rub. Even with the worst offenders removed from the payroll, your company's overall absence rate won't go down very much, because most absences are caused by otherwise fine employees who simply play the system for all it's worth. They regard allowable "sick days" as unscheduled vacations, to be taken when it suits their convenience. Their absence rates never approach the levels that would start you using the progressive discipline system. So the system misses the people who cause the bulk of the problem.

What about rewarding people who come to work regularly? Does that cut down on absenteeism? Probably not, at least after people grow accustomed to it. The system provides a bonus to people who would probably have come to work regularly without the bonus, and denies a bonus to those who would rather take some days off than pocket some extra cash. Unless very large cash awards are involved, most people value their free time, and their freedom to choose when to work and when not to work, much more highly than they value a few extra dollars.

One Absentee at a Time

You can't control absenteeism with policies that apply to everyone, because the problem has many different causes. Instead, you have to deal with individuals. That means that each supervisor has to be motivated to get absenteeism under control in his own department. If supervisors are not, the problem will just persist. No one else can really do much about it.

Most people with above-average absence records will fall into one of three groups, and each calls for a different treatment. Probably the largest group are the habitual absentees, next, conformist absentees, and third, escapist absentees.

Habitual Absentees

Habitual absentees are people who are easily overwhelmed. Life's little difficulties are just too much for them. They learned long ago that the easiest way to deal with stress is to go back to bed. They are not faking. They feel genuinely, but vaguely, unwell. They'll probably feel better tomorrow, when they'll dutifully come back to work. Meantime, they'll rack up some of the worst absence records in the company, second only to those hopeless characters who overstep the line and get fired. You wouldn't want to fire the habitual absentee anyway, because when they do come to work they are usually reliable and diligent.

You *can* motivate a habitual absentee to come to work more often, and the method is disarmingly simple. It's also a bit tedious, because it has to be used every day, forever, without fail. So the real motivation problem is not with the absentee but with you. You have to make the method part of your own daily routine.

What you have to do, preferably early in the day and then again near the end, is to *compliment* the habitual absentee for coming to work. Tell him how much you appreciate his presence, and how important he is to his fellow workers. If he comes in on a day when the weather is bad, congratulate him for his loyalty. Don't be afraid of overdoing it. Lay it on good and thick. And do it every day, forever. You might say something like, "I'm sure glad to see you here today. We really need you every day. You're a great worker, when you're here!" Next day, use a variant on the same theme, and the day after that, yet another variant. Don't be afraid of being repetitious. That's better than letting him feel neglected.

If he should miss a day, tell him how badly he was missed, and spell out the hardships that you and his colleagues had to endure without him. You might say something like, "We really got into trouble yesterday, because you weren't here. Some of your buddies had to do your work as well as their own. They were really tired out at the end of the day." In other words, send him on a guilt trip. Don't feel guilty about doing that. He deserves one.

The important point is to give him lots of attention. The last thing you want to do with a habitual absentee is to ignore him. That will only convince him that he doesn't matter, and that neither his presence nor his absence is noticed. In that case, why should he struggle in to work when he's not really feeling up to it?

The prescription, you may have noticed, is not very different from what you would use with a child. You gently encourage or mildly admonish, but you never ignore. There's a reason for that. The habitual absentee has never grown up, and by this stage of his life he probably never will. Someone else has to remind him that he really can do what is asked of him, and of the harm he causes when he doesn't do that.

The method works as long as you use it, and it stops working when you stop using it. Properly handled, a habitual absentee's absence record will get down to around the departmental average and stay there, *as long as you continue the treatment*. That's an excellent payoff for you, since you'll be investing minutes of your own time and buying back days of his. The return on your investment is astronomical.

Conformist Absentees

Conformist absentees are also conformists about everything else in life. They take their cues from the group, and do whatever the group is doing. If the average absence rate in their department, say, is once a month, they'll be absent once a month. In most cases, you are dealing with an overgrown adolescent who hasn't made the transition yet from a high school mentality to one of adult responsibility.

An easy way to cut his absence rate is to transfer him to a department with a lower-than-average absence rate. Typically, this means transferring a younger person into a group of older people. You could also transfer this kind of absentee into any small group. People who work in small groups are more interdependent than people in large groups, so absence rates tend to be lower. Your objective, in both cases, is to give the conformist absentee a low absence rate to which he can now conform.

If you can't solve the problem with transfers, your challenge is to help this person grow up faster than he otherwise might. This calls for some private, straight-from-the-shoulder, man-to-man or woman-to-woman talks. The idea you want to convey is that the time has come to stop thinking of the organization as an adult "system" that has to be defied or beaten. You might say something like, "Wake up. You're not in school anymore. This is the real world. We're all working for a living, and we've got real work to do. I want to be able to count on you, and so does everybody else around here. So, can I?"

What conformists really want more than anything else is respect. You have to show them that the smartest way to get that is not by following the mindless crowd but by showing other adults that they can be relied on to do their part.

Escapist Absentees

The *escapist* absentee stays away from work because he hates it. It's as simple as that. He is typically the victim of a bad match between his capabilities and his job. We've already reviewed this problem in chapter 9, where we noted that the human mind does not tolerate boredom very well.

If a mind isn't given enough to do, it naturally wanders off in search of something better to do. It may wander into fantasy and daydreams, or it may wander into mischief, or, as in this case, it may wander off the work site altogether. The problem is not with the individual, but with the job.

It is also a self-correcting problem, in that people who are stuck in jobs that bore them this much will probably quit them soon enough. But that also means the loss of someone who would probably not have stayed away from a higher-level job. The only real cure is to move that individual to a job that demands all the abilities he's got. Unfortunately, some managers are reluctant to take a chance on someone with a bad absence record. So escapist absentees are left to languish a while longer in jobs they cannot tolerate, and eventually they are lost altogether.

Defectors

The groups we have considered until now are all "sick," so to speak. They are motivated to escape from work, or even from life as most people live it. This final group, however, consists of people who are quite healthy. The awkward fact is that in the healthy act of preserving their own sanity, they create a difficult problem for management.

How do you motivate defectors not to defect? First, you need to know what motivates them to do that. Then you either eliminate the cause, or, if you can't, you resign yourself to a high turnover rate.

Most people who voluntarily leave one job will get a better-paying job, so the usual conclusion is that they left primarily because of money. However, provided there is any market at all for their skills, getting an offer of higher pay is not difficult. The new employer will assume that you expect more money, and for your part, you need a higher level of pay to justify such a radical move. So the real question is not whether you were dissatisfied with your pay but what made you enter the job market in the first place.

Money is only rarely the answer to that question. That's because there really is a job market out there. There is supply and demand, and there are real buyers and sellers who deal in human talent. Personnel departments are acutely aware of that and make it their business to know the market price for people with various skills and various levels of experience. Companies must remain competitive with each other's pay rates or risk both the loss of key people and the inability to hire new people. So unless something is radically wrong, there probably is not a lot of difference between your current salary and what you could command elsewhere.

There are two different answers to the question of what starts a job search. For blue-collar workers, the single most common reason is a desire to escape supervisors whom they consider unfair, overbearing, or disrespectful. The easiest way to reduce blue-collar turnover would be to replace the supervisors who generate the most complaints. However, management tends to admire the same supervisors that employees loathe, precisely because they are tough and uncompromising.

Among professionals and managers, the most common reasons for looking at outside job opportunities are lack of job satisfaction and lack of advancement opportunities. When these people complain of doing dumb work, or of getting nowhere fast, they are prime candidates to become ex-employees as soon as they can make more satisfactory arrangements elsewhere. The only effective solutions to the problem are career management, which was discussed in chapter 7, and job redesign, which we discussed in chapter 9.

Turnover creates replacement costs. If it produces a shortage of key talent, it can limit a company's ability to exploit its competitive advantages. To personnel managers, who regard turnover as a rejection of all that they have wrought, it is the unkindest cut of all.

Nevertheless, turnover isn't all bad. It has its positive side. It keeps fresh talent and new ideas flowing into a company. It probably spares the company from severe, intractable, long-range problems. The frustrated employee who, for whatever reason, cannot escape from the source of his frustration, is probably doomed to becoming demotivated, embittered, and inattentive to his work, or even actively hostile to it.

Suppose someone asks you the classic motivation question (Remember? "How do you motivate somebody who . . . ?"). In this case, it's about a long-term employee who is for all practical purposes unfirable but has been trapped in a succession of unstimulating jobs, and whose performance has finally dwindled to where he fits the description of the previous paragraph. If that's the question, your questioner has achieved the ambition of everyone who ever had to deal with an expert, by asking the unanswerable question. I suggest that you simply congratulate him.

It is much better to avoid this problem than to have to solve it. Unless it is within your power to change one or more of the conditions set by that version of the classic question, you're dealing with someone who *can't* be motivated. And that's the main reason why defectors, despite the temporary inconveniences they create, are not such bad problems after all. They spare you from the greatest frustration that a highly motivated motivator ever has to face.

CHAPTER
——— 14 ———

BAD BOSSES

Bad bosses actually reduce the effectiveness of the people who report to them. They do this by blocking initiatives, frustrating ambitions, and in some cases by terrifying their subordinates into taking no risks whatever. Of course, the easiest way to take no risks is to follow directions blindly and make no decisions of one's own. If you should encounter that problem in your dealings with, say, a retail store, or a company from which you buy a service, you may very well have run into a symptom of the bad-boss problem. You may not be dealing with a blockhead, but with an intelligent employee who is scared stiff.

Good bosses, on the other hand, enable their people to do better work. Mediocre bosses have no particular effect, one way or the other, on what their subordinates produce.

It's hard to say how many bosses are really bad. In part, it's a question of definition. Managers who are disliked or unpopular do not necessarily harm their subordinates' work. Still, bad bosses are a very persistent part of our folklore, and where there's that much smoke, there must be some fire. There is not much hard evidence to indicate how widespread it really is, but it is certainly not an uncommon problem. If you haven't encountered a bad boss yet, sooner or later you probably will. They are at least *that* common.

In this chapter, we're going to look first at the causes of the bad-boss problem, and at the more common attempts to deal with it. Then we'll look in some depth at the one method that really seems to work. After that, we'll look at what you might do if you have a bad boss, and finally at the interesting question of what to do if *you* are the bad boss.

What Makes Bad Bosses Bad?

Bad bosses are almost never *all* bad. In the real world, totally incompetent bosses have a low survival rate. Instead, most bad bosses have an uneven competence profile. They are usually very good in the technical aspects of their jobs, or in tasks that require specialized knowledge or skills. In other words, they are good at doing what their subordinates are supposed to do. They are just not good at managing them. A bad sales manager, for example, probably is (or was) a really super salesperson. A bad engineering manager probably is (or was) an exceptionally capable engineer. Indeed, those strengths were probably the main reasons why bad bosses were selected for managerial jobs in the first place. The problem is that their technical virtuosity tends to blind us to their lack of skill in building and maintaining relationships. The bad boss is a lopsided manager whose technical wizardry is offset by clumsiness in the motivational part of his job.

Don't read any cause-and-effect relationship into the combination of high technical skill and low motivational skill. There isn't any. If you look at a large number of managers, you will find examples of just about every combination of these two abilities. Indeed, the real winners among them will be strong in both aspects. Most managers, however, are ordinary mortals like you and me. They bring to their jobs some great strengths and some not-so-great strengths. In some cases, they bring actual weaknesses. These are usually overlooked or tolerated because of the value placed on their strengths.

That is the origin of the bad-boss problem—the failure of too many managers to realize that the essence of managing is to multiply your own effectiveness. You do that by causing as much work as possible to be done by others. Because of that failure, too many managers overvalue the ability to merely *do* a job, and undervalue the ability to get *others* to do it.

Typically, a bad-boss-to-be outshines all of his or her colleagues in lower-level jobs, and on the strength of being a better worker than the rest is promoted to a supervisory job. This is where a cruel deception takes place. Bad bosses do not delegate. That's partly out of contempt for the lesser abilities of their subordinates, and partly because they don't know how to teach or inspire them to do their work properly. Instead, bad bosses undertake to do most of their department's work, especially the most critical or demanding parts, themselves. They frequently rationalize this with the correct, but irrelevant, observation that they know better than everyone else how the job should be done.

That takes a heroic effort, but for a while at least they can actually compensate for their deficiencies as motivators with tremendous effort and diligence. This brings them even more admiration and further promotions. No one inquires too closely how, or at what cost, those spectacular results were obtained. No one notices that the bad boss has not been managing at all, but instead has been playing super-salesperson or super-engineer or super–what-have-you. The irony is that they are highly motivated nonmotivators.

The problem finally becomes acute when bad bosses are promoted to a level where there are so many subordinates in the chain of command below them that they can no longer compensate, with their own efforts, for what so many people are not permitted to do, or have lost interest in doing. When the bad-boss problem finally reaches this stage, management is likely to respond to it in one of three ways. None of them is effective.

Bad Solutions for the Bad-Boss Problem

By far the most common reaction to the bad-boss problem is to minimize it, deny it, or turn a blind eye to it. The bad boss's defenders and apologists will stress the huge, possibly irreplaceable strengths that he brings to the job. Then they will add that a little discontent on the part of the troops is probably inevitable, and certainly not something to which we should overreact. Or they will dismiss as preposterous the suggestion that the bad boss is probably having a "net negative" effect on the organization's work. (That is, what is subtracted from the subordinates' accomplishments may actually exceed what is added by the bad boss's personal contributions.) Finally, they may simply choose not to notice a problem that has not yet boiled over, and which in any case appears to have no easy, obvious solution.

The second response is to apply an educational Band-Aid. The bad boss will be sent to one or more of the many executive programs offered by universities or management institutes. The hope is that by poring over textbooks, or listening to a professor, the bad boss will learn how to be a good boss. That is naive. The bad boss's problem is not a lack of knowledge but his entrenched habits. Indeed, the bad boss who returns from one of these programs can probably quote motivational theories and rattle off current academic buzz words as nimbly as any newly minted Ph.D. But bad bosses don't need to stuff their heads with highfalutin concepts. They just need to *act* differently.

A variation on the educational approach has been to send the bad boss to a sensitivity-training session. As the name implies, the object of this method is to heighten an individual's awareness of how his behavior is interpreted by others. This method reached a peak of popularity several years ago, from which it has since receded. It is controversial for many reasons.

The basic problem with sensitivity training is that constraints of time and money limit it to one session of about one week's duration, usually with a group of fellow students who are strangers to each other, and with no provision for follow-up. As a result, the sessions may be eye-opening or even thrilling, but carry-over effects to the bad boss's job are seldom observed.

The third common response to the bad-boss problem, although a distant third compared to the first two, is to lose patience with the bad boss and fire him. The problem with that method is that you lose all of those great technical strengths, which in many cases really *are* irreplaceable.

So the bad-boss problem is very tough indeed, because it has serious consequences and no easy solution. It originates in one of the oldest and most persistent fallacies in management, the idea that people who do their own work well have thereby demonstrated their fitness to manage others. That just isn't so.

We are all familiar with the same principle in another context, but somehow we seldom see the connection. In sports, we commonly observe that great players seldom become great coaches. We have no trouble understanding that two different sets of skills are involved. The same is true of doing a job and managing other people who do that job. But the analogy escapes us, so we still hand out managerial jobs chiefly to those who have done their own jobs well, without regard to whether they have demonstrated any aptitude for leadership. (See chapter 8.)

This fallacy has such a grip on the managerial mind that it has already outlived several generations of motivation experts, and will probably outlive several more. Let me explain. When I was a graduate student (which was not recently), I had an elderly professor who was getting ready to retire. When he lectured to us about the error of blindly promoting the best workers, he sighed and said that it had been identified as a fallacy when *he* was a graduate student (and that was even less recently). George Santayana was right. Those who cannot remember the past are condemned to repeat it.

Don't let that happen to you. When you are asked to recommend people for promotion, remember that managerial jobs are not rewards to be granted to those who are merely deserving. Managerial jobs are jobs, not rewards. They have particular demands, especially regarding the ability to influence the way others do their work. The best way to avoid the bad-boss problem is to nip it in the bud. That way you can avoid the tortuous and uncertain process of attempting to repair a bad boss, which I shall now describe.

Repairing a Bad Boss

There *is* a way to fix the bad-boss problem. It is expensive, and it works only under certain conditions; the outcome is never certain. Still, it might save an otherwise irreplaceable manager, and might turn a bad boss into a moderately good one. Because of the high cost and the need to offset it against sufficiently large benefits, it has been used (so far) only with high-level executives. Theoretically, it could be used with anyone, but I will limit myself here to what I have actually experienced.

The first few times that I was asked to work on a bad-boss problem, I failed miserably. But I had enough sense to figure out what I had done wrong, and my next few attempts were at least more promising failures. Eventually I got it right. I won't bore you with my early attempts to find my way up the learning curve. Instead, I'll tell you the conditions you've got to have for the technique to work. Then I'll describe the technique by sharing some cases with you.

There is one absolute prerequisite. The bad boss *must* want to change. The motivation must be very strong. Occasionally, a bad boss will realize that further advancement is out of the question unless he becomes much more skilled with people. More likely, however, the CEO will call in the bad boss and make him an offer that he can't refuse: "I'm calling in a consultant to help you to become a better leader. I want you to cooperate fully with the consultant, or leave the company. That's it. You have no other alternatives."

That may seem harsh. But to become a better boss, a bad boss has to undergo a very difficult transformation. To have any hope of making it, he has to be determined and disciplined. Without real fortitude and resolution on the bad boss's part, the method isn't going to work. Obviously, this means that you've got to begin by selling the bad boss on the need for change. In most cases, only the individual's peers or superiors can do that job.

So what can the bad boss's subordinates do? They've got to get to their boss's peers or superiors. Does it take guts to do that? Yes. That's one reason why so many bad bosses are still bad. No one has dared to tell them, or to tell anyone else, that they're bad.

Once that first major hurdle has been overcome, you have to find a consultant with whom the bad boss feels compatible. That's an intuitive judgment that the consultant and the bad boss can make, together, in a few hours. As for the consultant, some experience in psychological counseling would be helpful. More important characteristics are maturity, an ability to listen, and knowing the difference between what you are hearing and what you want to hear.

You can't change a bad boss's behavior by focusing entirely on his behavior. You've also got to focus on everyone with whom the bad boss interacts. You'll quickly discover that a bad boss's subordinates have become experts at bringing out the worst in their leader. The reverse is also true. You've got a bunch of vicious circles to break, and it's best to break all of them if you can. So the problem to be solved is a group problem, and not simply a bad-boss problem.

Typically, neither side recognizes the extent to which it is causing the behavior it finds objectionable on the part of the other side. For example, bad bosses may insist on intervening in the work of subordinates. That's because they're convinced that no one can do the job better than they can. After a while, subordinates become accustomed to not finishing their own work, because their boss finishes it for them. So they turn in work that is incomplete, or inaccurate, or even sloppy, convinced that it doesn't really matter because their boss will change it anyway. The boss, of course, uses their slipshod work as a justification for staying so deeply involved in it. The result is "reverse delegation," a highly inefficient distortion of rational work flow, in which the work of many lower-paid subordinates is transferred to one highly paid superior.

Major changes in the bad boss's personality are simply not in the cards. But we don't need major changes to improve the way in which subordinates and a bad boss work together. Small, narrowly focused changes can do the job, if they're carefully selected.

Suppose we asked several of the people with whom you work to list the things you do that they wish you wouldn't do. We'd eventually get a short list on which there was fairly high agreement. The same would be true if we asked them to list the things you do that they really appreciate. Each of us, in other words, has a more or less distinct behavioral "signature" by which other people tend to recognize us. In seeking to improve the way in which a group works with a boss, we concentrate on those "signature" actions, especially the negative ones. The idea is to stop people from bringing out the worst in each other.

To do that, we need a fairly precise description of what we want you to do, or not do. For example, we can't say that you should "listen better," because that's too vague. You wouldn't know what to focus on. Instead we might say, "Stop interrupting." Then you'd know exactly what we wanted you to do.

Timing is one of the keys to success in this process. I learned that the hard way. First, the counselor has to visit fairly frequently during the initial stages, at least once a week, to keep everyone's attention on what's expected of them *now*. You can't treat it as a postponable item, because that damned consultant is going to be here in just a few more days, asking everybody if everybody else actually did what they said they'd do.

Second, the process has to continue for at least a year. Positive behavioral changes are usually evident in most people after a few months. That's the easy part. The difficult part is sustaining those changes and making them permanent, instead of just reverting to old patterns. That calls for persistence. You don't let attention wander away from what everyone has come to expect of everyone else. A complacent belief that "the problem is already solved" is the great enemy of behavior change.

The counselor is going to use plenty of *feedback*. That's up-to-date, reliable information on how the people with whom you work actually interpret your behavior. On every visit, the counselor gathers everyone's impressions of everyone else's performance during the preceding week, boils it down, and then gives each individual the feedback report.

Most people go through life without ever getting *any* feedback. That's one reason why our behavior tends to be so persistent. Hardly anyone knows what he's doing that other people really wish he wouldn't do. Two fears are often expressed about the use of feedback. One is that social dynamite will be ignited, and that relationships will be destroyed by too much candor. I've never seen that happen. It turns out that most people are better liked than they realize, and less disliked than they fear. Also, most people can handle feedback constructively, without becoming angry or resentful. That's another way of saying that most people are more adult than other people think they are.

The other fear is that some people can't take much candor and may be pushed over the line into mental illness. The shocks involved in learning about yourself are relatively mild, but someone who was not in good mental health to start with might have trouble coping with them. That's why it's a good idea to use a counselor with some background in psychology. Anyone who seems too timid or too defensive should be excused from this process.

The next two cases are drawn from my files. Names and places have been changed, but otherwise the events are described as they happened. The first case was only a partial success. (In the real world, to partially improve a bad boss isn't doing badly at all.) Also, you can learn from a partial success, and do better the next time. The second case, which actually benefited from the first, was almost completely successful.

SOUTHERN STEEL PRODUCTS, INC.: GEORGE BALLARD

When the company formed a new Southeastern Region, the president's choice for its general manager was George Ballard, a dynamic salesman in his late thirties. Ballard had joined the company only six years earlier and had risen rapidly to a middle-level position in sales management. His appointment was controversial, because it rocketed him past several more senior managers, including his own former boss. But the president had seen Ballard in action, handling difficult customer problems with great skill. He was convinced that Ballard was the best person for the job.

However, during the president's first few visits to the region's headquarters in South Carolina, he sensed that Ballard's relationship with his staff had become severely strained. He noted that Ballard made most of the staff's decisions for them, leaving them sullen and resentful. The president felt personally responsible for this situation, but because he thought of Ballard as his protégé, he was reluctant to confront him directly. That is why he decided to call me in. He wanted me to deal with Ballard for him.

He asked me to go to South Carolina to "save" Ballard. "George has done a superb job in everything except running his staff," the president said. "That's where he just goes in and swings a two-by-four to get what he wants. I don't think he realizes the extent to which he is feared." I said I was willing to try, provided Ballard was also willing. The president assured me that he would take care of that.

On my first visit to South Carolina, Ballard introduced me to each member of his staff by explaining that person's job to me in detail. He hardly gave any of them a chance to say a word of their own. Suddenly, after three or four such introductions, he switched tactics and began letting the staff members explain their jobs to me. Later, when we were alone in his office, I asked him to explain his sudden change. He replied, "My instinct is always to take charge of a situation. But then I remembered why you are here, and I thought it would look better if I let them explain their own jobs." I asked him why he felt he had to "take charge." His answer was, "Any time someone hesitates, or wants to think for a minute, I feel that I have to fill the vacuum that they are leaving. I want to keep things moving."

I noted that the region's business was expanding, and that sooner or later he would need the support of his staff to run it. He said that he understood that. "But the emotional side of me says, 'Let's just roll right over them and get things done,' even though the intellectual side of me knows that in the long run, that isn't going to work." I asked point-blank if he really felt that way, or was simply trying to please me. He replied, "Well, the boss seems to think that you are the answer." I said that if there was an answer, it was in him, not me. Nevertheless, I was pleased by his candor. So I suggested that I visit him and his six staff members once a month for six months. He agreed without hesitation, and the first round of interviews was held shortly thereafter.

I began each interview by saying that our purpose was to make the team as a whole more effective, rather than just to "fix" Ballard. In any case, Ballard would need the team's help to change, just as they would need his help to regain their confidence in themselves. I then put three questions to each of them about the other six people in the group. (1) What does this person do that you find helpful? (2) What does this person do that hampers your work? (3) What does this person not normally do that you would find helpful? I thus collected eighteen perceptions of each individual by his fellow team members and used them to prepare a feedback report for each of them.

Next, we held a general meeting. Each person would disclose to the group as much of his own feedback report as he cared to reveal. I was there to see to it that no one got hurt and that the meeting did not get sidetracked. The purpose of the meeting was to set some goals for everyone. Each would agree to try to change certain specific aspects of his behavior during the next months, in an attempt to become more useful to his colleagues. The *quid pro quo* was that each of his colleagues would try to accommodate his requests of them.

I began the discussion by saying, "You are all highly qualified for your jobs. The subject of this meeting is not how to do your own jobs better, but what each of you can do to make everyone else on the team more effective." It was agreed that Ballard would share his feedback report first. He read it aloud in its entirety:

On the positive side, you are seen as energetic and enthusiastic. You are also seen as being open to new ideas, *when* your staff can get you to listen.

The main criticism by far is an apparent lack of faith in your subordinates. You are seen as not respecting their opinions, and as not believing that the difficulties they tell you about are as serious as they claim.

You are also seen as unable to control your own energy. You impatiently take over tasks that others have begun, not because they are being done badly, but because you seem to need constant activity. Your attention is so fixed on your immediate goals that you ignore your subordinates' feelings.

One of your more annoying habits is not showing up for scheduled meetings with your subordinates. This implies that matters which they consider important are not important to you.

The next hour was spent in a heated discussion. Ballard denied nothing, but said he was surprised at the intensity of the reaction to what he considered minor incidents. His finance director then spoke up: "You thought they were minor, George, because you never thought about us at all. The only things you cared about were shipments and collections, and whether the damned invoices had gone out by five o'clock." Open comments like this impressed Ballard far more than the feedback report, because it took courage to make them.

Presently Ballard said he would put the following commitment in writing (which he subsequently did):

I will listen harder to you in order to understand what you are trying to tell me. When you tell me that you are running into obstacles, I will trust you. I will not barge in and take over your work. I will stay out of your area of responsibility unless you ask for help. I will attend as many scheduled staff meetings as possible.

The practical problem at this point was to motivate Ballard to keep his promises. Everyone knew that I would return to South Carolina five more times, and that I would check everyone's perceptions of everyone else's behavior during the preceding month. No one, least of all Ballard, wanted to be accused of not keeping his promises to the others. That proved to be quite an adequate motivator, at least for a while.

Ballard's feedback reports at the next few meetings were promising. His staff felt that he was more relaxed, which made it easier for them to work with him. They felt he had made a visible effort to control his impulsiveness and that he was beginning to run the region through them, instead of trying to do everything himself. This pattern continued through the fourth meeting.

Ballard postponed the fifth meeting, claiming urgent business elsewhere. The meeting was finally held three weeks late. His feedback at that meeting showed some signs of backsliding. One staff member said, "If you want to get his attention, you have to be prepared to put your job on the line. Otherwise, he's too preoccupied with other things to listen." Another said that Ballard "was looking over my shoulder again, checking my decisions. He seems to want to review everything."

When I saw Ballard privately, I asked if he felt that he had already "solved" the problems I had been asked to help him with and was now turning his attention to other matters. He denied that. I told him that maintaining the gains he had achieved would be tougher than anything he had done so far. That seemed to impress him.

However, Ballard postponed the sixth (and final) meeting twice. It might never have been held at all if the president had not insisted on it. The feedback reports indicated that Ballard was trying spasmodically to live up to his promises but was largely preoccupied with external matters.

When I met with the president to review the case, I told him I had learned some things that hadn't been apparent to me at first. His own reluctance to confront Ballard and his use of me as a surrogate were part of the problem. Ballard's ambitions were so strong that no one, myself included, could have motivated him as well as the president could. I told him that the only way to preserve the gains Ballard had made and to prevent further backsliding would be for him to become actively involved.

The president agreed to do so, and Ballard did manage some further improvements in his working relationships with his staff. For example, with Ballard's consent, the president would take selected members of Ballard's staff to lunch during his visits to South Carolina, and he used those contacts to form his own opinions of Ballard's progress. The mere fact that the president was doing this provided Ballard with an adequate spur. The president seldom referred to these luncheon meetings during his conversations with Ballard.

The other lesson I learned from this case involved timing. Ballard needed more support in maintaining his new methods than I was able to provide in six monthly visits. More frequent visits over a longer time period would have had a better chance of success. You live and you learn.

MONARCH REFRIGERATOR CORPORATION: EDWARD LAMBERT

I was called in by Monarch's personnel director. He had been concerned with Ed Lambert for quite some time, because there had been a steady stream of requests to transfer out of Lambert's division, and no requests to transfer in. Periodic attitude surveys indicated that the division had the lowest morale in the company. He had spoken to Lambert about these matters several times, but Lambert had dismissed them as unimportant.

Then the division's sales began to slip. Monarch's president had investigated personally and found that the basic problem was slow response time in Lambert's office. Too many decisions required his personal approval, and some were made too late to stave off competitive advances. After consulting with the personnel director, the president laid down the law. He demanded that Lambert get help. Clearly, the president felt that Lambert was worth saving. Otherwise, it would have been simple enough to just fire him.

When I met Lambert for the first time, it was obvious that he had mixed feelings about me. He had little choice but to cooperate, if he wanted to keep his job. On the other hand, he also wanted me to exonerate him of the accusation that he had been an inexpert manager. So he sought to convince me that the stories I had heard about him had been exaggerated. His motives were first to convince me that he was right, so that I would leave as quickly as possible.

Lambert had risen through the ranks, largely because he had an encyclopedic knowledge of the division and a phenomenal memory for detail. He insisted on approving virtually all decisions made by his immediate lieutenants, and in some cases by people as many as two management levels below them. The evidence was apparent the minute we walked into his office. There were piles of paper everywhere, all awaiting his review.

I asked Lambert why he burdened himself in this way. He replied that he often found fault with his subordinates' work and had to send it back for revision. He was determined that no instructions would be sent out to the field organization unless the staff work was perfect.

"Ed," I said, "you are trying to be your own staff. That just overloads you and underloads them." To my surprise, Lambert suddenly pulled out a notepad and began to jot down what I had said. He also switched from lecturing to asking me questions. "What can I do?" he asked. "My subordinates' work is full of mistakes."

I replied, "We'll have to find out *why* they make so many errors. Maybe we can minimize them. If you weren't so bogged down, trying to be your own editor and your own proofreader, you might have more time to run this division."

From that point onward, our relationship changed. Instead of regarding me as an arbitrator between him and his president, Lambert began to treat me as a tutor. In all of our subsequent meetings, he took notes of what I told him, much as a student might do in a classroom.

Months later he told me, "I decided that if I had to deal with you, I might as well get something useful from you." That proved to be a very constructive move on his part.

On my next visit I met privately with each of Lambert's principal lieutenants. One confessed that Lambert frightened him with thinly veiled threats of firing him if orders were not carried out to the letter. Accordingly, he adopted a "low profile" with Lambert, meekly doing as he was told and keeping his own ideas to himself. Another was a "good soldier" type who had always obeyed orders unquestioningly. He simply continued that lifelong pattern when he was with Lambert. The third initially regarded me as "a spy from personnel." Even after he began to trust me, he worried that the division might be ridiculed because, "We could not solve our own problems without calling in a shrink."

All three shared a common unwillingness to confront Lambert directly with the problems he had caused for them. They also had a common tendency to submit incomplete work to him, because they knew he would change it anyway. They knew that if they questioned his judgment, he would launch into a long, detailed, self-justifying monologue. Rather than sit through any more of those, it was easier to just keep quiet and let Lambert have his way.

I held a meeting with all three of them, without Lambert, and accused them of being part of the problem. "Sure," I said, "Ed is a fussy guy. He's a detail junkie. But if you send him incomplete work, that just feeds his belief that he's got to check everything. And if you won't tell him how much he frustrates you, how is he to know? The problem originates with Ed, but you're making it worse. We can't change Ed unless you change, too." That clearly shook them up.

I then suggested that Ed, his three lieutenants, and myself hold a joint meeting one week later. The purpose would be to bring into the open the points that everyone had been making with me privately. Then we could set some mutually agreed goals to begin changing everyone's established patterns of behavior. Ed agreed enthusiastically. The lieutenants agreed with some apprehension.

Prior to the meeting I did some further interviewing with a few middle-level managers who reported to Lambert's lieutenants. I also spoke to a few senior secretaries, because I knew that they usually had good insights into the attitudes of clerical and administrative employees. The complaints I heard were common enough. They spoke of little or no recognition for good work, too few chances for advancement, and unequal workloads between departments. You can hear that sort of thing in almost any company. What was unusual, however, was a strong feeling that it would be futile to try to get management to correct any of these problems.

Indeed it had been futile. The reason was that Lambert's lieutenants, who were well aware of the simmering discontent at lower levels in the division, simply had not passed the complaints on to him. They were convinced that he would interpret them as a personal attack, and that he would respond with another of his lengthy tirades. So various small morale problems had gradually festered throughout the division. In time, the conviction that management simply didn't care about such problems became the biggest morale problem of them all.

It was now clear why so many employees had sought transfers, and why the attitude survey results had been so negative. It was also clear why Lambert was convinced that the personnel director had exaggerated the scope of his division's problems. His lieutenants, out of fear of how he reacted to criticism, had left him in the dark. He had been flying blind.

At the meeting, Lambert was by far the most candid of the participants. Of course, he also had the strongest motivation to get something constructive out of the meeting. He acknowledged that he had stifled dissent, and that by so doing he had cut himself off from information about the state of morale in the division. His lieutenants conceded that they had chosen not to challenge him, even when they felt he might be wrong.

I then asked them to make a conscious effort to begin acting differently toward each other in certain specific ways. I asked Ed to listen carefully to any disagreement with his views and to postpone any response at all until at least the following day. He agreed. My purpose was to avoid the lengthy harangues that had been so inhibiting to his lieutenants. I also asked his lieutenants to speak up frankly when they disagreed with him. They also agreed, although with obvious reservations.

For the next several months, I visited the division weekly. I usually began by checking in with the lieutenants to get their views on what had happened since my last visit, especially between them and Lambert. Then I would spend a few hours with Lambert himself, reviewing the week but also planning for the future.

After a few weeks, Lambert asked my opinion of a plan to appoint one of his lieutenants "chief of staff," to screen all paperwork that required his (Lambert's) approval. The chief would make sure that nothing reached Lambert's desk that was not already crisp, complete, and accurate. That would enable Lambert to make a prompt yes-or-no decision on each proposal, without having to plough through all of the supporting details. I thought it was a marvelous idea and encouraged him to implement it. A few weeks later, he did.

Meantime, the reports I received from various sources in the division indicated that Lambert had really begun to delegate. Decisions were being made fairly rapidly, and in varying degrees his lieutenants had begun to influence those decisions. Perhaps as a result, sales and profits were up, and requests for transfers out of the division were down.

When I agreed to work with Lambert, the company had given me a one-year retainer so I would have enough time to lock in the changes and to prevent the kind of backsliding that had occurred in the case of George Ballard. My visits gradually became less frequent, because I did not want Lambert or his lieutenants to feel that the changes they had achieved depended on me.

As the end of my contract approached, the president asked me for an evaluation of Lambert's progress. To answer him as objectively as possible, I prepared a list of nine questions for Lambert's lieutenants to answer. Each was based on actions that had characterized "the old Ed," and to which they had objected most strenuously when I first met them. For example, I asked whether, during the preceding two months, they had seen Lambert countermand an order they had given to one of their subordinates, or launch into one of his lengthy monologues, or imply that he would view any disagreement with his views as an act of disloyalty.

Of twenty-seven answers (nine questions to three managers), there were twenty-one favorable replies; three were "borderline" (Lambert had begun to act in the old way, but checked himself); and three cited repetition of the old patterns. I told the president that this was a very good result, since less than a year before Lambert would have received twenty-seven unfavorable ratings.

I also complimented the president for having forced the issue in the first place. While Lambert had shown uncommon open-mindedness and determination, there would have been no change if the president had not demanded it. The president replied that his alternatives had been pretty bleak. Lambert was the most knowledgeable person in the division, and he did not want to lose him if he could avoid that.

After that I had occasional informal contacts with Lambert or his lieutenants. From what I can gather, most of the changes have persisted, although there has been occasional backsliding. The most impressive report of all came from the personnel director. In a recent attitude survey, Lambert's division had the highest morale rating in the entire company.

From these two cases, and others not reported here, I have drawn two main conclusions about the bad-boss problem. First, under certain circumstances, this kind of problem can be largely corrected. Second, most organizations are still reluctant to correct it. That's a pity, but that's the way it is.

Living With a Bad Boss

Bosses, as individuals, may be nice people. They can also be tyrants. But the reason they are so often disliked is not so much their personalities as their role. Your boss's responsibilities put him in direct conflict with your natural desire to do whatever you jolly well please.

By definition, a boss limits your freedom. Worse still, a boss has authority over you, and can reward, punish, and control you. So we treat our bosses cautiously, regard them warily, and note their deficiencies quickly. That's one reason why it's not easy to be a good boss.

Thus, the mere fact that you may dislike your boss does not make him, or her, a bad boss. That would only be true if your boss's effect on your work was negative. Bosses are not required to win popularity contests. They are required to get work done, and done well, by others. It is only when they can't deliver on that fundamental requirement that we can label them as bad bosses.

If you really have a bad boss, you face the same options that your boss's superiors face. You can try to escape, or make the best of it, or try to help your boss to change.

Escape is the route to follow if you're convinced that your boss is both hopeless and intolerable. You can escape by transferring to another department in the same company, or by leaving the company altogether. Your best hope of a transfer is to find a department that needs you more than your present department does. Your problem then is to persuade your boss that as far as he is concerned, you are replaceable. If that doesn't work, your only escape route is out the front door. That is not a decision to be taken lightly.

But if you're really convinced that your boss is a permanently entrenched obstacle to your growth, the time has come to start checking out the job market. However, a word of caution: don't be so desperate to escape from your bad boss that you leap at a second-rate job offer. Make up your mind to tolerate your boss until something really superior comes along. Then, and not until then, jump.

The second option is to make the best of a bad situation. Distasteful as it may be, that could very well be your best option. There are ways to minimize the discomfort of working under bad bosses. They can be humored. That is, you can give them whatever they insist on, even if that has to be at the expense of work that you consider more important. Or you can busy yourself with the details of your job and ignore your boss as much as possible.

Another possibility is to make some off-the-job activity, such as a hobby, the center of your life. In that case you can regard both your job and your boss as necessary evils that support your hobby. The pity of it is, of course, that by adjusting to a bad boss in these ways, you'll be doing less for your company, and for your own career, than you're capable of doing. That's part of the cost of a bad boss.

Bad bosses are usually just as able to learn as anyone else. The problem is that no one dares to teach them, or even to suggest that they have something to learn. You can help a bad boss to make small improvements if you're subtle, and also fastidious about preserving his or her dignity. Frontal assaults on a bad boss's self-esteem are out for everyone except the CEO.

The best way to get a bad boss's attention is to know what goals are highest on his or her agenda and to suggest a better way to achieve them. Your goal is to teach your boss to act differently. However, you do not want to be so tactless as to suggest that your boss needs to change. Instead, propose ways in which *you* can serve your boss better by doing your job differently. You want to be in a position to send soothing signals to your boss. What you want your own behavior to bring out in your boss's behavior is, if not the best in him or her, then at least something better. So you change your boss's behavior by changing your own first.

For example, suppose your boss has the unlovely habit of countermanding your orders to your subordinates (as Ed Lambert did). You might say, "Boss, from now on, whenever I want one of my people to do something that is not routine, I'll check with you first. I'll tell you what I want and why I want it. You can give it your blessings or tell me why you want something else. In an emergency, I'll make the best decision I can, and then notify you right away. Would that be all right for you?"

You'll find that constantly checking your decisions is going to be burdensome, but then so will your boss. If he or she is reasonably bright, it will soon be apparent that most of your proposals are sound, and that it's safe to give you some leeway. You'll also be tactfully eliminating the "NIH" problem, which all too often is the real reason why bosses object to their subordinates' decisions. That stands for "Not Invented Here" and simply means that many people (not just bosses) feel more comfortable with decisions they've helped to shape than with those made entirely by others.

Another way to deal with an overly attentive boss is to try to standardize your decision processes and persuade him to let you adhere to them. Your objective is to call him in only for unusual problems, or important decisions for which the available information is ambiguous. Make sure that on each such occasion, you present him with a recommendation and not just a problem. Your objective is to keep him out of your hair by assuring him that most of the time you'll be doing your job exactly as he would, and that when you can't assure him of that you'll bring the problem to him.

Are You a Bad Boss?

These are the signs that should make you suspicious. First, do you find that most of the people you supervise are incompetent? When you find replacements for them, are the replacements also incompetent? True, there are lots of incompetent people out there. However, most organizations screen them out quickly enough. Frankly, the odds against one manager collecting so many incompetents are pretty long. You ought to entertain the possibility that what you regard as ingrained inability is simply their way of reacting to your management style.

Another clue is transfer requests. Ed Lambert ignored these because he didn't know what was causing them. His people were voting with their feet, trying to escape from an unhappy workplace. If the number of people working under you who "want out" is persistently above average, you've got a problem. Better make sure that the problem isn't you. And don't dismiss that possibility lightly.

Yet another clue is a total lack of dissent. If your subordinates clam up when you ask for questions, it's either because you invariably explain yourself with total clarity or because they're afraid to tell you what they think. Take your choice. If you think it's the lucidity of your prose, you may have missed your calling. You might make a better author, or speechwriter, or playwright, than a boss.

Here's another set of clues to look for. Are you working extra-long hours, in an attempt to keep up with an ever-increasing workload? Is one reason for that increase a lack of qualified people to whom you could delegate some of your work? Despite your effort, is productivity (however that may be measured in your department) steadily slipping? If you've got all of these symptoms, a prime candidate for being the central cause of all of them is—you guessed it—you, dear reader.

If any of these clues start you wondering whether you might be a bad boss, don't keep your worries to yourself. Ask for feedback, starting with your superiors, who have nothing to lose by being candid with you. Next, try your peers, who have relatively little to lose. Don't be surprised if they express their criticisms so softly as to be nearly imperceptible. They won't want to hurt you, and they certainly won't be looking for any confrontations with you. Instead, they'll hope that you'll pick up their hints, without them having to come right out and say that you're a bad boss. So if you ask for feedback, listen hard for implications and subtleties in the answers you get.

Suppose you arrive at the conclusion that you, of all people, are a bad boss. What can you do to improve? You'll be terribly tempted to try the "New Year's Eve" gambit. That is, you'll solemnly resolve to become a better boss, and you'll start out with the best of intentions. But you know the fate of most New Year's resolutions. The problem is that your habits are likely to be ingrained, as are the habits of the people who know how to bring out the worst in you. My advice won't surprise you. Go find yourself a competent counselor, and tackle the problem head on.

A final word. There is still a certain stigma attached to seeking help. The prevailing mythology holds that real bosses solve their own problems, and that anyone who can't do that shouldn't be a boss. That's nonsense. Smart bosses know the difference between the problems they can solve by themselves and those they should hire experts to solve for them. The issue is not who solves the problem, but who solves it best, and whether it is solved at all.

And what should you do if someone snickers that you were so muddled that you had to turn to a "shrink" to extricate you from your problems? You should never reward ignorance by noticing it. An ignoramus was meant to be ignored.

CHAPTER
15

POLITICS AND INFIGHTING

Conflict between members of the same organization has a much worse reputation than it deserves. It can, of course, be a royal pain in the lower abdominal tract, especially for those poor souls who find themselves continually fighting with their colleagues over such things as influence on decisions, and over resources like manpower and money.

Whatever its causes, internal conflict consumes time, drains energy, and is almost universally disliked. For these reasons, academics have usually assumed that it is bad and have searched for ways to cool it off, or even to prevent it altogether. So it may come as a surprise that some conflicts are deliberately created by management—and for very good reasons. Other conflicts are unavoidable, because of external factors that no one really controls, or because of the need to periodically rearrange the way in which a company is organized.

There are at least three kinds of conflict to be found in organizations. It can occur between groups, as a function of their differing missions. We'll begin this chapter by looking at that kind of problem. But conflicts can also occur between individuals, because of differing assumptions about what is appropriate in a given situation. Much of this type of conflict is really caused by differences between the cultures in which the clashing individuals grew up.

We'll deal with "culture conflicts" in the second half of this chapter. Finally, there are "personality conflicts" between individuals who can't stand each other. Since it would take another book to describe and analyze those, we won't cover them here at all.

Starting Fights That Never Finish

Conflict is rather like body temperature. It's a sign that the organization is alive and that its people are doing what they are supposed to be doing. Believe it or not, they're often supposed to be fighting with each other.

As long as the temperature doesn't turn into a fever, as long as vital departments don't break down in the heat of battle, the fact that members of the same corporate team are fighting each other is normal and healthy. Not comfortable, not fun, not something that most of them wouldn't gladly avoid if they could. Nevertheless, from the organization's standpoint, a few good fights are an indication that all is well. That's why it's much wiser to manage conflicts than to try to stamp them out.

Management creates conflict in order to make better decisions, and also to prevent waste, dishonesty, and a terrible problem that goes by an equally terrible name: suboptimization. That's management's "S" word. It means attaining certain goals at the expense of other, equally important goals.

Let's look first at decisions. The higher you go in management, the more you'll find yourself making decisions about which you know very little. When you're making decisions on behalf of the entire organization, you'll have to integrate facts and opinions that are produced for you by many kinds of specialists, such as scientists, lawyers, publicists, and accountants, to list just a few.

Therefore you'll need a method to make sure that all of these specialists have done their homework, so they can do a proper job of advising you. You also need to be sure that you're not favoring a weak argument that has been smoothly presented over a stronger argument that has been poorly presented. You can accomplish both of these purposes by putting your advisers into competition with each other. Let them fight it out for the prize of having you make the decision they want you to make.

The box that follows contains an example of constructively managed conflict.

THE CASE OF THE CLASHING LIEUTENANTS

A few years ago, one of my client companies ran into a problem that many other companies would envy. They had seriously underestimated the demand for a new product and found themselves quickly swamped with more orders than they could handle. The general manager of the division that made the product called a meeting of his staff to decide what to do.

You might think that the sales manager would be ecstatic, but he wasn't. He was aghast. The last thing in the world he wanted was to disappoint loyal customers. He also feared that competitors, knowing that he couldn't deliver the new product quickly, would offer "me-too" products that might cut into his sales. His solution was simple. Hire more workers and run the factory around the clock, thereby tripling production. That would enable him to catch up with demand in less than a year.

"Not so fast," said the personnel manager. She was worried about the long-range implications of going on a hiring binge. "What happens after you've caught up? Your sales will flatten out, and we'll be stuck with hundreds of extra people on the payroll, whom we won't need."

"That's easy," replied the sales manager. "Fire them. Lay them off. Give them severance pay. Aren't you supposed to know all about that sort of thing?"

"I do, and there's no way that could work," replied the personnel manager. "The union would shut us down. It's almost impossible to get rid of redundant people as it is. If we have to increase production temporarily, I think we should subcontract it out. Let somebody else do it for us."

The general manager had often complained that he knew little about labor relations. But at this point, he looked the personnel manager in the eye and said, "Wait a minute. It can't be that bad. Are you exaggerating a little, perhaps? Would they really shut us down over something like that?" "Yes, I think they would," she replied. "OK, then prove it," snapped the general manager.

The personnel manager took a deep breath. "You only have to read the contract," she said. "After six months, full-time employees are entitled to all of the job security provisions. We've already tested that clause in arbitration, and we lost. No, they've got too much invested in that clause to let us get away with layoffs. I'm sure they'd strike."

The general manager nodded. "I understand," he said. "All right, let's continue." Although he was still no expert in labor relations, he had satisfied himself that his personnel manager could substantiate her opinions and was not exaggerating. Later in the meeting, he used the same tactic with the sales manager, challenging one of his opinions to see if he could support it.

At this point, the production manager entered the argument. "I'm against subcontracting," he said. "We can control quality in our own shop, but it's hard to get a subcontractor to do it right, especially with high-volume production. He's going to cut corners and try to get by with marginal materials. He'll hire the cheapest labor he can find. That's the only way he can come in with a low enough bid and still make a profit for himself."

Next, the chief accountant offered an opinion. "We goofed in not forecasting this product right," he said. "But that's water over the dam. We made a mistake and we're stuck with it. The problem now is to not make everything worse. So let me ask an embarrassing question. What's wrong with just running our factory the way we are, on only one shift? Why not let the customers wait? Frankly, I like the idea of a big backlog of orders."

The sales manager fired back. "You don't appreciate the importance of customer loyalty," he said. "Don't forget that the customer pays for everything, including our salaries. How am I going to explain why one customer gets the product, and another has to wait? They'll be up in arms. All those years, when we patiently built up their loyalty to us, will go right down the drain."

At this point the general manager took over. "I think I understand the problem now," he said. "There probably isn't a risk-free way out of this. Still, I want to run the smallest possible risk with our customers, while at the same time running the smallest possible risk with the union."

Turning to the manufacturing manager, he said, "I'll accept your judgment on the quality problem, because you know much more about it than I do." Then he turned to the sales manager and the personnel manager. "That means that both of you are going to have to run some risks, whether you like it or not. I'm going to pin each of you down. There must be some minimum number of new people we can hire without getting into big trouble with the union. And there must be some minimum number of customers we can risk antagonizing. The question is, what are those numbers?"

The debate continued for several more hours, but its outcome was foreshadowed by the general manager's strategy of optimizing between the sales and personnel considerations, instead of maximizing one at the expense of the other. He arrived at that strategy because each of his lieutenants, by clashing with each other, had clarified the problem for him. They had exposed both their own strongest arguments and the weak points in each other's arguments.

It was a grueling meeting, and no one left it feeling elated. But it had served its purpose. By putting his staff members into direct conflict with each other, the general manager had forced the essence of the problem to the surface, where he could act on it.

The Rules of the Game

You can improve the quality of your decisions by making your advisers into adversaries. They will force each other to be well prepared with facts and figures, and they won't let each other get away with half-baked arguments. They won't enjoy the process, but that is not the purpose of decision making.

This is why any major decision that is not preceded by a battle royal is, almost by definition, a dangerous decision. Whenever several professional specialties can offer insights into a decision, each perspective must be pitted against the others to determine the relative priority that each should have over the others.

However, deliberately induced conflict can be carried too far. You must never let your advisers forget that this kind of competition is only a means to better decision making. It is not an end in itself. That means that there is a time to argue and a time to close ranks. You do not prove yourself to have been right merely by predicting, correctly, that your colleague's strategy will fail. Your prediction is only right when your colleague's strategy fails despite your own best efforts to make it succeed.

Preventing Waste and Dishonesty

Consider purchasing agents. They are a company's first line of defense against waste. Their job is not to provide the company's managers with exactly what they want, but with something that is good enough and costs less. That often leads to battles, especially with technical specialists who insist that nothing less than pure unobtainium will do for their projects.

Also consider safety inspectors. In some companies, they are authorized to shut down production until hazardous conditions are put right. That brings them into direct conflict with foremen, who are charged with getting the product off the factory floor, and onto the loading dock, as quickly as possible.

In both cases, management puts its people into conflict with each other to be sure that neither of two important goals overwhelms the other. You don't want to buy gold-plated materials when nickel-plating, or even no plating, would do just as well. Neither do you want to buy something simply because it's cheap, only to discover that it's also inadequate. Also, you don't want employees to be hurt, maimed, or even killed for the sake of meeting a production schedule. But neither do you want to miss that schedule when there is no serious risk of injury. The way to balance these concerns is to give someone a stake in protecting each of them, and let them fight it out.

Management also creates deliberate conflict to keep its employees honest, or to convince outsiders of that. For example, most financial managers begin their careers as internal auditors, poking into the records kept by various operating units. They're on the lookout for inefficiency, inaccuracy, and even fraud.

The real purpose of auditors is not to detect skullduggery, but to prevent it. Only rarely do they uncover anything more nefarious than clerical errors. But part of the reason for that is simply that they're on the job. Everyone knows that those nosy auditors will be combing through their records, hoping to win some glory for themselves by uncovering someone else's malfeasance. Rather than become the auditor's next victim, most people try a little harder. They'll make sure that their records are accurate, and that supporting documents are available.

The conflict between auditors and the people they audit is usually low key. Suppose, however, that the auditors discover (or think they discover) something out of line. When that happens, the fur flies and the language becomes a bit robust. No one enjoys it. But the truth is likely to emerge, and that's what counts.

The Dreaded "S" Word

Now, what about "suboptimization"? I wish there were a shorter word to describe what that means, but I haven't found one.

You recall that it means achieving one goal at the expense of other goals that may be equally important, or even more important.

For example, you can spoil your customers with more service than they need. You can guarantee same-day delivery of any order, no matter how small. They will no doubt like that, but they won't necessarily appreciate it. That isn't ingratitude on your customers' part. It's just a proper understanding of what's important to them and what isn't.

Meantime, in order to provide that service, you'll need extra trucks, extra drivers, and you'll have to swallow increased insurance, maintenance, and fuel costs. So you will have made your customers marginally more happy, and you will have inflated your distribution costs out of all proportion to what was gained. That's suboptimization.

Or you can cut your training costs by hiring people who are brighter, or better educated, than their job requires. They'll learn the job quickly, with little or no formal instruction. You can cancel a lot of training classes, and you'll look like a hero when your budget is reviewed.

But those overqualified people won't last long. They'll be bored stiff, and most of them will be gone in a matter of months. So your recruiting and hiring costs will increase as you bring in replacements, and then replacements to replace the replacements, through what proves to be a revolving door. The losses can easily outweigh the gains. That, too, is suboptimization.

Our dreaded "S" word is nearly always the result of too little conflict. It's what happens when one group dominates the rest of a company and the other groups roll over and die.

For example, if you were to ask a group of sales representatives what is worse than losing a sale, you are likely to be met with incredulous stares. To them, *nothing* is even remotely as bad as losing a sale. But any accountant can show you that making a sale that loses money, without providing some compensating benefit (such as a toehold in a potentially profitable market), is worse than no sale at all. After all, you're not in business to lose money. But in companies that are dominated by their sales departments, you will find lots of such sales. Their market share will be spectacular, mostly because it has been bought with their own profits.

It's a question of time before such companies have to match their prices to their costs, or start eating their losses. The problem is usually more complex than just a dominant sales department. In a case like this, the financial department would also be part of the problem.

When a valid point of view gets no attention, it's usually because its advocates are not respected. That's why no one listens to them. To make such a company healthy again, you have to restore a balance of influence. You have to strengthen the financial department enough so that it can take on the sales department and win at least as many battles as it loses.

So much for conflicts that management sets (or should set) deliberately. Now let's consider conflicts that beset us without our help, whether we want them or not. These are the conflicts that come, so to speak, with the territory.

Cultural Differences

Excuse me, but here we go again into semantics. *Culture*, in popular usage, refers narrowly to the pastimes of the elite, such as opera and ballet. But we're going to use the word in its much broader, anthropological sense. For us, *culture* will include everything inside the heads of people that unites them as a group. *Culture* includes traditions, values, attitudes, shared memories, and just about everything else that binds a group together.

We feel comfortable with people whose culture we share. Why? Because they think like we do. They understand us, and we understand them. We can communicate with them, and that turns out to be one of life's greatest comforts.

The most important thing to be said about cultures is that there are a lot of them. There are a lot of ways to look at life and at how it should be lived. When you meet people from a different culture, you're likely to find that they don't think the same way that you do. What's even more disconcerting is that they don't always act in ways that you consider appropriate. And it may amaze you, or amuse you, to learn that they think you're rather peculiar yourself.

The second most important thing to be said about cultures is that you can't ignore them. Not if you want to be a manager in what's left of the twentieth century, and in what we can foresee of the twenty-first. One glaring reason for that is what economists call the "globalization" of business. Almost 30 percent of everything that is bought, sold, or bartered in the entire world already crosses borders, and that figure is constantly growing.°

As a manager, you can hardly avoid doing at least *some* business with people in other countries. If you want that business to be profitable, you'd better learn something about how they think. You may be dealing with people for whom *now* means "eventually," for whom *exactly* means "approximately," and for whom *certainly* means "maybe." You may be dealing with people for whom *yes* means, "I know that you want me to say 'yes,' so I'm nodding my head and smiling at you and saying 'yes' to you, solely to make you happy. Yes, yes, yes."

Above all, you had better learn that cultures have an ultra-tenacious grip on the people who participate in them. That means that you ignore cultural differences at your peril. You can't simply persuade, or even coerce, people into giving up their culture if they don't want to. The Soviets, for example, spent seventy years trying to get their citizens to give up religion, before they gave up the effort themselves.

Riding Honcho in Europe

Americans are in a particularly unfortunate position when it comes to dealing with other cultures. Our mass media and our educational system have created a "mainstream" culture that blankets an entire continent. North America is the only place on earth where you can travel for thousands of miles without having to change your cultural assumptions, or your language, even once. That's provided, of course, you stay within your own socioeconomic sector; for example, the world of airports, hotels, and offices, or conversely, the world of truck stops, motels, and warehouses. In that sense, there are really several American cultures. But within each of them, many Americans tend to be naive about other cultures, or other sectors of their own culture, and are unprepared for the enormous diversity in the rest of the world.

I had a memorable encounter with lack of preparedness for cultural diversity several years ago while I was in Europe on an assignment

---

°The International Monetary Fund gave the figure as 29.5 percent in 1989.

for an American multinational company. I was asked to attend a meeting of the general managers of each of the company's European subsidiaries. The meeting was addressed by an American executive who had been sent over to explain a controversial new policy change. He was a very accomplished man who had, until then, never been outside the United States. He strode confidently to the podium, loosened his necktie, and said, "OK, now, I'm going to ride honcho on this new policy over here. And believe me, as policies go, this one is a lulu. Like, no kidding, boys and girls, this one is for real!"

I was seated in the audience between a Swede and an Italian. The Swede, who understood colloquial American English fairly well, squirmed uncomfortably. The Italian turned to me with a mystified expression. I could only whisper, "I'll explain later."

I was embarrassed for my countryman. Implementing a radically new policy is hard enough, but he had made his job much harder by convincing his audience that he was a buffoon who need not be taken seriously. At one stroke, he had confirmed all of the worst prejudices that Europeans harbored about Americans: that we are brash, over-confident, and undereducated. It took several weeks of hard work to undo the damage, to persuade him to be more circumspect, and to persuade the Europeans to consider the policy separately from their feelings about its principal booster.

You don't need a passport to run into cultural differences. You can often do that by just driving across town, to where those "other" people live. Right here in America there are plenty of your fellow citizens who have little in common with you beside citizenship itself. But they have a great deal in common with each other, such as lifestyles, attitudes, and outlooks on life.

The more different those lifestyles, etc., are from yours, the more difficulty you're going to have in dealing with those "other" people, especially as employees. But if you're a manager, you're responsible for motivating everyone in the chain of command below you. That includes people whose culture may be very different than yours.

The most publicized cultural conflicts arise between different racial or ethnic groups. But there can also be conflicts between groups with different income and educational levels. I ran into that when I was still a young and relatively naive consultant (see the box on p. 244).

It would help to digress here for a moment about the sociology of the American labor force. The great socioeconomic sorting shed in American life is the college campus. Those who manage to spend four years of their young lives at one of these places are shepherded onto a high plane of affluence and privilege. Those who never get near a college campus, especially those who never graduate from high school, are shunted onto a lower plane.

Each group mingles almost entirely with people like themselves. So they really constitute separate cultures, in the sense that we are using that word here. The college graduates become the managers and the professionals, and the non-graduates become the skilled workers and the laborers. The lives of the two groups almost never intersect, except when their work requires it.

A HARD ACT TO FOLLOW: THE CASE OF THE "GRAY HATS"

An oil company had asked me to survey the opinions of its refinery workers, prior to bargaining on some measures designed to improve productivity. Several years before, the company had brought in engineering consultants who had worn distinctive gray safety helmets and were remembered by the workers as the "gray hats." Those consultants had recommended massive reductions in the workforce. That had led to a bruising strike from which the company ultimately had to back away.

This time the company took what both they and I considered a more sophisticated approach. The survey would reveal employee attitudes toward the kinds of changes that were contemplated. Mostly, these involved training the workers for more technically advanced, better-paid positions. Then, an extensive communications program would be developed to win them over gradually to the new plan. Only then would it be implemented.

Because the plan would actually benefit the workers, we felt that all we had to do was clarify it and clear up a few misunderstandings. Our intentions were pure and our methods were rational. How could we go wrong? Well, we found a way.

We decided to inform the union of our plans, but solely as a courtesy. We did not seek their cooperation, because we didn't have to. What we proposed to do was well within management's rights. Nothing in the contract prohibited the interviews and questionnaires that the survey would require. The union leadership, however, thought differently.

What we had at the oil refinery was a group of college graduates making what they thought were altruistic plans about a group of non-high school graduates, most of whom still nursed bitter memories about the last group of outsiders that had been foisted upon them. And the non-graduates, to phrase it as their leaders did, were not about to let those bastards in the front office pull another fancy trick on the union's hard-working membership.

We announced that our first step would be to interview a small sample of workers. On the day when we were to begin, a mimeographed flyer was handed to all workers as they entered the refinery gate. It read as follows (grammar and spelling are verbatim):

> The Company is putting on a program where hourly people, as well as salary people, will meet in a small group and air their complaints. These complaints might then be put in the form of questions and every one will be asked to answer them. The research group will then feed them into computers and the results would give the Company an idea where changes might be made.
> "THE UNIONS POSITION IS AS FOLLOWS"
> The Company is advised of problem areas almost on a daily basis. The Union also knows what the problems are. The Company could save themselves an unnecessary expense by simply sitting down with the Union, discussing those problem areas in an effort to resolve them. The Union feels that *no outsider can really solve our problem.*
> You, the members, must realize that if the Company wants to put this program into effect, they will. But, they cannot force you to take part in it. If you wish to take part in this program, the Union cannot stop you, so the decision is really yours to make.
> "YOUR EXECUTIVE BOARD DOES NOT RECOMMEND" this program, and has this bit of advice for you. If you decide to take part, just remember, what you say could hurt you later on. THE JOB YOU SAVE COULD BE YOUR OWN.
> If its true (and we're not saying that it is) and the company can make you attend the meeting, that is one thing, but they cannot force you to answer questions. Think before you do anything, your job could be at stake.
> "REMEMBER THE GRAY HATS THAT WERE HERE A FEW YEARS AGO"

The flyer had its intended effect. Many of the workers who were invited to interviews simply never showed up. Most of those who came sat tensely through our explanations. We handed out copies of a letter, signed by the refinery manager, guaranteeing that no participant would be harmed. We asked if they had any questions, and there were none. Then, to prove our sincerity, we announced that anyone who did not wish to stay for the interviews was free to leave. Virtually all of them rose silently from their seats and did exactly that. Our survey was effectively scuttled.

One could look at this case as simply a clumsily handled exercise in labor relations. But it was more than that. Obviously, we should not have circumvented the union leadership. However, they probably did not have the information we were seeking. We needed to know how workers felt about the skill requirements of their jobs and the extent to which their talents were being utilized. Those topics are not ordinarily discussed in the course of union business meetings.

The basic problem, however, was the mistrust and suspicion with which the workers regarded their management. That was aggravated by their experience with the "gray hats," but it had even deeper roots. The contrast between the rewards of the well educated and the less educated conveys a powerful message to both sides. To managers and professionals, the message is that we live in a meritocracy and we're doing this well because we deserve it. To skilled workers and laborers, the message is that those damned college graduates use their educations to deceive us and victimize us and as a result they take a lot more than they deserve.

In other words, the workers were predisposed to interpret the survey as another manipulative assault, even without the help of the "gray hats" and even without our inept handling of their union. They were predisposed because their culture was in conflict with ours. So they simply dug in their heels and refused to cooperate. They stopped us cold. The highly sophisticated survey never happened. We had completely underestimated the width of the cultural chasm that separated the workers from the professionals and the managers.

It might have been possible to win the union's cooperation if we had first spent a great deal of time discussing the problems that each side had with the other. However, when leaders get too far out in front of their followers, the leaders can suddenly find themselves out of a job. They can be accused of having been fooled, or even of having "sold out." So the power of shared ideas, or even of shared prejudice, is often enough to restrain leaders who may have begun to escape from those shared beliefs.

Cultures are that powerful.

Changing the Organization

Conflict is also thrust upon us when we decide to change the way in which a company, or any part of it, is organized. The issues here are what should be done, and by how many people, located where and reporting to whom. What is at stake is nothing less than influence on decisions and control over how the organization uses its resources. Or to condense all of that into one word, the issue is *power*.

Power is reshuffled whenever a company reorganizes. Careers hang in the balance. That is why the issue of what the next organization chart will look like is never regarded with cool, intellectual detachment. On the contrary, it arouses passions. Arguments are marshaled for and against all of the various alternatives under consideration. Not surprisingly, these tend to be self-serving.

Those who benefit from the status quo will defend it as tried and true. Why leap into the dark, they will ask, and risk the perils of the unknown, when we have here a proven system that has done the job for us time and again? They will prove conclusively that the deficiencies of the existing organization have been exaggerated, and are in any case due entirely to a few minor problems that will be cleared up by Friday afternoon at the latest.

Those who expect to gain from a change will attack the *status quo* as obsolete, inefficient, and out of touch with the times. They will prove, just as conclusively as their opponents, that huge benefits are within reach, or that horrendous dangers will be averted, if only we can break out of this antiquated monstrosity of an organization.

If the current organization is centralized, they will speak of its strangling bureaucracy and its unresponsiveness to the urgent needs of our troops in the field. If the current organization is decentralized, they will speak with the same conviction of duplication of effort, lack of coordination, and of the right hand not knowing what the left hand is doing.

It is precisely because the infighting over reorganization can be so divisive that companies tend to postpone the issue until the need for change is undeniable. It is also why management consultants are called in for presumably impartial opinions, which strengthen management's hand in dealing with whichever side eventually loses the struggle.

A RINGSIDE SEAT AT AN INTERNAL FIGHT

A few years ago, I had a ringside seat at just such a struggle when a multinational pharmaceutical company asked me to help sort out its organizational options. The company was already quite decentralized. The question posed to me was whether it should decentralize even further, or move in the opposite direction by pulling most decision making back into its headquarters.

I quickly realized that the president had sought my help primarily because he had a massive political problem on his hands. The organizational issues, while complex enough in their own right, were of secondary importance.

As I visited the corporate headquarters and the various regional and subsidiary headquarters, I heard the same arguments that the president had heard. Without exception, they were serious, carefully thought out, and well supported by facts and figures. But the executives at corporate headquarters argued for centralization, and the executives who were stationed overseas argued just as cogently for decentralization.

For example, an executive at headquarters said, "Why do we need to interpose a regional headquarters between us and the subsidiaries in each country? Especially now, when telecommunications are so good? We have fax, we have telex, we have everything. I can pick up the phone and talk to any general manager, anywhere in the world. The middleman in the regional headquarters simply gets in the way. Let's face it, the regions are redundant. Who needs them? We certainly don't."

But one of that executive's counterparts, who was stationed at a regional headquarters in Latin America, offered a very different opinion. He said, "You must never forget that we make our money in the subsidiaries. That is where we actually sell our products. Corporate headquarters sells nothing, and neither do we. So the key question is, who can best help the subsidiaries?

"To answer that question," he continued, "you must go to the subsidiaries, and look at them up close. And what do you see? Tremendous differences between one subsidiary and another. Argentina, for example, is not the same as Brazil, and Brazil is not the same as Colombia. And there are not only differences between countries. Things are so volatile in this part of the world that Argentina today is not the same as Argentina was yesterday."

Then he concluded his argument. "So how can you help these subsidiaries? First and foremost, you need in-depth experts who know each country. You can't run a worldwide business by sitting in New York City, trying to manage forty-eight Argentinas all over the world. That's why we need regions like this one, with experts who are close enough to the countries to really understand what is going on."

I began to realize that we would need some kind of standard against which to measure all of these arguments. Late one afternoon, listening to the president expound on the strategic problems facing the company, it dawned on me that an organization's structure had to support its strategy. In this case, the company needed to maximize its cash flow for several more years, until new products would be ready to replace those that were already in the field. So the test for any organizational argument was, how would it affect cash flow in the next few years?

Following that reasoning, the company scaled down both its headquarters and its regional operations. Headquarters became much less involved in detailed reviews of subsidiary operations. The regions were converted into resource centers to which the subsidiaries could turn for help, if they wanted it. Tight regional control over the subsidiaries simply ceased. Because there was less work to do in both headquarters and the regions, manpower reductions at both led to significant savings. The subsidiaries were given ambitious goals and left largely on their own to achieve them. Most of them rose to the occasion.

From a purely economic perspective, the reorganization was a success. But from a broader perspective, the results were mixed. Many people whose work was found to be redundant, or even unnecessary, had to leave the company. Some actually found better positions elsewhere, and so considered the reorganization a blessing in disguise. Others had to accept jobs that were less desirable than those they had left. To them, the reorganization was a disaster. As for my consulting project, all that can be said for it is that it gave the company an economic rationale for changing its structure, which protected top management from otherwise inevitable charges that it had made the change on the basis of favoritism and bias.

Inevitably, conflict bruises most of those whom it touches. That includes the managers who sometimes stir it up deliberately. Even so, it is better to face conflict head-on than to pretend that it doesn't exist.

What's the best way to deal with people *inside your own com-*

pany whose interests seem to collide with yours? Try reasoning first. Both sides may need to do some thinking about precisely what their interests really are. Perhaps that apparent "collision" isn't inevitable. Is each side really entrenched in all of its positions, or is there room for a deal to be struck? Can you find a way to live together? The conclusion that you can't should never be arrived at lightly.

If reasoning doesn't work, you have to escalate the conflict. At some point in the hierarchy above you, there's a common reporting point. That is, there's an executive who presides over both your department and the people with whom you have your quarrel. That's where the buck stops.

Get the quarrel onto that person's desk as quickly as possible. And prepare yourself to live with whatever decision is handed down, whether you like it or not. That's because if you can't live with an adverse decision, you really have to leave. There is a time to argue, and then there is a time to close ranks.

CHAPTER
16

THE GREAT FLAP
OVER ETHICS

Every ten years or so, the media seem to rediscover some basic facts of business life. For example, that the rat race doesn't bring out the best in everyone. That there are liars, cheats, and thieves among us. And that, in the daily scramble to make a buck, get ahead, or outwit the competition, some people don't play by the rules.

As facts go, those are not very attractive, but neither are they particularly new. Nevertheless, after uncovering some particularly horrendous scandals, the media will announce that an ethics crisis is upon us. What follows is predictable. The loss of old-fashioned virtue will be publicly lamented. Business schools will be blamed for having graduated class after class of amoral technocrats. Ethics professors, often a threatened species on college campuses, will find themselves suddenly in demand. New cottage industries will spring up and flourish for several years, helping companies to restore their moral tone with ethics seminars, or by publishing codes of ethics.

But media-generated crises are transient. After a while, readers

NOTE: This chapter is based in part on two articles by the author: "Why 'Good' Managers Make Bad Ethical Choices," *Harvard Business Review* 46, no. 4 (July–August 1986); and "Managing Ethics from the Top Down," *Sloan Management Review* 30, no. 2 (Winter 1989).

and television viewers tire of the same old stuff. Editors hunt for something new with which to galvanize public attention. The crisis fades. After a long enough interval, it will return and restart the cycle.

Meantime, the ethics *problem*—which is not a "crisis" at all, but a nasty, awkward, constant fact of business life—endures. It was here long before its latest rediscovery by the media, and it will be here long after the next one comes and goes. The unfortunate truth is that misconduct in business organizations is like the lowly cockroach. It is a plague that we can suppress, but never eliminate. We are concerned here with the practical question of how you can suppress it.

Fuzzy Thinking and Muddy Waters

If "ethics" is understood as an inquiry into how people *should* conduct themselves, it is a problem for philosophers. But if it is understood as an attempt to make an organization's people behave themselves as well as they can, it is a problem for managers. The practical question is how to minimize the amount of lying, cheating, and stealing that we have to put up with. All of that involves influencing behavior, so what we really have is a problem in motivation. That is how we will treat it here.

The most common approaches to business ethics are not very helpful, because they misdiagnose what is wrong. The problem is not that moral standards have fallen, or that ethics professors don't teach enough courses, or that all we need to do is get rid of a few bad apples, or that we can solve the ethics problem by simply spelling out, on paper, what you can and can't get away with. Nevertheless, these ideas are so common that we'll have to dispose of each of them before we can deal with business ethics as a problem in motivation.

How Good Were the "Good Old Days"?

Let's begin with moral standards. Would it really help if we could return, somehow, to "good old-fashioned morality"? After all, our sense of what is right and what is wrong is the cement that holds civilization together. It is what distinguishes us from savages.

No one in his right mind believes that we could even live together without some kind of morality.

The problem with a "return" to old-fashioned morality is that there is no convincing proof that we, or our forefathers, were ever really there. We have no reliable evidence that the moral level of society is actually lower now than it was in the past. No one has ever measured morality, so we have nothing but anecdotes with which to compare one era to another. But if you tried to compare then and now, you'd have no way to prove that your comparisons were realistic, or fair.

Suppose you went ahead and compared anecdotes anyway. Sure enough, you'd find that our generation has its Wall Street insider scandals. But you'd also find that our fathers and grandfathers had their Teapot Domes and their robber barons. Any good business history text will serve up scandals just as juicy as today's, if not juicier. You could even make a case that, overall, we're better behaved today than Grandpa's generation was, back in the good old days.

Of course, the counter-argument would be that we're still not good enough. That's certainly true. But the point is that no one can say for sure whether the *general* level of business morality has declined, or whether we've simply become more expert at detecting, and bewailing, a smaller number of lesser rascals. So next time you read that business ethics have fallen to an all-time low, take it with a grain of salt. The truth is that nobody knows.

Can Wisdom Make You Good?

What about turning to philosophers? Some of the greatest minds of all time have wrestled with defining the shoulds and should nots of this life. And some of today's best professional minds are devoted to the study of what those great ethicists have taught us. Could we not just dip into that deep reservoir of wisdom and find some principles that could be taught to managers? Yes, of course we could.

But would managers who were armed with that wisdom become more ethical themselves? And would they be better able to instill some ethical guidelines into the hearts and minds of the people who report to them? Perhaps. And then again, perhaps not.

There are two problems here. Ethics, as a specialized branch of philosophy, isn't for everyone. Many would find it too abstract, too lofty, and too dull. Managers, who often have to make decisions quickly, may find that philosophical ethics are too cumbersome and time-consuming to be useful.

But there's another problem. Managers who have done things that others found inexcusable were not, for the most part, amoral or unprincipled. They suffered, instead, from an all-too-common psychological quirk: they were out of touch with their own standards when they needed them most. It simply never occurred to them, when they were deciding what to do, that there was anything wrong, or even questionable, about what they were doing.

Ethics are seldom actually rejected or cast aside; most people are not that callous. But it is much too easy to overlook the ethics that we already know. Ethical problems are seldom obvious, especially when we aren't looking for them. And, let's face it, we seldom are. We have too many other things to worry about.

To make people *behave* more ethically, it would not help much to teach them what the great minds of history have thought about ethics. That would make them wiser, perhaps. But acquiring wisdom is not the same as behaving oneself. Wisdom is only useful if it is accessible at the very moment you need it. Otherwise it is just background knowledge to be stored away in the back of your brain. If you don't recognize that the problem under your nose is an example of what you studied in your philosophy class, you'll be oblivious to the ethical questions that it raises. Later, someone who reviews what you did may decide that you (yes, *you*—lovable, well-intentioned you) were unscrupulous.

Of course, that accusation would be unfair. You've probably got your share of scruples. But in this instance, they weren't handy when you needed them. Your conscience was simply unconscious. That's not just a play on words. It's a reasonably accurate description of a common psychological condition.

The human conscience usually works well enough when it's working at all. But typically, it only works part-time. Why? Simply because we have other things on our minds, like pleasing the boss or getting the job done. That's why, when there are ethical problems right under your nose, it may not dawn on you that you had better consult your conscience. But, alas! That's how most decisions are made that are later judged to be unscrupulous. And the fact that you may have made that decision blindly, mindlessly, even naively, doesn't change the judgment.

The Ethics Trap

You should face the fact that if you are a manager, there are people who are motivated to judge you. There are nosy reporters, crusading district attorneys, vengeful subordinates, and your own boss, to name a few. There really is an ethics trap out there that is all too easy to fall into, especially when you are preoccupied with getting your job done. So the question is, how can you give your job the attention it deserves and still steer clear of the trap?

Can we save you by making you study ethics? Probably not. You don't need more wisdom nearly as much as you need a practical way to connect the wisdom you already have to what you are doing. You need a warning signal that tells you in no uncertain terms that *this*, right in front of you, is an ethical problem, and you had jolly well better deal with it as such. If we could be sure that your conscience, and everyone else's, was on the job whenever it was needed, we could all sleep much better at night.

The best way to do that is to charge certain people with remaining constantly alert, on behalf of everyone else, for ethical problems. We need people whose job it is to point those problems out, and to make sure that people think them through. We need people whose pay, advancement, and even job security depend on how well that perpetual watchdog function is performed. What we need, in other words, are a few good managers. Not ethicists, not philosophers, but a few properly instructed managers. We'll have more to say about those proper instructions later.

Throwing Out the Dirty Rotten Scoundrels

And now, what about the "bad apple" theory? This is the idea that nearly everyone is good, and that when bad things are done they are nearly always the work of a few nefarious, good-for-nothing scoundrels. If that were true, all we would have to do is hunt them down and weed them out. We could just fire them and forget them. Then, because good people are always good, we could also forget about all of this ethics stuff.

But the truth is not nearly so simple. Yes, there are some people who will try to get away with whatever they can whenever they can. But there aren't really very many of them, and they account for only a small part of the ethics problem. Most of the time, the culprits are perfectly ordinary people who were exposed to more temptation, or more pressure, than they could handle. Or they found themselves amidst people who were taking bribes, or falsifying records, or dipping into the petty cash box, and they simply joined the crowd.

The bad apple theory has two big defects. First, it focuses on a relatively small part of the problem. Worse, it directs attention away from the larger part of the problem. It encourages managers to live in a fool's paradise. Our greatest exposure to inexcusable behavior does not come from petty crooks or even from big-time embezzlers but from ordinary people with clean records who have earned our trust—so far.

There aren't that many crooks or embezzlers in the first place, and they usually reveal themselves sooner or later. Petty crooks acquire police records, and big-time embezzlers become overconfident and push their luck too far. But the woods are full of straight, respectable people whose ethics have never been tested by temptation or by pressure. Many of them might not pass such a test if it was given under compromising conditions. It's all those ostensibly good apples that we have to worry about if we really want to suppress most of the misbehaving that goes on inside organizations.

Semantics Are Not the Answer

You can't make people ethical by simply telling them exactly what is ethical and what is not. You can't write ever-more-precise guidelines to fit every conceivable situation and then expect people to stay within those guidelines. We can't save ourselves by overdosing on semantics.

The rule-writing approach to promoting ethical behavior has two problems. One is practical, and the other is psychological. The practical problem is that any comprehensive list of dos and don'ts would soon fill several volumes. No one but a lawyer would read through all that verbiage, or give it the critical analysis it deserved. The lawyer, of course, is well paid to do that, but the rest of us have better uses for our time. So unless you want everyone with an ethical problem to consult a lawyer before making a decision, you can't count on rule-writing to keep your company out of ethical problems. It simply costs too much.

The psychological problem with writing lots of rules is that a written rule, no matter how fussily and precisely it is written, always invites a test of exactly how far it can be pushed before it is breached. It tempts people to seek the very edge of the permissible. Because they are under pressure to be as efficient as they can, they will seek to use every last advantage without quite stepping over the thin line into what is labeled as unethical.

The problem is that the line between what you can and can't get away with is never really thin. It is necessarily fuzzy, because rule writers can never guarantee that whoever judges your actions is going to interpret the rules the same way you did. So if you decide to find out how far a rule can be pushed before you overstep it, sooner or later you are going to overstep it. Like the wily embezzler who becomes too clever and is eventually caught, you will become too impressed with the flexibility of that rule, and eventually you will break it.

Codes of ethics should be written in loose, general terms. That way they can be kept brief, which makes them more likely to be read. Of course, general rules require interpretation. The best advice on how to interpret them is to be very conservative. If a question even arises as to whether something you might do would be unethical, the question itself guarantees that someone, somewhere, would consider it unethical if you did it. So the common-sense rule is, "When in doubt, don't."

That may seem like fainthearted advice. If everyone facing a risk simply covered their posterior, wouldn't that take the enterprise out of free enterprise? No, it wouldn't. Contrary to popular mythology, managers are not paid to take risks. They are paid to know which risks are worth taking.

One risk that is definitely not worth taking is the risk of ruining the rest of your career. That's why, if someone asks you whether some loosely phrased rule applies to his specific situation, the best answer you could give would be to ask another question: "Why should you be the test case?" And your best answer to a dare-devil subordinate's question of "How far is too far?" would be, "Don't try to find out."

Why Good People Do Bad Things

When ordinarily well-behaved people behave unethically, they have usually talked themselves into a serene belief that they are doing nothing wrong. They have fallen for their own rationalizations. (That's another two-dollar word. A rationalization is a handy excuse. We use it to persuade ourselves that a rule, which we know perfectly well, does not apply to our particular case.)

Rationalizations are, of course, self-deceptions, and they are usually deliberate. The reason we fall for a thin excuse is that we are looking for one. Our real intention is to do something that we know is questionable. So we look for an easy way to disconnect our conscience temporarily, much as we might turn off a hearing aid in order to avoid hearing what we don't want to hear.

The most common rationalizations are that a rule doesn't "really" apply in this instance, or that you are "expected" to do something "slightly" unethical because it will help the company, or that it is "safe" because no one will ever know what you did. Any of these excuses can be quite convincing to someone with a strong incentive to break the rules.

The Real Ethical Dilemma

How can you tell if a rule "really" applies to what you are doing? How can you avoid crossing a line that is almost never defined precisely? The only safe answer is not even to move in the direction of the line. Here is where the *real* ethical dilemma begins to emerge, however. Because if you constantly played it safe, and never tested the limits of what you could and couldn't get away with, you'd risk being considered inefficient, or even gutless, by your superiors.

Your superiors will hardly ever ask you directly to do something that both you and they know is wrong. But they can also communicate with you obliquely, should that suit their purposes. They could leave you to draw your own conclusions about what they are careful not to say. They could give you the impression that they are very interested in obtaining certain results and that they will not be very interested in exactly how you manage to achieve them. They could manage to let you know that there are certain things that they don't want to know.

In other words, your desire to please your superiors could be turned against you. If you are foolish enough to let that happen, you could suddenly find yourself in the market for a nice, convenient rationalization.

But beware. This game can turn nasty. If you are ever accused of crossing the fuzzy line between right and wrong, those same superiors who keep pressing you to do more, or to do it better, faster, or less expensively, may turn on you. They may blame you for exceeding their instructions, or for ignoring their warnings. So the best way to determine whether a rule "really" applies to what you are doing is to let your boss decide.

When what you might or might not do is questionable, let the burden of decision rest on someone who is paid to make the tough decisions. Make your boss earn his pay. To understand how that simple step protects not only you but also your boss and the entire organization, you have only to put yourself into your boss's place. That would happen if, for example, one of your subordinates came to you and said, "Boss, I'm just not sure it would *really* violate our conflict-of-interest rules if one of our vendors took me to lunch. Wouldn't that be all right?"

If you agreed, you'd have given your blessings to at least the appearance of bribery. Even if you had your own reasons for wanting to cultivate that vendor, you'd be smart enough to tell your subordinate to pay for his own lunch. You can't openly condone what policy prohibits. Neither can your boss. That's why bringing the question into the open keeps both of you honest. Leaving it in the realm of hints and winks and innuendo tempts one of you to break the rules, to the silent applause of the other.

Taking Small Risks Too Often

The belief that unethical acts can serve a company's best interests nearly always results from a parochial idea of what those interests are. The company's overriding priority is not to maximize every quarterly profit, but to survive. Credible threats to survival have to take precedence over short-term gains. Companies that did not take those threats seriously have been forced into bankruptcy, or cut down to mere fractions of their former size, by government regulators.

For example, consider Alpha Industries, a manufacturer of microwave equipment in New England. A few years ago, Alpha paid a substantial sum to a manager at Raytheon, ostensibly for providing Alpha with marketing advice. But at the time, Alpha was seeking an Air Force subcontract from Raytheon. Air Force investigators charged Alpha with bribery. Alpha was indicted, its contracts were suspended, and its profits promptly vanished. During the same year, the Pentagon suspended 453 other companies for similar contract violations.

Why did so many managers put their companies in such jeopardy? Probably because they miscalculated their chances of being caught. Conscience alone does not deter everyone. For example, First National Bank of Boston pleaded guilty to laundering satchels of $20 bills worth $1.3 billion. That takes a lot of satchels. I once had to carry $15,000 worth of $20 bills in my attaché case, and I could barely cram them all in.*

Literally thousands of satchels must have passed through the bank's doors before the scheme was detected. That kind of heavy, unnoticed traffic breeds complacency. You become convinced that your game is perfectly concealed and that your risk is negligible. Sooner or later you become careless, and your own carelessness trips you up. Small risks that are taken too often eventually become big risks. You may be tempted to say, "All right, then just how often is too often?" But you already know the answer. "Don't try to find out."

---

*Lest you think I was laundering ill-gotten gains, here is the story of my own "suitcase full of money." I had presented some seminars in a country where corruption was rampant, so I insisted on cash payment in U.S. dollars. That's why my attaché case was stuffed. When I arrived in the U.S., I declared the amount to the customs agent, who automatically alerted the IRS to watch for the income on my next tax return. I scrupulously obey American tax laws. Whether that is ethical or merely prudent, I leave to you. On the other hand, I am not so scrupulous about the laws of corrupt dictatorships. My client probably obtained that pile of twenties on the black market.

Managing Misbehavior

You can't hope to wipe out skullduggery altogether, but you can cut it down to manageable size. To keep most people on their best behavior most of the time, you need a two-pronged approach. First, you try to eliminate the conditions under which unethical acts are likely to occur. That helps the honest majority to stay honest. Second, you try to deter those who are exposed to those conditions anyway. That persuades all but the most desperate, daring, or stupid of the dishonest minority to keep their hands out of the cash register.

Three conditions can put the ethics of otherwise honorable people to a severe test. It's a lot easier to eliminate these conditions, or at least minimize them, than to try to figure out who will pass the test and who will flunk. The conditions most likely to strain your ethics are: unusually high rewards for good performance, unusually severe punishments for poor performance, and implied approval of what is formally forbidden.

Unusually High Rewards

How high is an "unusually high" reward? You probably wouldn't risk the loss of your reputation, or your prospects for advancement, merely to influence your next salary increase. It would depend, of course, on the probability that you might be caught, on how harmless you considered the act required to earn the raise, and on exactly how nice that raise was. But in general, you would not sell your soul to the devil for a price that the devil would consider a bargain.

But suppose the devil raises his bid? Suppose he reasons that every man has his price, and every woman has her price, so that getting you to compromise your ethics becomes a mere exercise in negotiation? Suppose you could acquire so much money that it could earn more, even if you invested it conservatively, than the highest salary you could hope to command? Suppose your ill-gotten money could earn more passively than you could earn actively, and honestly? (That's my definition of being rich.) Suppose you could become *that* rich by merely bending some of your fundamental principles a little bit?

Suppose, in other words, that we put you to a terrible test. Principled as you may be, clean as your record may be, prudent and cautious as you may be, would you pass? And if you did pass, would it be your principles that led you away from temptation? Or would it be a nagging concern that such a bonanza could not be concealed, and would arouse suspicions? We don't know, and could not know unless you were actually put to that test. But it is wiser never to know the answer, by deliberately keeping you from that kind of temptation. Precisely because you don't know if you are corruptible, you will be wary of corruption.

The most recent of our many "ethics crises" was launched by the great binge of corporate acquisitions during the 1980s. Many an investment banker was put to a severe ethical test, not unlike the one I've just described. Some found themselves pushed far beyond the limits of their scruples. Huge sums danced and dangled before their eyes, and could be had by merely betraying a few rules of the game. Some succumbed, and at least some of those were caught. It is easy to sneer at those who were exposed, and to dismiss them as moral midgets. But would you or I have behaved differently in the face of enormous temptation? We don't know, and it is better that we never find out.

That is why it is wise not to put extreme temptation in the path of even the most honorable people. Huge bonuses and commissions can distort one's values, in much the same way that too much power can corrupt one's standards of decency. You can motivate people without corrupting them, simply by keeping their rewards within the bounds of reason. It is sufficient to help people earn more money faster than before. You don't have to make them rich beyond the dreams of avarice overnight.

Unusually Severe Punishments

Unusually severe punishments have the same distorting effect on one's values as unusually high rewards. If people are desperate to avoid what they regard as a calamity, they will go to whatever lengths they must to avoid it. That can include a little lying, cheating, and stealing, if need be. One's conscience will be anesthetized by terror, so the dirty business can be done. For most people, the calamity to be avoided at all costs, and therefore their greatest vulnerability to being corrupted, is the loss of their job.

Your job is almost certainly your most valuable asset. It is probably worth more than all of your other assets put together. To calculate what your job is worth, you only need to determine the sum that would have to be invested at current interest rates to yield your pre-tax salary, plus the cost of purchasing your employee benefits at non-group rates. Even for people with modest incomes, that sum is enormous. (When interest rates are low, as in a depression, that sum is stupendous.)

Now, suppose you were confronted with the possibility of losing all of that. Let's also suppose that you couldn't readily replace it, because the economy has slowed down. And let's add the realistic assumption that some very special people are absolutely dependent on you, and that you've got debts to pay and a fairly expensive lifestyle to support. What would you be willing to do to avoid that catastrophic loss?

Perhaps your moral standards are as rugged as an oak. Perhaps you can stare bankruptcy in the face and say, with Shakespeare, that he "who steals my purse steals trash . . . but he that filches from me my good name, robs me of that which not enriches him, and makes me poor indeed." Stirring words, those, and a very profound thought. But under that kind of stress, with kids to feed and a mortgage to pay, would you say them? Or would you find yourself echoing Alfred P. Doolittle, the cockney dustman in Shaw's *Pygmalion:* "Middle class morality! I can't *afford* it, Guv'nor!"

Again, we don't really know the answer, do we? And it is best that we never have to find out. That is why threats that one's job is at stake, or even hints of threats, should never be used to "motivate" people. You might just motivate them to do something inexcusable, something that would make your company's reputation look just ghastly, if what they did ever came to light.

Implied Approval of the Forbidden

Finally, ordinarily good people can be induced to do bad things if they find themselves in circumstances in which the distinction between right and wrong is blurred. This is where the example set by one's superiors becomes important. You can elicit illicit behavior simply by misbehaving yourself, or by overlooking other people's misbehavior, or by condoning it. Your subordinates will draw the logical conclusion that whatever you do, or agree to, must also be sanctioned by your own superiors, or else done with their connivance. What can be wrong, then, with doing something that "the company" seems to tolerate, even if it might seem a little bit questionable to an outsider?

This kind of reasoning can lead whole departments to falsify their time cards, or to inflate their expense accounts, or to augment their home workshops and offices with the company's tools and supplies. It can lead to certifying defective work as having passed inspection and attesting to inspections that never took place. It can lead to innocent people being killed by products that never should have left the factory.

This is a more difficult problem to deal with than excessive rewards and excessive punishments. With those two forms of ethical entrapment, the action needed to avoid them is clear-cut. But with implied tolerance of questionable practices, the required action is mostly a matter of self-discipline, and of constant watchfulness over your own attitudes. The most important point is to be sure that you are not being seduced by conformity.

If your conscience doesn't care for what everyone else is doing, you should not assume that your conscience must be naive. It's the only conscience you've got, and if you let it be tucked in and put to sleep you will have become, for all practical purposes, unprincipled. And your only excuse for doing what you know you shouldn't do would be that everyone else was doing it too.

Without principles, without standards, we sink too easily to the lowest common denominator. And that can be pretty low. Much lower than you would want to sink. So keep your conscience wide awake. Consult it at least as often as you check your wristwatch. Without a wide-awake conscience, you become the contemporary moral equivalent of the death camp guards who pleaded, after World War II, that they had only obeyed orders and done what everyone else was doing.

Putting It All Together

Now, let's summarize where we have been until now. To keep an organization ethical, you must first minimize the exposure of its people to the three circumstances that can lure them into being unethical. The first two of these are excessive rewards and excessive punishments, both of which are motivationally unnecessary and ethically compromising. The third is the absence of conspicuous disapproval of unethical acts, or worse still, the example set by managers who engage in such acts themselves.

Several tricks have been proposed for enabling you to keep your conscience on the job. Any of them will work if they are used, but only you can see to it that they are actually put to work. All of them involve imagining what it would be like if the action you are contemplating were to be exposed.

Lee Iacocca, for example, proposed this test: "Would you want your mother to switch on the six o'clock news tonight, and hear on nationwide television about what you had done?" Another test is, "Would the boy or girl you once were be proud of what the man or woman you have become is about to do?" The fact that your mother does not actually hear about you on the six o'clock news does not make your action any more justifiable than if she heard. As for what that boy, or that girl, knows about you: don't kid yourself. He *knows*, and so does she.

Deterring the Dastardly

Our first line of defense against unethical conduct is each individual's conscience. We have to do everything we can to keep it awake. The second line of defense is to eliminate or minimize the circumstances that can overwhelm a conscience, or deceive it, or put it to sleep. Now we come to our last line of defense, which is to put in place deterrents that will stop those who are not restrained by conscience from doing what we don't want anyone to do; or at least to make them stop and reconsider.

There are three things you can do to make sure that very few reasonable people, regardless of temptation, would risk an unethical act. First, you can draw a clean line between the behavior you'll tolerate and the behavior you'll have to punish. Those distinctions are a necessary first step, but by themselves they are not enough. Nevertheless, that first step is about as far as most organizations care to go.

The second step is to invest time and money in making sure that those distinctions are understood and remembered. The third step, by far the most drastic and controversial, is to put the fear of God into would-be violators by conspicuously raising the risk of exposure. Relatively few organizations have gone so far as to take that third step. But then, relatively few have taken the second step, either.

The clear line is usually drawn with a published code of ethics. These are becoming so common that it's hard to find a large or even medium-sized company that doesn't have one. Codes of ethics have some important advantages—they can clarify issues that may have been murky, and they can go on record with principles that might only have been vague and implicit in the past. A good code of ethics spells out the rules by which everyone in an organization is expected to play. All that is useful and good.

But what if a code of ethics is published with great fanfare, distributed to everyone, and afterward mentioned only occasionally, if at all? It will be filed and forgotten. It will offer about as much protection as a disconnected burglar alarm. A code of ethics is only as useful as your efforts to keep it in the forefront of everyone's attention. Alas, in too many organizations, that effort ceases when the booklets have been distributed. Absent that continuing effort, codes of ethics can be little more than public relations gimmicks. They can also be used by companies to disown employees who overstep that line, especially as the passage of time obscures it.

Ask most companies what they are doing to stay ethical and they'll present you with a copy of their ethics booklet. The code itself is always admirable and often eloquent. But if it is not enforced, you have to suspect that it is intended to impress critics more than employees. If the company is ever accused of conniving, it can wrap itself proudly in its code of ethics, call a press conference, and say, "See for yourselves how pure we are."

Suppose some poor fool has broken the rules and is caught. He may have been driven by overly ambitious performance goals, or pressured by superiors who demanded results at any cost. The code of ethics he has violated may have sat quietly on his bookshelf, gathering dust and unmentioned by any of his superiors, for years. But because the code had been given to him, he can now be safely abandoned. His superiors can say, "You had the code, and you broke it. So it's all your fault and not ours. We warned you. Good-bye."

The point is that codes of ethics can be used for dastardly purposes, *if* they are not continually emphasized. And that takes both time and money.

Most organizations are much more willing to spend money than to allocate time for a new project. The reason is simple. A bank can lend you money, but no one can give you more time. Forty hours a week is what you usually get. The more you demand beyond that, the more people will object that you're imposing on *their* time. And because of Parkinson's Law ("Work expands to fill the available time"), those forty hours are already filled to the brim with whatever they are already doing.

Ask for one or two of those hours, every few months or even once a year, and you'll be told that everyone's time is already overfilled. "What we don't need," you'll be told, "is one more bureaucratic demand on time that we don't have to spare. Besides, we've already heard about that ethics stuff, so we don't need to hear anymore."

But we tend to forget about what we don't hear about. What's more, we draw conclusions about what we don't hear about. If something isn't important enough for your boss to repeat, you probably won't consider it important enough to remember. If your boss continually tells you to get your work done, but seldom if ever adds that you should get it done ethically, the boss's priorities will seem clear enough. And it's your boss's priorities, not the brave words in the company's code of ethics, that will probably command your attention.

Ethics codes need to be reviewed with everyone periodically, and preferably in the most *in*efficient way—in small discussion groups, in detail, and at least quarterly. The booklet on the bookshelf can't do the job alone. Ethics, like any finely tuned machine, need preventive maintenance every so often.

Whistle-Blowers and Tattlers

The fate of so-called whistle-blowers has been well publicized. These are the people who call attention to the real or imagined misdeeds of their colleagues, or even of their superiors. They usually find themselves treated as traitors, ostracized, and subtly induced to leave. Are they unsung heroes or grudge-holding fault-finders?

Probably a bit of both. To accuse someone publicly of wrong-doing breaks whatever trust may previously have existed between you, and makes any future relationship tenuous at best. The fear of strained relationships, or of retaliation, is enough to deter many people who know, or think they know, that someone else is up to no good. So whistle-blowing takes guts. Or desperation. Or being just plain mistaken about the facts.

There's the rub. It's impossible to generalize about what motivates whistle-blowers. Some of them are heroic, but others are merely self-righteous.

However, one generalization about whistle-blowers is not only possible, but essential. We need them, because they keep the rest of us honest. So it is in the best interests of organizations to protect its whistle-blowers. The mechanisms for doing that belong in a legal textbook, not a book on motivation. Whistle-blowers serve as a kind of auxiliary conscience for the rest of us, and like our own consciences, they achieve their purposes primarily by making us uncomfortable.

Two Consciences Are Better Than One

When you select people for positions in which their ethics are likely to be tested, that very fact demonstrates your confidence in them. But don't be overconfident. Be prudent and hedge your bets. You can reinforce both your confidence and their ethics by acknowledging that you're leading them into temptation, and that you're well aware of it.

To help them live up to their own standards, let them know that you're going to keep a friendly eye on them. You're going to drop in from time to time, unannounced, to take a look at what's going on. You'll make it clear that this does not imply distrust in *them*. Emphasize that you would not have entrusted them with this tricky assignment in the first place if you had any serious questions about their integrity. Rather, what you don't trust is the situation itself. That's why you feel obliged to help them deal with it honorably.

If people are in a position to be bribed, or to help themselves to other people's property, or to surreptitiously break a rule that you don't want broken, you owe it to them to be watchful, and to let them know you're watching. Two consciences can be better than one. Your watchfulness reduces any temptation they might feel and reinforces their ethics with a strong dose of reality. That gives them two powerful reasons to behave themselves.

First, it feels good to have done the right thing when the wrong thing beckoned. It's nice to *deserve* to feel righteous. (Not many people can, because not many people's righteousness is ever tested.) Second, it hurts to be caught doing something wrong.

By far the most painful way to hurt ordinarily honorable people is not to fire them, or even to jail them, but to expose their misdeeds. For someone who has any pride at all, humiliation is the most awful punishment, because it strips away that pride. Shakespeare was right. Take away someone's reputation, and you make him poor indeed.

Helping Honest People Stay Honest

To make sure that ethical people remain ethical in the face of temptation, you raise the risk of exposure. Your purpose is not to catch more crooks, but to dissuade honest people from becoming crooks. That's why you want to be quite candid about the existence of procedures that are designed to expose unethical conduct. You would not be so naive as to reveal exactly when, where, and how those procedures will operate. But you'll make no secret of the fact that you have confidence in your methods, and that anyone foolish enough to test them will be sorry.

Whenever a specialist in motivation recommends a "negative" approach like this one, it raises eyebrows. After the last few paragraphs, your eyebrows may be raised too. You may ask, "Is this the same author who told us, only a few chapters ago, that threats can be counterproductive?" Yes, it is.

There's an important difference between threatening people who don't achieve performance goals and threatening people who try to achieve their goals by breaking the rules. The first threat pressures people to forget their ethics. The second one pressures them to remember. Sometimes the ends justify the means, and this is one of those times.

That's why you want it to be known that you have ways of uncovering people who forget their ethics. And if your checking turns up no evidence of wrongdoing, don't conclude that you've been an incompetent sleuth. It's much more likely that you've been a competent motivator. You will have helped honest people to stay honest. In this bad world, that's no small achievement.

Instructions for Ethical Watchdogs

Finally, what about those "proper instructions" to managers who serve as ethical watchdogs, making sure that no one overlooks the ethical implications of their work? They are fairly simple, and they would read something like this:

1. You are responsible for making sure that everyone under your supervision not only becomes familiar with our code of ethics, but that they remain familiar with it, permanently. If they forget the code, or misinterpret it, or fail to realize that it applies to what they are doing, it's *your* fault. You will be held accountable. This should motivate you to make sure that none of that happens.

2. In the normal course of working with your subordinates, find time to ask them if there's an ethical aspect to whatever they're doing at the moment. Your purpose is to sensitize them to how often ethical issues are encountered, and with how easy it is to overlook them. When no immediate ethical implications can be found, choose one of the principles in the code, and ask your subordinate to discuss how it could apply to him or her. That serves the same purpose. Do this at least weekly. Your conversations on ethics will seldom require more than a few minutes.

3. Whenever your people are under heavy work pressure, or have been told that their performance must improve, or are exposed to people who may wish to "buy" their cooperation, be especially inquisitive as to exactly how they are carrying out their duties. Be conspicuously inquisitive. You're not an undercover investigator. You're an above-board manager who is charged with *preventing* dishonesty.

4. Your own example is all-important. Your integrity must be unquestioned. If a pattern of unethical conduct persists among your subordinates, that raises the question of whether they are simply following your example. It is your job to make sure that does not happen.

PART IV

MOTIVATION IN
THE REAL
WORLD

CHAPTER
—— 17 ——
MOTIVATION SYSTEMS

A "motivation system" contains all of the behavior-shaping influences that affect an organization, both past and present. It includes methods that are currently in force that were consciously designed to motivate, like salaries. But it also includes the lingering effects of former motivators. Sometimes these motivational "ghosts" can be stronger than all of the current motivators. A frequently seen example would be memories of how a company treated its employees in the good old days (or bad old days, as the case may be). The past can work for you or against you, but it's always there, and you ignore it at your peril.

For example, consider once again the "Case of the Gray Hats" in chapter 15. Management was frustrated by the fact that the union representatives were unable to anticipate whether the rank and file would approve or reject a contract offer. Thus, each proposed settlement was really a leap in the dark, and it was hard to say whether the contract details were too generous or not generous enough.

My proposed "solution" was to try to talk with a cross-section of the union members, in hopes of discerning the reasons underlying their preferences about the issues on the bargaining table. Management was willing to try it, and even persuaded the union leadership to go along with the idea. But I was stopped cold by a group of activists within the union, who spread the word that I was probably a "management spy."

Actually, I would have been both a management *and* a union "spy," since I had insisted that the results of my interviews be shared equally between management and the union. But having that label pinned on me was enough to discourage most of the union members from meeting with me. In that case, we were unable to overcome the lingering effects of the past. But the lesson is that the past is always there, and must always be taken into account.

The Context of American Motivation

The effectiveness of a company's motivation system depends on how well it fits its context. In our case, that context is the structure of American society and the dynamics that animate it. A motivation system that can tap into those dynamics, and channel them, can become enormously effective. A system that ignores those dynamics, or tries to suppress them, will not do much motivating in the land of the free and the home of the brave.

That is why a brief glance at American society and the "American dream" is in order here. Compared to other countries, and with respect to the distribution of wealth and power, the United States has the most fluid society in the world. People are constantly moving up, down, or sideways. Getting ahead is the national sport, falling behind motivates strenuous attempts to recoup what was lost, and getting nowhere is, for those who suffer that fate, a dirty little secret.

The concept underlying the American "way of life" is that your fate is in your own hands, that there are no artificial barriers placed in your way, and that you are free to become whatever you have the wit, endurance, and luck to become. Granted, there are some Americans, especially among minorities, for whom that concept is not a reality. But by and large, the American culture creates huge advantages for those who want their lives to be defined by their accomplishments rather than by the circumstances of their birth. That is why so many Americans who were born into the lower middle class find themselves today in the upper middle class, or even the upper class.

That massive upward movement is what America is all about. It is the net result of millions of individual triumphs and tragedies. It is both a cause and a result of the huge postwar expansion of the American economy. It has made us the envy of the world. And it has created opportunities that the shrewdest American companies have cleverly exploited. All those highly motivated, upwardly aspiring people needed a vehicle to lift them to the wealth and power to which they aspired. And the companies needed highly motivated people to power their drive to corporate growth. It was a perfect match.

There are, of course, many Americans for whom "getting ahead" is not an attractive alternative. Some dismiss it as the "rat race." Others are content as long as they don't fall behind. They illustrate the fact that there is really more than one American dream, and that the ideal of finding wealth, power, and fulfillment through one's work is only one of many such "dreams."

Nevertheless, I would argue that bettering one's station in life, both in terms of improving on your origins and outdistancing at least some of your contemporaries, is the predominant American dream. It probably affects more people than any other vision of what is possible and desirable in contemporary American life. More important, since the end of the Great Depression and World War II, it has fueled the greatest economic expansion in the history of the world.

The Best Motivation Systems

My observations of motivation systems in American companies have led me to believe that the most effective ones owe most of their success to six policies, all of which respond in some way to key elements in the "American dream." They are: (1) selectivity in hiring, (2) generous pay and benefit programs, (3) encouragement of long-term employment, (4) flexible implementation of policies, rather than rigid rules, (5) cooperative unions, or no unions at all, and (6) a conscious policy of putting employee motivation above all other priorities. It is interesting to note that some of these policies, especially numbers 3 and 4, are similar to features in Japanese motivation systems that have been noted by other observers such as William Ouchi.°

A word about policies. In large organizations, policies have much more of an effect on motivation than individual managers can have. Policies determine what managers are encouraged to do and what they are discouraged from doing. They even determine who gets to be a manager in the first place. That is why it is hard to overstate the importance of policies. Some day, you may get up to the level where policies can be set, or changed. If you do, that will present you with your best chance to make major, long-lasting improvements to the motivation system of your company. Until then, your job is to implement the existing system as intelligently as you can. Meantime, you can evaluate that system by comparing it to the six policies that characterize companies that achieve consistently high motivation among their employees.

Selective Hiring

The companies that do the best jobs of motivating are not interested in trying to motivate just anyone. They are quite fussy about whom they hire, and they are primarily interested in attracting those who are easiest to motivate. So they try to make themselves interesting to people who have already begun to climb.

The best way to do that is to play hard to get. You screen people so extensively, and you hire so selectively, that being hired by a company as selective as yours becomes a distinction in itself. In effect, it confers membership in an elite club. And that membership helps to generate tribal thinking of the "one for all and all for one" variety. "Members" are proud to be associated with superior people.

But is that consistent with the "American dream"? Is not the American culture supposed to stress equality, with liberty and justice for all?

Don't kid yourself. If you have equality of opportunity, which *is* the American dream, you can't have equality of results, which definitely is not the American dream. It is precisely to foster in-

°William Ouchi, *Theory Z: How American Business Can Meet the Japanese Challenge* (Reading, MA: Addison Wesley, 1981).

equality of results, for both their employees and themselves, that the smartest American companies are so choosy about whom they hire. They want the brightest and the best, and they especially want more than their share of those who are easiest to motivate.

Generous Pay

The primary reason why the smartest companies pay salaries that are well above the market is to be able to attract and hold people who can get more work done, and do it better, than ordinary people can. In that sense, higher salaries can actually be more economical than lower salaries, because the kind of people whom higher salaries attract can get more work done per payroll dollar.

High pay also gives these companies an abundance of job applicants, which permits them to skim the cream of the labor market. It also contributes to an elite "image" for the company, which pulls in lots of people who will want to work their way up the company hierarchy. High pay is also a sound defensive measure, because it increases the premium that other companies have to pay if they want to lure your employees away.

There are also secondary advantages to high pay. It makes your employees less likely to become interested in unions, and for that matter it makes unions less interested in your company. After all, union organizers have to stay within their budgets, just as corporate managers do. Smart organizers target companies that seem to present the greatest vulnerability to being organized. Most unions have better uses for their time and money than trying to organize companies with high pay scales.

Long-Term Employment

In American firms, long-term employment is usually based on three implicit understandings:

The *first* is that the company will not fire you merely because there is no work to do. If your job must be eliminated, the company will retrain you for another job. You can only get fired for gross violations of written policies. Getting your boss mad at you is not, in itself, a firing offense.

Second, your part of the implicit "bargain" with the company is honest, unremitting effort. While the company would not fire you for redundancy, it will certainly fire you for shirking.

The *third* implicit understanding is that you are encouraged to plan on having your entire career with the company. The company's internal communications media constantly remind employees of their benefits, their prospects for interesting assignments at various stages of their working lives, and eventually for a comfortable retirement.

In recent years, many firms (notably on Wall Street and in Detroit) have not kept their part of the implicit bargain. Thousands of people who had signed on, so to speak, for the duration of their careers suddenly found themselves out on the street, abandoned to the vagaries of the labor market. The motivational effect on those who were *not* let go is usually devastating.

There are two common reactions. Some become fearful and slow down their work, as if that could somehow prolong it. Others become cynical, polish up their résumés, and begin a quiet, patient, persistent job search. Most of those will eventually leave.

Nevertheless, long-term employment policies by themselves are no guarantee of high productivity. The civil service, for example, cannot point to extraordinary levels of productivity. Nor do these policies necessarily deter employees from leaving, especially to become bigger managerial fish in smaller corporate ponds.

Still, long-term employment policies have three important motivational effects. They eliminate any tendency to do less work, especially during recessions, for fear of working oneself out of a job. They increase willingness to do more than is ordinarily required, because the company does not thereby gain unfairly at the employee's expense. And they contribute to a company's elitist image, the effects of which we have already noted.

Flexible Controls

Some American companies are run as much by their policy manuals as by their managers. The intent of a manual is to ensure that managers behave consistently. Manuals seldom actually tell a manager precisely what to do; rather, they list which factors to consider in a decision. In some companies, however, the manual becomes, in effect, a substitute for managerial thought rather than a guide for it. This is usually because of fear that exercising too much discretion will expose the manager to criticism, or even worse.

Thus policy manuals pose a dilemma. On the one hand, consistency really is important. One thoughtless, impulsive supervisor, or one discourteous salesperson, or one purchasing agent who accepts favors from vendors, can undermine years of effort to build positive relations with employees, customers, or suppliers. The problem is to somehow attain enough uniformity without ignoring extenuating circumstances. That kind of fine balance is always difficult to achieve.

But the answer does not lie in adding more pages to the policy manual, because the problem is seldom in the phrasing of the rules or guidelines. Rather, it is a question of trust. The underlying problem is not how to read the policy manual but how to read your boss's mind.

If managers fear that their superiors might criticize decisions that tried to take circumstances into account, they will protect themselves by ignoring those circumstances and sticking rigidly to the rules. Thus, even when in theory the policy manual was only intended to guide, in practice it can turn into iron-fisted control.

In American companies that do the best job of motivating, policy manuals tend to be brief and sparely written. They concentrate on general principles, rather than on detailed lists of dos and don'ts. Managers are taught to be less concerned with uniformity than with responding appropriately to each problem as it arises. There are some "thou shalt nots," of course: for example, about revealing confidential information. But in general, these manuals are less concerned with spelling out what to do than with defining which goal to pursue. The choice of method is left to the manager.

A deliberate lack of spelled-out, confining rules and the consequent reliance on managers' judgment are a concrete expression of trust. Of course, every so often someone abuses that trust. That is the price of having adaptive, flexible, imaginative managers. It isn't nearly as steep as the price of management that blindly follows the rules even when it encounters circumstances for which the rules were never intended.

Some managers are terrified by the lack of clear-cut guidance for every decision. Their primary motive is fear of having to answer for their own decisions. Faced with loosely written policies, they "delegate upward" by constantly asking their superiors what to do. If that problem cannot be corrected quickly, through coaching or training, it probably cannot be corrected at all. The best solution is to replace these managers as quickly as possible with someone who is willing not only to make decisions but to live with them and learn from their consequences.

Cooperative Unions, or No Unions

Companies that do a good job of motivating tend to have no unions, or unions that avoid confrontational tactics. This is no coincidence. Keeping unions out, containing them, or even decertifying them is often an explicit assignment given to personnel departments in such companies.

Unions are controversial. Most managers despise them. On the other hand, unions would not exist if many workers did not consider them necessary. Few people, unless they have had very sheltered lives, are completely unbiased toward unions. So before I pursue the topic any further, let me state my own biases. That will help you to weigh the arguments I am about to present.

I can state my attitude toward unions in three short sentences. First, I would not want to live in a country that had no unions, because I believe that unions help to keep managers honest. Second, I would prefer not to be a manager in a unionized company, because I know that having to deal with unions can be very frustrating. Third, I believe (contrary to what most union organizers and labor relations managers believe) that most working people are not easily duped and know perfectly well whether they need a union to protect them against their management. From that last statement flows a corollary. I believe that any company that becomes unionized in this day and age probably deserves it.

Back to those personnel departments that are charged with keeping unions out. They usually stress the idea that "third party intervention" (their euphemism for unions) is unnecessary. To prove that, these companies provide their employees with as much as or more than the union can in wages, benefits, and protected grievance procedures. All that comes without the necessity of paying dues and without the danger of interrupted income due to strikes. Critics would say that such a company bribes its employees to keep them from unionizing. The company would respond that it is managing its people intelligently and needs no help from self-appointed busybodies whom their employees do not need.

Of course, unions can offer employees some things that management can't, such as collective bargaining and the leverage inherent in a strike threat. These companies would counter that such things are important to the worker only when management is untrustworthy or dishonorable. They go to considerable lengths to demonstrate that they are neither.

Why do these companies work so hard to avoid unions? After all, the effort is expensive. Contrary to popular belief, the primary purpose of keeping unions out is not to keep wages down. These companies probably have at least as high a total compensation cost without unions as they would with them, if not higher.

In searching for an explanation, I am reminded of what I was told many years ago by a friend who was a psychiatrist. He told me that there are two kinds of reasons why anyone does anything. There are the good reasons, he said, and then there are the real reasons. There are three good reasons for avoiding unions if you can, and I'll list them here. Then I'll tell you the real reason management goes to such lengths to keep unions out of their companies.

The first "good reason" is the avoidance of so-called work rules. These are restrictions written into the union contract on how, when, and where a worker's labor may be used. Work rules make each employee indispensable, regardless of how much or how little work needs to be done. The effects of work rules are overstaffing, delays, lack of flexibility, and low productivity.

The second "good reason" for wanting to avoid unions is to be able to fire people who are hopelessly or incorrigibly unproductive. While there are usually very few such people in a company, they tend to be conspicuous and to set a poor example for employees who do not have a strong work ethic of their own. Just as a strike is the union's ultimate weapon, firing is management's ultimate weapon. Management considers it a necessity, in order to get rid of a small, irresponsible minority. Unions counter that the right to fire is like a license to kill, and that having such a weapon brings out the worst in entirely too many managers.

Both sides have a point. That is why managers have to be highly disciplined themselves, with or without unions. When they are not, employees may be justified in feeling that they need to be protected against their bosses.

The third "good reason" for wanting to shut out unions is that the exercise brings out the best in managers. Staying union-free puts a premium on decency and fairness. It gives an advantage to managers who can cultivate these qualities and inhibits those who like to throw their weight around. If you can break away from confrontational tactics, you can start using positive motivators, with all of their productivity advantages. So a benign side effect of keeping unions out is that you'll probably have a more highly motivated work force.

So much for the good reasons. The underlying reason, or if you will, the "real" reason, for management's anti-union zeal is that unions are a terrible affront to managerial pride. A union contract states, in effect, "You management people can't be trusted. So we're going to put handcuffs on you to make sure that you don't play any more dirty tricks on our people." The handcuffs are bad enough, but what really hurts is the implication that managers are just a bunch of bullies wearing neckties. What fuels the anti-union crusade is resentment of the implied insult, and a need by managers to prove that they are professionals and not bastards.

Motivation über Alles

The annual reports of most corporations include a few lines of boilerplate that hail the company's employees as its "greatest asset." However, relatively few companies treat their employees that way, especially during recessions. The typical reaction to a decline in business is to trim employment first and dividends last. Companies that lead in motivating do it the other way around. If you have built a winning team, the last thing you want to do is break it up.

If motivation really is your top priority, there are three things you'll have to be prepared to do, come hell or high water. The first is to keep everyone on the payroll, even when business is bad. The best way to do that is to keep the organization lean, so that when business is good everyone has too much to do. Instead of staffing for peak workloads that always recede sooner or later, you staff so that everyone will have plenty to do when there isn't much to do. You cover the difference with temporary employees or by subcontracting.

Keeping the permanent organization as small as possible has lots of advantages. It minimizes your exposure to layoffs, which is the single most corrosive element in employee relations. That, in turn, builds loyalty, which pays off when recruiters try to pirate your people away. It enables you to be selective in hiring, because you're never looking for more than a handful of people. It enables you to pay the kind of salaries that attract the best people in their professions, because your payroll won't be swollen by masses of redundant people. It makes internal communication faster and more reliable, because there won't be impossible numbers of people with whom you have to stay in touch.

The second necessity, if you're determined to put motivation first, is avoiding morale problems. Because of the insidious way in which those problems grow, you have to go looking for them before they become obvious. Obvious morale problems are often too far advanced to treat, or at least to treat quickly or inexpensively. That means periodic full-scale attitude surveys in which everyone has a chance to comment on everything. Above all, it means doing whatever must be done to clean up whatever problems the surveys may reveal.

The third component of a "motivation comes first" policy is propaganda. You want to make sure that everyone knows that the organization is committed to them, provided only that the commitment is mutual. The company's goals and values have to be reiterated, restated, repeated. Let no one think that this is just another company. Keep reminding them that your company is not merely better than other employers, but that it's different.

Why have a "motivation first" policy? Because it enhances and preserves your greatest asset. Can you afford it, especially when sales and profits are down? Only if you want to be able to compete with your toughest competitors when sales turn upward again.

Does it really pay off? That depends on whether you manage all of your other assets as intelligently as you'll be managing the greatest one. Some companies that did a wonderful job of motivating have nevertheless disappeared, because they did a less than wonderful job of planning, or pricing, or marketing, or controlling costs. Having conceded that, I'll still say that weak motivation systems are a much more common, and more deadly, problem than weak systems in the other arenas of management. To cite just two recent examples, a strong motivation system was not enough to save People Express, but a weak motivation system undermined and eventually brought down Eastern Airlines.

CHAPTER
—— 18 ——

MOTIVATING BIG BLUE

You should take all ratings of "best-managed" companies, including the one that will be featured in this chapter, with a grain of salt. True, you can ask so-called experts, including business school professors, consultants, and even managers themselves, to name the companies that they admire the most. What they usually admire is a company's current position in its markets, which could be fortuitous, rather than its internal management practices, about which they usually know nothing. Hardly anyone has a firsthand, in-depth acquaintance with more than a few companies, and those who do are not necessarily wise or discerning.

Consequently, most of what the "experts" can share with you is nothing more than third- and fourth-hand gossip, based mostly on reputations that may or may not be deserved any longer, if indeed they ever were. You must also reckon with public relations departments. A reputation for good management does not hurt the price-earnings ratio of a company's stock, and some of those reputations may include a certain amount of puffery.

Nevertheless, I'm going to cite IBM as an example of a company whose motivation system works very well with Americans. For all I know, there may be other companies whose motivation systems work even better. But the advantage of IBM, for my present purposes, is that I know it well. I was employed as an internal consultant for eight years, during a period when IBM was growing very rapidly.

IBM shows up on most lists of "best-managed" or "most-admired" companies. That is partly because of its spectacular growth. But it is mainly because the company dominates the computer industry, and because the computer has become a kind of metaphor for the era in which we live. However, being well known and highly regarded does not mean that a company's motivation system works well. You can only determine that by firsthand observation.

I had a unique opportunity to assess the company's motivation system, because that was my job. During my years with the company, I interviewed a few thousand IBMers personally, and used the company's computers to analyze the questionnaire responses of tens of thousands of others. What follows was neither authorized by the company nor cleared with it in advance. They are simply my own views as to why IBM has been able to motivate its people as effectively as it has.

And it *has*. Make no mistake about that. Despite its well-publicized problems in breaking into new markets, and the inevitable ups and downs of its quarterly profit-and-loss statement, IBM's overall record is still the envy of its industry—and most other industries. That record is no accident. It is the deliberate result of bringing together tens of thousands of highly motivated men and women and giving them a working environment in which their talents could thrive.

A RIDE ON A SKI LIFT

Perhaps the best way to begin this review is to recount an incident that occurred several years after I had left IBM. I was on vacation at a ski resort in Colorado, standing in one of the many long lines that led to a chairlift. The line moved slowly, and I looked about to see who my companion on the lift might be. To my surprise, one of the skiers standing near me was an IBM vice-president. So we greeted each other like long-lost brothers, and made the usual remarks about how small the world was.

Then, as we settled into the chair and began our long ride up the mountain, he turned to me and said, "Now, look. You've been out of the company for a few years, and you've had a chance to compare us with lots of other companies. And you've got nothing to gain or lose, because I'm not involved in any consulting contracts you might want. So you can be completely frank. What I want to know is, how good are we, really? You know, most IBMers have never worked for another company, so we have no basis for comparison. But now you do. So tell it to me straight. How good are we?"

I looked out at the mountains, and then at him. "All right," I said. "I'll tell you. Look. You know, and I know, that IBM has one of the world's greatest internal propaganda machines."

He winced, but I continued.

"You constantly bombard your employees with the same messages. 'We are different,' you tell them. 'This is not your average company. We are better. We treat people right. We'll do anything to take good care of our customers, and we treat our own people with dignity. So IBM is special. If you work for IBM, that makes you special, too.' That's the propaganda. You know it as well as I do."

He looked me straight in the eye, and his expression hardened.

"And all I can tell you," I continued, "after having had a chance to compare IBM with a lot of other companies, is this. The IBM propaganda is true."

He grinned.

I know a little bit about a lot of motivation systems, and a lot about a few of them. There may very well be some companies out there whose motivation systems work as well as IBM's, or even better. If so, I haven't encountered them yet. Also, some of my observations of IBM may be dated. However, based on what I can glean from my own informal network of friends and acquaintances within the company, the motivation system hasn't changed that much since I was there myself.

Motivation in Perspective

One last disclaimer before we begin. It is important to avoid overstating the effect of IBM's motivation system, because it was only part of a larger managerial system in which the emphasis was always on excellence.

For example, IBM's financial controls have always been strong. Managers were not permitted to add new employees, even when they needed them, faster than the revenue growth that would pay for them. Also, IBM's service for its products was legendary. Many customers cited the service rather than the products themselves as their main reason for ordering IBM equipment. Further, the company's sales force was renowned for its zeal and tenacity. It overcame another company's one-year monopoly with what was then the only computer on the market. And IBM's sheer size enabled it to take risks and absorb losses that many other companies could not have faced.

Having said all that, the fact remains that the wisest policies can fail if they are not properly implemented. The financial controls had to be held in place by dedicated men and women. The maintenance service had to be provided by a highly skilled field organization. The sales force had to be rallied and inspired. In brief, IBM could not have grown into what it is today if it had not had highly motivated employees to carry out its plans on a day-to-day basis.

However, not all IBM employees were highly motivated, at least not while I was there, and I doubt if all of them are highly motivated today. But in so large an organization, it is not necessary for *everyone* to excel. It is only necessary that *enough people* in the right jobs want very much to do their jobs superbly, and in IBM *more* than enough people were that highly motivated. Indeed, far more IBMers (in percentage terms) had strong achievement and influence motives than employees in most of the other companies I have had an opportunity to examine since then.

What accounted for the unusual effectiveness of IBM's motivation system?

The Motivational Context

In the preceding chapter, we noted that to work effectively, a motivation system must respond to needs that are common in the population from which its employees are drawn. We also noted that there are many needs in the working population in as huge, diverse, and restless a country as the United States.

In order to understand how IBM succeeded in motivating so many people so well, we have to re-explore the American motivational context, this time at a somewhat deeper level. Lots of people "got ahead" in IBM, but they could also have done that in many other companies. But there are other needs out there that are almost as strong, which IBM succeeded in satisfying better than any company I have seen before or since.

My best guess as to the unfulfilled needs that motivate a majority of Americans, and to which most American motivation systems do not respond effectively, are these:

First, most Americans prefer to be dealt with separately as distinct individuals, rather than as one among many. While they may or may not succeed in distinguishing themselves, they consider it important that they have a chance to do so. To make a name for oneself, to leave a mark, to be singled out for some kind of favorable recognition; these are all deep-seated needs that are bred in abundance by the American culture.

Second, most Americans would prefer, if they could, to deal only with trustworthy people. If they could, they would shun sleazy, sly, or dishonest people altogether. While they can guard their own interests if they have to, they would prefer not to have to.

Third, they need a cause. They want to associate themselves with one or more ideals that transcend mere self-interest, but without sacrificing self-interest.

Fourth, they want to be part of an organization that is recognized for being exceptional in what it stands for, what it accomplishes, how it conducts its business, and whom it hires. They want to bask in reflected glory.

In brief, what too many American companies overlook about too many Americans is that they are closet idealists. That is also why so many American companies are out of touch with their own culture. It is, finally, the reason why a few American companies, including IBM, have been able to achieve much higher motivation levels than most other companies.

The IBM Motivation System

The IBM motivation system has ten key components, each of which responds to one or more of those four powerful American needs.

1. The company is in a position to be very selective about whom it hires.

2. Managers are severely constrained from treating any employee arbitrarily or harshly.
3. Employees can appeal managerial decisions that they feel are unfair to them.
4. Rapid advancement for many individuals, especially during the early stages of their careers, is the rule.
5. All employees are salaried.
6. The company offers high pay and benefits.
7. The company is committed to avoiding layoffs.
8. There is a commitment to keeping employees technically and professionally up to date.
9. There are regularly scheduled employee attitude surveys.
10. The internal propaganda is relentless.

I'm going to have more to say about some of these elements than others. In some cases I want to share some personal experiences with you. In other cases, however, the concept has already been covered in detail in previous chapters, so it needs no repetition here.

To put these components of IBM's motivation system into their own context, I'm going to use another anecdote. IBM used to sum up its philosophy of motivation with a catch phrase, "respect for the individual." I would rephrase it as "treating real people, warts and all, in the right way." Here's an example of how that philosophy was implemented.

RESPECT FOR THE INDIVIDUAL

I was recruited into IBM by the company *psychiatrist.* He was a full-time employee who was asked, through his professional contacts, to find a psychologist to study the motivation of the IBM sales force. That turned out to be me. His usual duties, however, were to see to it that IBM employees or their dependents who needed psychiatric help, ranging from simple counseling to hospitalization, received the most competent care available in their communities. Today, such services are called employee assistance programs and have become commonplace, but in those days, mental health services for employees were practically unheard of.

Many companies still prefer to act as if their employees had no anxieties, no marital problems, no substance dependencies, and no occasional passages through rough emotional seas. They maintain that pretense even when those conditions affect job performance, as they usually do. The IBM approach to emotional disorders was much more straightforward. The underlying assumption was that these things happen to people, even to the best of people. The company wanted its employees to have the best possible care for any condition, be it emotional or physical, that could handicap their performance. It was as simple as that: no evasions, no pretenses that IBMers were not as human as everyone else, and certainly no suggestion that emotional disorders carried some kind of stigma that required them to be hidden at all costs.

There is no satisfactory way to measure the frequency of emotional disorders. However, in my judgment the emotional illness rate in IBM was *less* than in most other companies. That was in spite of the stresses for which IBM became famous, such as frequent relocations of families and relentlessly long hours of work. (Two of the company's internal jokes were that "IBM" stood for "I've been moved" in the United States, and in German-speaking countries, for *immer bis mittenacht*, which translates as "always until midnight.") On the other hand, very few IBM employees felt trapped in dead-end jobs, or subjugated to the petty despotism of a boss about whom they dared not complain. Both of those problems are common in many other companies, and both can undermine emotional health.

Therefore IBM did not *need* a psychiatrist for its employees more than other companies did. Rather, it *chose* to have one, because it was willing to face the fact that when you employ more than 100,000 people for periods of up to forty years or more, some of them, some of the time, are going to need that kind of help. To this day I don't understand IBM's computers very well, but I know sophistication and compassion when I see them. It was that combination that first got me intrigued about the company.

Selective Hiring

The trick to selective hiring is not merely to screen a great many candidates in order to hire only a few. It is to attract a disproportionate share of the best candidates in the first place. IBM did this by sending its most successful younger managers, rather than professional interviewers, on recruiting trips to college campuses. Most of these managers were only a few years older than the students they interviewed, so it was easy for the students to look upon the managers as role models.

That was exactly what IBM wanted. The managers were not there to pick and choose among the students. They were there as bait, to make IBM look especially attractive to students who might be motivated to emulate them. The picking and choosing was done later, by the professionals; but they chose from an applicant pool that had already attracted an unusually high percentage of achievers.

The purpose of selective hiring was not merely to get good people, but to encourage the feeling of having joined an elite team. This is sometimes called the "Yankee effect," a reference to the old New York Yankees back in the days when they always won the World Series. It was said then that if you put a bush league player into a Yankee uniform, he'd suddenly start playing like a major leaguer, because he wanted to deserve that uniform.

Similarly, your status in your community was enhanced if you were one of IBM's chosen few. Being on the team also made you want to live up to its performance standards. So indirectly, but powerfully, selective hiring had a motivational effect of its own.

Managerial Restraint

One of the unwritten rules among IBM managers, recounted with special emphasis to the new ones, was, "If you really want to risk losing your job, just have one subordinate submit one justified complaint that you've been unfair, or that you've treated him disrespectfully." Virtually all IBM managers got the message right away, and most of them never forgot it. Having a bit of authority can bring out the worst in some people, especially if they are not accustomed to it. But I almost never saw any managers in IBM who had let their authority go to their heads.

The message that the employees got was that they were each held in high esteem, and that they were not to be abused. The concept was drummed into IBM managers in many ways, ranging from simple courtesy (which was the norm in most manager-employee relationships) to a protected right to appeal any managerial decisions that affected you. The very existence of such a right caused it to be used rarely. Most managers, knowing that subordinates could go over their heads if they felt they had to, worked hard to keep their relationships in good repair. On those few occasions when employees did appeal a decision, their appeals were taken very seriously.

After I left IBM, whenever I told managers in other companies about IBM's restraints on its managers, many of them were incredulous. Their expectations included gross abuse of managerial lenience, near rebellion, and outright chaos. In fact, the great majority of IBM's employees were quite cooperative. The point they proved was that people can behave themselves without being held in line by threats. Of course, there were the inevitable exceptions, and they were dealt with briskly, but humanely.

The "Open Door" Policy

This was the protected grievance channel. Those who felt that a superior's decision about them was wrong could appeal over that superior's head, without fear of retaliation. For example, when I worked at corporate headquarters just outside New York, a complaint arrived from an employee in Oregon who had not been satisfied with his performance appraisal, or with the reviews given to his appeal at successive headquarters levels in Los Angeles and New York City.

Together with other staff members, I spent several hours reviewing the voluminous file before turning it over, with our recommendation, to the executive vice-president. In that particular case, we felt that the manager was probably right and the employee was probably wrong. Nevertheless, the manager had not followed the strict letter of the company's policy. The executive vice-president ruled in favor of the employee, and his manager was reprimanded.

It might seem that with their managers held to such exacting standards, IBM's employees might be tempted to abuse their privileges, and that poor performance might be tolerated. Yet quite the contrary was true. The company's management trainers stressed that there was no inherent conflict between productivity and morale. Managers were expected to keep *both* of them high. In the language of the "managerial grid," IBM was practicing a 9,9 management style even before Blake and Mouton came along to give it a name.*

---

*R. Blake and J. Mouton, *The Managerial Grid* (Houston: Gulf Publishing, 1964).

Rapid Promotion

Perhaps the most powerful motivator that IBM had in those days was the lure of promotion. At the time, IBM was one of the fastest socioeconomic escalators in the world. It carried tens of thousands of ambitious young men and women, many from humble origins, straight to the affluent upper middle class, and in only a few short years. This, of course, appealed to the "getting ahead" syndrome in the American culture. IBMers knew that the reward for good performance would be quick entry into the ranks of management.

It was common knowledge in those days that a few years of IBM managerial experience had more salary-commanding power in the job market than an MBA from a prestigious business school. Thus IBMers needed very little urging to perform at the top of their abilities, because they wanted to get one of those managerial jobs. It was very much to their personal advantage to do their best, regardless of whether they ultimately chose to stay with the company or to leave it.

Many, including me, eventually left. Most became executives in other companies, or started their own businesses. But there are two important points to be made about this turnover. First, despite the loss of many good people, IBM retained more than enough other good people to keep right on growing. After I left the company, I would scold clients who had not invested enough in their management development systems by telling them that "IBM has a third team that can beat your first team."

The company's policies created a talent surplus which, while it made those losses inevitable, also enabled the company to absorb them. A talent surplus is a by-product of enabling people to grow as fast as they can. It is easy to get "hooked" on the blossoming of your own talents. In this case, company growth stimulated individual growth, which in turn stimulated more company growth, and so on, until company growth itself eventually, and inevitably, slowed. So many people were excited by their own growth that IBM easily survived the loss of some very talented employees. (Some of them, indeed, were talented enough to establish companies of their own that later competed quite successfully with IBM!)

The second point to be made about IBM's turnover is that most of the company's "alumni" are remarkably loyal. Only rarely does one encounter the kind of bitterness or disgruntlement that is often found among the former employees of other companies. Most ex-IBMers felt that their years with the company were well spent. They left to become bigger fish in smaller ponds, or were lured out by singularly lucrative pay packages, or because they recognized that every time one is promoted in a company as richly endowed with talent as IBM, the competition for the next promotion becomes even fiercer.

Salaries for All

All IBM employees, from the janitors to the chief executive officer, are paid a salary. Some are also eligible for various bonuses, but no one receives an hourly wage. All that may sound like a lot of administrative detail, but its motivational impact is enormous, for two reasons, one obvious, the other not.

The obvious reason is personal budgeting. Workloads may fluctuate, but salaries don't. You can count on them and plan your expenditures accordingly. Also, salary income tends to be higher than wage income that is calculated at the same hourly rate, because it is not subject to interruption. Obviously, IBMers liked that.

However, the not-so-obvious reason is probably more important. While money may not be much of a motivator, it is an extraordinarily potent communicator. Nothing gets a message across quite as powerfully as a paycheck. But the "message" does not depend so much on the numbers on the check as it does on how they are calculated.

A salary is an implied commitment to pay you at a fixed rate, regardless of how the company itself may fare. It is the company's way of putting its money where its mouth is. A salary says, in effect, that "while we may not need you all of the time, you are so important to us that it more than repays us to keep you available all of the time." An hourly wage conveys an altogether different message, no matter how high the wage itself may be. That message is, "We don't want you here unless you are needed at the moment, because when you are not needed, you are just a useless burden to us."

So a salary recognizes how indispensable you are, while a wage emphasizes how dispensable you are. The implications for personal dignity and respect could not be more different. IBM's motives for eliminating hourly wages were self-serving, because it greatly reduced any attractions that unions might have had. But the effect was a big boost in positive motivation. IBM factory workers and others in similar jobs felt good about themselves, because the company valued them so highly.

High Pay and Benefits

When I worked for IBM, people outside the company had a rather exaggerated idea of how well we were paid. That was a classical "halo" effect. That is, the company was known to be selective in whom it hired, and its products were successful in the marketplace, so it was simply assumed that it also excelled in all other respects as well, including pay. While our pay did rank pretty well compared to the outside market, it did not really exceed the overall market by that much. More money could be had elsewhere, especially from competitors who were desperate to hire trained people in scarce specialties.

Those competitors did succeed in poaching some IBMers. But not many, because if you left IBM, you left a lot. For example, benefits.

IBM's benefits were *very* good. The company prided itself on introducing new benefit programs that other companies later copied. Some examples were full-salaried leaves of absence for employees who wanted to teach in minority schools, or early retirement, with partial continuation of pay, for employees who would begin new careers as academics.

The objective of the pay policy was to attract and hold good people. The objective of the benefits policy was to make continued employment so comfortable that you wouldn't really think of leaving to work elsewhere.

I was hired by IBM precisely because management wanted to look at its pay program from a realistic perspective. In the precomputer days, an IBM salesman's commission was the first month's rent on the machines he placed with customers. (All salespeople were male in those days.) The reward for each sale was a few hundred dollars, and that was an effective incentive. But with the advent of computers, the first month's rent could be tens or even hundreds of thousands of dollars.

The company realized that it would have to change its system for paying the sales force. But it didn't confine itself to figuring out some new pay formulas. Instead, it asked how important pay really was (all mythology and so-called common sense aside) to the specific group of people (about two thousand of them, at the time) who constituted its sales force. So the company hired me to make a motivational survey of that group.

I wasn't about to interview all of them. That would have taken forever and wasn't really necessary anyway. Instead we drew a 10 percent sample, and in six months of hard work I had long, probing chats with all two hundred of them.

The upshot of all that, with respect to pay, was that these were pretty sophisticated people. They wanted money, all right, but they wanted power, prestige, and nonfluctuating incomes even more. In other words, their number-one incentive was not their current income, no matter how handsome it might be. Promotion was what they were really after. Knowing that, the company did not have to escalate salesmen's incomes to unheard-of levels simply because the price of their products had shot up dramatically.

The "Full-Employment" Policy

This was a policy commitment to not lay off employees due to cyclical declines in business. That policy was one of the main reasons for IBM's restraints on hiring, even when business was booming and most employees had more work to do than they could handle. The company preferred subcontracting, or even lengthy backlogs in the factories, to hiring employees who might become redundant next time the economy turned down.

The full-employment policy is probably the main reason that IBM, despite its size, is totally union-free in its domestic operations. But there are also subtler effects. You don't generally see adversarial attitudes between IBM managers and employees. That makes it much easier to experiment with new methods. Because no one is dispensable, there is more of a "one for all and all for one" spirit in IBM than one finds in many other companies, and less of an "us *versus* them" attitude by managers and employees toward each other.

Everyone's Up to Date in Big Blue

Nearly every IBM employee receives some kind of formal classroom training every year, whether they work in a fast-changing branch of high technology or simply need to be reminded of what they may have known once and then forgotten. IBM's training budget actually exceeds the entire operating budget of some big universities. Training is an expensive motivator. But it pays off.

You could justify this massive expenditure for operational reasons alone. After all, the company's products are close to the leading edge of their technology, and the company's people have to support those products. But the policy of investing heavily in education also has two important motivational effects.

First, when you are surrounded by constant technological change, it's very reassuring to know that your employer won't let you become obsolete by default. IBM learned that lesson the hard way, but it never forgot it. When one of the "new generations" of computers was introduced, the company had plans drawn up to retrain all of its maintenance people on the new system. But through one of those inexplicable oversights that occasionally happen, no one bothered to inform the troops of what had been planned. They began to have visions of going the way of the blacksmith and the buggywhip maker. Soon they were up in arms, demanding that they not be left behind in a technological backwater. A very red-faced management had to admit that it had failed to announce that they had already done the right thing. To make up for their error, they accelerated the retraining program.

The second motivational effect of a commitment to training is that it increases the market value of IBM employees. Some took advantage of that by defecting to other employers with all of that training freshly stored inside their heads. But most saw IBM's commitment to training as an incentive to stay, because they realized that what they had just learned would also become obsolete in its turn. They could see far enough ahead to realize that the next round of training, and all of the rounds after that, also had to be weighed in the balance. As long as they stayed in IBM, they could command top dollar with other employers whenever they chose to leave. Once they left, however, their next employers were less likely to be able to keep them technically up to date from that point forward.

Attitude Surveys and Training

IBM was one of the first major companies to launch a program of regularly scheduled attitude surveys for all employees. These surveys are usually conducted annually and give everyone an opportunity to express their views on employment-related matters, typically through questionnaires. Merely measuring morale is not the major purpose of the surveys, however.

IBM's attitude surveys are primarily intended to *enhance* morale. When they identify some factor that could depress morale, which could be anything from minor complaints about air conditioning to major complaints about promotion opportunities, the appropriate group of managers is told to do something about it. They are required either to correct the problem or to give employees a satisfactory explanation of why it can't be corrected.

Managers are not judged on whether their subordinates voice complaints. Human nature being what it is, an absence of complaints would be unnatural, even at IBM. Rather, the managers are judged on the effectiveness of what they do to eliminate those complaints.

The ultimate purpose of an attitude survey is to pinpoint what you have to do to get better results in the next survey. There will always be complaints, but when I was at IBM we used to distinguish between good complaints and bad ones. A good complaint was a new one, and what made it "good" was that it hadn't had time to fester, so it was still easy to fix. A "bad" complaint was an old one that had persisted from a previous survey. That meant that the manager had done nothing, or at least nothing effective, about it.

IBM managers whose subordinates persistently produced "bad" complaints were in the company doghouse unless it could be shown that the problem was beyond their control. So they had an incentive to be responsive to the data that the surveys generated. And that responsiveness was the main motivational effect of the attitude surveys. The message was that when you feel strongly enough to complain, it's somebody's job to listen. And that "somebody" is very likely to be your boss, or your boss's boss.

Propaganda

Now it is time to recall my ride on the ski lift, when I spoke to the IBM vice-president about the company's "propaganda." I'm sure he understood that I was not using that term in its corrupted modern sense, which implies blatant lies and exaggerated quarter-truths. Rather I meant it in its original sense, to mean persistent repetition of a few important themes.

There is an old maxim among teachers, and others who communicate for a living, that the best way to make your point memorably is to "tell them what you are going to say, say what you said you would say, and then tell them what you just told them." In other words, use repetition.

IBM used internal publications, bulletin boards, training programs, executive speeches, and any other opportunity that presented itself to remind employees, again and again, of two ideas that were central to the company's culture. First, that the company made a fetish of doing things right. There was nothing shoddy or second rate about its products or its services, nothing you would ever want to conceal or have to apologize for. Second, that the company's commitment to doing the right thing applied with special emphasis to two groups of people: its customers and its employees. The company made it clear that it expected a lot of its employees, and that they in return could expect a lot of their company.

The message was woven into so many memos, bulletins, notices, and articles that you could hardly ignore it. That's what made it propaganda. But it was confirmed by your everyday experience. That's what made it convincing.

DECENT TREATMENT FOR HAND-PICKED PEOPLE

If I had to summarize the effects of something as complex as IBM's motivation system in only six words, those are the six I would choose.

IBM managed to convey the idea that its people were not ordinary, but special, and that they deserved to be treated accordingly. You were special to begin with, because a very choosy company had chosen you. But you were also special because some of the company's own image, including its spectacular success and its reputation for doing things right, rubbed off on you. The company was regarded by outsiders with a certain awe, and to varying extents, so were its employees.

All that made you want to live up to the company's reputation. It made IBMers want to stretch their talents and reach for new heights of achievement. Working at the top of your abilities was the commonly accepted norm in IBM, and, just as in every organization, most of us wanted to conform to the norm. (You can see the same phenomenon in schools. In some, nothing less than grades of A are socially acceptable, while in other schools a "gentleman's C" is quite acceptable. If you transfer students from one school to another, their grades usually rise or fall to fit the new norm. In IBM, the equivalent of an A was considered standard.)

Of course, this performance-enhancing effect did not reach everyone. But it did influence a very substantial part of the whole. When you have that kind of motivation surging through tens or even hundreds of thousands of people, the effects on things like earnings per share and price-earnings ratios can be dramatic. And they were.

So the ultimate motivational effect of being made to feel that you were special was a big boost in performance. But the effect of expecting decent treatment was equally important. Top management held middle and lower management to very exacting standards of supervisory conduct, and the employees knew it. Managers could reprimand, warn, and even fire their subordinates. But those were all tools to be used in a strictly professional manner, rather than perquisites of the manager's job. And no IBM manager was a law unto him- or herself, because employees had a well-advertised right to go over their manager's head whenever they felt the need to do so.

The effect, especially on employees who could compare IBM with previous employers, was a general relaxation of wariness and tension. IBMers might be edgy because of workload pressures, but they almost never had to look over their shoulders to see whether their boss was out to get them, because that wasn't the way most bosses worked. Energy could be focused entirely on the job without having to divert part or all of it to self-defense. So the ultimate motivational effect of confidence in your boss's decency was an undiluted, undiverted flow of all of your abilities into your work.

IBM in Perspective

I have chosen to emphasize the positive aspects of IBM's motivation system because those are the parts that are worth studying and emulating. However, I hope I have not created the impression of uncritical adulation of my ex-employer. IBM did some things that I thought were rather dumb. But there were not many, and they were not very important, and they certainly were not worth studying or emulating. Above all, they came nowhere near canceling out the positive effects of the ten elements I have already reviewed.

But to prove my point, here are some examples of IBM's non-invincibility in the motivational field. First on the list were the company's sophomoric songs in praise of itself, which employees were once expected to sing lustily at company meetings. Those had begun to fade, mercifully, when I was in the company, and are mostly part of the company's semiofficial nostalgia today.

Second, the company promoted the huge, expensive, and somewhat ostentatious "conventions" of employees who had met certain performance standards, such as the famous One Hundred Percent Clubs. Salesmen were invited to these gala meetings for having achieved sales quotas that were set at levels that permitted about 80 percent of the sales force to meet them. Therefore the real incentive was not to go to the convention, but not to be left out. The meetings themselves were valued mostly for opportunities to swap stories with colleagues and to do some networking. The speeches by company executives were usually predictable and therefore not very memorable, especially if you had already heard them once or twice. The main effect, overall, was to preserve a tradition that was largely obsolete.

The company was also capable of ham-handed attempts to enforce unnecessary conformity. For example, it once decreed that all salaried employees at company headquarters had to punch in at time clocks when they arrived for work, because some of them arrived habitually late.

I will not include IBM's famous dress code in this brief list of motivational lapses, even though the dark suits, white shirts, and conservative ties or scarfs are the objects of derision outside the company. Within the company, the "uniform" is considered a status symbol that helps to set IBMers apart from the employees of less prestigious companies. I might add that the best definition of an appropriate dress code that I ever heard was given by an IBM manager: "Always dress so that no one at work notices how you are dressed." Your clothing, in other words, should not be distracting if your purpose is not to attract attention, but to get some serious work done.

To bring this chapter to an end, let me note that IBM's managers, despite their formidable reputations, were in fact ordinary mortals who occasionally did dumb things. Their great advantage was that they worked in a tradition that had already had most of the kinks worked out of it years before they joined the company. It was that tradition that enabled ordinary men and women to achieve one of the most remarkable bursts of motivation in modern industrial history. Quarterly reports may come and go, but IBM's overall record stands as a monument to what intelligent motivation policies can accomplish. We need more companies with records like that.

CHAPTER
19

THE GREATEST MOTIVATIONAL CHALLENGE

The greatest motivational challenge of them all is to keep yourself motivated under adverse conditions—that is, when you have nothing but your own motives to sustain you and the external motivators are either lacking or working against you. What can you do, for example, when you're persistently blocked from achieving your goals, you're paid less than you're worth, your job does not provide full scope for your talents, you've got a bad boss, and to add insult to injury, things are not so great in your private life?

Sounds like a nightmare scenario, doesn't it? Everything going wrong at once. Life isn't ordinarily that cruel. But any of these things could happen to you. If you are hit by one or more of these calamities, you're going to have to know how to manage your own motivation. That's a five-step process.

Step one is to remember who you are. Step two is to make a detailed assessment of your situation. Step three is to zero in on those aspects of your situation that you can do something about. Step four—the hard part—is actually to *do* those things. Step five is to keep your perspective.

Managing Your Motivation

Hamlet had it right. We really have a grand total of two choices in this life, and they keep on recurring. You can passively endure life's slings and arrows, or you can try to do something about them. This is also true of motivation. You can note, perhaps correctly, that your company or your boss doesn't know how to motivate you, or you can ignore that and supply your own motivation.

That choice is not as simple as it sounds. Sometimes a lack of external stimulation can be stultifying. This is what happened in "The Case of the Vanishing MBAs," back in chapter 9. For someone who is trained to think strategically and to solve multifaceted problems, the novelty of doing humdrum work wears off very quickly. Sometimes the best way to keep your internal motivation alive and well is to change the external motivators. That frequently means looking for a better-motivating job elsewhere. If for some reason you can't do that, you may have no choice but to accept a motivationally unfavorable situation, at least for the present.

"Supplying your own motivation" means deciding that, instead of producing as a *quid pro quo* for some kind of reward, you're going to produce because you want to, reward or no reward. It means a decision to achieve something mostly to prove that you can do it. Supplying your own motivation means that you're not about to turn in work that you can't be proud of, regardless of whether your company or your boss deserves it.

Some would say that by taking this attitude, you are collaborating in your own exploitation. That misses the point. If your work is a vehicle for expressing and perfecting your talents, and not just a commodity to be sold to the highest bidder, the best reason in the world for doing your work right is because it is yours.

Whatever your decision may be, it is important that you make one. The issue of for whom and how hard you should work is too important to be settled by default. You have to accept the responsibility for either supplying your own motivation or changing employers, or for consciously biding your time until you can.

Remembering Who You Are

You are what you want. There may be things you want to have, such as (I presume) wealth, or things that you want to be, such as loved by a few people and highly regarded by many, or things that you want to experience, such as triumph or adventure or even, perhaps, revenge. There are also things you want to avoid, such as illness or disgrace or losing your independence or your freedom. Whatever your own collection of wants may be, they define you as distinctly as your fingerprints do, because they shape the pattern of what you will attempt and avoid throughout your life. In other words, you are your motives.

Many people cannot articulate their motives, and may not even be aware of all of them. Usually, it isn't necessary that you have that much insight into what makes you tick. You can go on "ticking," so to speak, for decades without needing to know what drives the mechanism. But there are times when it really helps to have at least some knowledge of what your own motives are, because otherwise there is a danger that you might betray them. If you do, you might subsequently decide that you have been a failure, or at least that you have made a colossal mistake. Of course, both are to be avoided, if possible.

Anyone who has known you well for a long time can probably discern repeated patterns in your life. With a little candid reflection, you can probably see some of those patterns yourself. Are there some things you've persistently tried to get, even when the odds were against you? Are there some things that have always stopped you, because you couldn't bear what you might lose? Those repeated patterns are your motives. To some extent, you can pit one against another. You can decide, for example, that despite your desire to maintain your income, you're just not going to do that at the expense of your integrity and pride. (That's what chapter 16 was all about.) But never underestimate the strength of a motive that's already influenced your choices, again and again, throughout your life.

If you're stuck in a motivationally unfavorable situation, the basic question is how to be true to yourself. It's Hamlet all over again. ("This above all, to thine own self be true.") That's why

Shakespeare's classic still plays to standing-room-only audiences after more than three hundred years.

In other words, you have to resolve the tactical question of what to do in the light of the strategic question of who you are. And nothing reveals who you *really* are more clearly than the way you react to a hard choice, or to adverse motivational circumstances. Your real choice is to stand by your principles, come hell or high water, or to admit that those principles were a bit romantic and unrealistic and cut them down to a more human scale that you can live with.

Making a Detailed Assessment

Before you make a major decision that could affect the rest of your life, you'd better make sure that you've got your facts straight. It's easy to read more drastic conditions into your situation than are actually there. So go over that situation again, point by point. Exactly what is frustrating you, and how bad is it, really? Are you perhaps overstating your difficulties just a bit? Is there a positive side to your situation that you're overlooking? Are you, to be blunt about it, overreacting to some problems which, when seen in their proper context, aren't really all that bad?

Is there light at the end of the tunnel? For example, are some of the things that frustrate you likely to change? Is your pay *that* far below what you could earn elsewhere, and has elsewhere actually offered you a job? Are you giving more attention to the parts of your job that you do well, and not as much to the parts that could use more of your time and attention than they get? Is your boss merely ungracious and uncharming, rather than incompetent, and do you really have to be charmed in order to do your best work? If your personal problems are intruding into your work, wouldn't it be better to solve them than to blame them on your work, or your work on them?

It's only when you've subjected your complaints to a rigorous cross-examination and found that they survive unscathed that you know that you have to move on to the next step. But if you find you've been exaggerating your problems, the best thing to do is calm down, avoid doing anything rash, and forgive yourself for being just as human as anyone else.

What Can You Change?

Unless you're already pretty high up in your organization's power structure, you probably can't influence most of the external motivators that affect you. But you can probably influence some of them, and it may repay you to attempt to do that. Motivators tend to affect each other, so movement in some of them may very well create movement in others.

It's fairly common for a boss and a subordinate to emphasize different parts of the subordinate's job description. Thus you may feel that you're doing a wonderful job that your boss doesn't appreciate, while your boss, looking at the same set of facts, concludes that you're not doing well at all. If that's the problem, it's time to refocus your attention. Give attending to your boss's wishes a serious try.

But you also have to weigh another question, which is whether you and your boss are compatible. Sometimes your motives and your boss's motives will conflict. There could be an honest difference of emphasis. For example, you may be the "big picture" type, concentrating on concepts and leaving the details to others, while your boss may be the kind who watches the decimal points. We need both kinds of people in an organization, but they don't necessarily tolerate each other very well. Or the difference between you and your boss could be neurotic. He may have a need for others to submit to his will, and for your part, you may resist taking orders from anyone. In both cases, behavior is driven by needs that have little or nothing to do with the needs of the organization.

If the problem is compatibility, one of you will have to go. You will have to decide whether to wait your boss out, in the hope of his impermanence but at the risk of his finding a way to remove you first, or to leave as soon as possible. In the latter case, the rule is that you never go from somewhere to nowhere. That is, make sure that you have another job lined up, and a good one, before you bid your boss farewell and head out the door.

Apart from all of the poetic, idealistic things you've read about the virtues of persistence, there are some very practical reasons for refusing to give up your quest for whatever it is that motivates you. Once you give up, it's not so easy to ever try again. A tactical defeat is no disgrace, but a strategic defeat leaves you doubting your own abilities. It's one thing to bide your time and wait for a more promising moment, but it's quite another to declare yourself unfit for further competition. To avoid that, you should periodically reassess your goals and make sure that they aren't merely romantic. A man's reach should exceed his grasp, but not by too much—unless he is a fool.

Do It

Once you've settled the question of what must be done, you face the necessity of actually doing it. This is where the men are separated from the boys, and the women from the girls. This is where you find out whether you can live up to your own hopes and dreams or have merely been entertaining yourself with pipe dreams.

There are some tricks that can help. My own favorite way of making myself do what I know I must do is to use the analogy of diving. How do you work up the courage to jump off the edge of a pool into water that may be colder than you think? What I do in that situation is to lean forward until I must either spring away from the wall into the pool or fall flat on my face in the water. The act of leaning commits me to the dive. Similarly, most of the really difficult things that we have to do in this life begin with saying a few key words that, once said, commit you to say all of the others. They might be "Boss, I've decided to leave," or "I'm sorry, but I can't accept your offer," or any of a hundred other ways to announce a critical decision.

Some people announce their critical decisions by first building up to it, listing all of their reasons, and finally stating what is already obvious. Others end the anxiety quickly by stating their decision first and listing the reasons for it afterward. In most cases, what makes a decision difficult is fear of disappointing the person whom you have to tell. The usual reason given for listing your reasons first is that it softens the blow. My own view is that you can't soften the blow. If someone is going to be disappointed by your decision, he's going to be disappointed. The real question is whether he'll remember and understand your explanation, after the initial shock wears off. That means offering to discuss your reasons, if the other party wants to, as long as it's understood that your mind is made up and that you're past the stage of listening to pleas or counterarguments.

So if the time has come to do something drastic, rehearse your reasons, go see the person who must be told, lean off the edge of the pool, and dive. Say those few irrevocable words, and brace yourself for the sound and fury. Whether you give your decision first and then follow with your reasons, or vice versa, is a matter of individual taste.

Keep Your Perspective

People who are highly motivated tend to be impatient with the pace of fate and to overestimate the long-range impact of short-range problems and decisions. For these reasons, they tend to judge themselves too harshly and to blame themselves when they can't get all that they want exactly when they want it. Like everything else in life, high motivation has a cost, and in this case the cost is burnout. You can, in other words, motivate yourself right into disappointment and despondency, unless you keep your perspective about yourself and your ambitions. That is the ultimate form of managing your motivation.

Every now and then it pays to remind yourself that the world won't end if you don't reach all the goals you've set for yourself. Sometimes your real problem is that your goals are unrealistic, in which case you have to scale them down until they are within reach. Never confuse an adjustment with defeat.

To optimize your motivation, to get the most accomplishment with the least frustration, set your goals just beyond your reach, but no farther than that. Use your own past record as a standard, and try to exceed it, but not by much. Set your goals at a level where you have to lunge to touch them, where it's going to take extra effort and even a bit of struggle to reach them. But don't set them so far beyond your past accomplishments that you'd have to be lucky to reach them. Only gamblers and incurable romantics rely on luck.

Each time you succeed in reaching an extended goal, you can set the next one a bit higher. But only a bit. To keep yourself motivated, see to it that you keep succeeding. Most people know that motivation is one of the main causes of success, but relatively few realize that success is one of the main causes of motivation. That's why it's so important to prevent your ambitions from eluding your common sense. As long as you are the master of your motivation, and not its servant, you will be able to keep it indefinitely on the high plateau where it belongs.

INDEX